Political Theory: Methods and Approaches

Political Theory

Methods and Approaches

Edited by

David Leopold and Marc Stears

OXFORD
UNIVERSITY PRESS

OXFORD
UNIVERSITY PRESS

Great Clarendon Street, Oxford OX2 6DP

Oxford University Press is a department of the University of Oxford.
It furthers the University's objective of excellence in research, scholarship,
and education by publishing worldwide in

Oxford New York

Auckland Cape Town Dar es Salaam Hong Kong Karachi
Kuala Lumpur Madrid Melbourne Mexico City Nairobi
New Delhi Shanghai Taipei Toronto

With offices in

Argentina Austria Brazil Chile Czech Republic France Greece
Guatemala Hungary Italy Japan Poland Portugal Singapore
South Korea Switzerland Thailand Turkey Ukraine Vietnam

Oxford is a registered trade mark of Oxford University Press
in the UK and in certain other countries

Published in the United States
by Oxford University Press Inc., New York

© The several contributors 2008

The moral rights of the authors have been asserted
Database right Oxford University Press (maker)

First published 2008

British Library Cataloguing in Publication Data

Data available

Library of Congress Cataloging in Publication Data
Political theory : methods and approaches / edited by David Leopold, Marc Stears.
    p. cm.
  ISBN-13: 978-0-19-923009-9
  ISBN-13: 978-0-19-923008-2
 1. Political science–Philosophy.   2. Political science–Methodology.
3. Political science–Research.   I. Leopold, David.   II. Stears, Marc.
  JA71.P6313   2008
  320.01–dc22   2008011583

Typeset by SPI Publisher Services, Pondicherry, India
Printed in Great Britain
on acid-free paper by
CPI Antony Rowe, Chippenham, Wiltshire

ISBN 978–0–19–923008–2 (Hbk)
ISBN 978–0–19–923009–9 (Pbk)

10 9 8 7 6 5 4 3 2 1

☐ CONTENTS

⬚ ACKNOWLEDGEMENTS

The origins of this volume lie in the 'Text and Interpretation' class convened by the editors, and held in the Department of Politics and International Relations at the University of Oxford. The class was designed for graduate students starting the M.Phil. in Political Theory, and we are very grateful to all those who have participated in the ongoing conversation about methodology over the years that the course has run. We are also grateful to Dominic Byatt, Richard Dagger, Desmond King, and Mark Philp, each of whom played a crucial role in helping us to think of ways in which to bring something of that conversation to a wider audience. We have benefited from the support and advice of Bridget Taylor, and from the research assistance of Will Jefferson, Jeremy Millard, and Ben Saunders. The editors have learnt much about methods and approaches in political theory from discussions with all the contributors to this volume and also with many others over the past few years, including Duncan Bell, Daniel Butt, Geoffrey Hawthorn, Melissa Lane, Lizzy Pellicano, David Runciman, Helen Thompson, and Quentin Skinner. We thank them all for their insights, and look forward to future exchanges. Last but not least, the editors thank one another, for what has been a pleasurable collaboration.

☐ NOTES ON CONTRIBUTORS

Elizabeth Frazer is Official Fellow and Tutor in Politics, New College, Oxford, and University Lecturer in Politics, Department of Politics and International Relations, University of Oxford. She is the author of *The Problems of Communitarian Politics* (Oxford: Oxford University Press, 1999), and numerous articles on the subjects of citizenship and education, and ideals of political relationships. She is currently engaged in research projects on justifications of violence in political thought, and on citizens' resources for political conflict.

Michael Freeden is Professor of Politics and founding Director of the Centre for Political Ideologies at the Department of Politics and International Relations, University of Oxford, and Professorial Fellow at Mansfield College, Oxford. Among his books are *The New Liberalism: An Ideology of Social Reform* (Oxford: Clarendon Press, 1978); *Ideologies and Political Theory: A Conceptual Approach* (Oxford: Clarendon Press, 1996); and *Liberal Languages: Ideological Imaginations and 20th Century Progressive Thought* (Princeton, NJ: Princeton University Press, 2005). He is editor of the *Journal of Political Ideologies* and is currently completing a book on the political theory of political thinking, as well as developing approaches to the comparative study of political thought.

Sudhir Hazareesingh is CUF Lecturer in International Relations in the Department of Politics and International Relations, University of Oxford; Fellow in Politics at Balliol College, Oxford; and Fellow of the British Academy. Among his books are *Political Traditions in Modern France* (Oxford: Oxford University Press, 1994); *From Subject to Citizen* (Princeton, NJ: Princeton University Press, 1998); *Intellectual Founders of the Republic* (Oxford: Oxford University Press, 2001); and *The Legend of Napoleon* (London: Granta, 2004). He has also written extensively on various aspects of French political and cultural history. He is currently working on a book on the Gaullist myth in contemporary France.

Iwao Hirose is Assistant Professor in Ethics in the Philosophy Department and the McGill School of Environment, McGill University, and Research Fellow in the Centre for Applied Philosophy and Public Ethics, University of Melbourne. When he drafted his contribution to this book, he was the Donnelly Junior Research Fellow in Ethics at University College, Oxford. His recent publications include 'Aggregation and Numbers', *Utilitas*, 16 (2004), pp. 62–79; and 'Weighted Lotteries in Life and Death Cases', *Ratio*, 21 (2007), pp. 45–56. He is currently working on a book entitled *Moral Aggregation*.

David Leopold teaches political theory in the Department of Politics and International Relations, University of Oxford, and is a Fixed-Term Fellow in Politics at Mansfield College, Oxford. His recent publications include *The Young Karl Marx: German Philosophy, Modern Politics, and Human Flourishing* (Cambridge: Cambridge University

Press, 2007); 'The State and I: Max Stirner's Anarchism', in Douglas Moggach (edited), *The New Hegelians* (Cambridge: Cambridge University Press, 2006), pp. 176–99; and 'The Structure of Marx and Engels' Considered Account of Utopian Socialism', *History of Political Thought*, 26/3 (2005), pp. 443–66. He is currently working on some issues raised by utopianism in both the history of political thought and contemporary political theory.

Daniel McDermott is University Lecturer in Political Theory in the Department of Politics and International Relations, University of Oxford, and a Fellow in Politics at Keble College, Oxford. His recent publications include 'Fair-Play Obligations', *Political Studies*, 52/2 (2004), pp. 216–32; and 'The Permissibility of Punishment', *Law and Philosophy*, 20 (2001), pp. 403–32. He is currently completing a book on the moral justification of punishment entitled *Retributive Justice*.

Lois McNay is Reader in Politics in the Department of Politics and International Relations, University of Oxford, and a Fellow in Politics at Somerville College, Oxford. Her books include *Foucault and Feminism* (Cambridge: Polity Press, 1990), *Gender and Agency* (Cambridge: Polity Press, 2000), and *Against Recognition* (Cambridge: Polity Press, 2007). She is currently working on ideas of gender and agency in social and political theory.

David Miller is Professor of Political Theory in the Department of Politics and International Relations, University of Oxford, and an Official Fellow of Nuffield College, Oxford. His books include *On Nationality* (Oxford; Clarendon Press, 1995), *Principles of Social Justice* (Cambridge, MA: Harvard University Press, 1999), *Political Philosophy: A Very Short Introduction* (Oxford: Oxford University Press, 2003), and, most recently, *National Responsibility and Global Justice* (Oxford: Oxford University Press, 2007). He continues to work on problems of social and global justice, and on the nature of citizenship in multicultural societies.

Karma Nabulsi is University Lecturer in the Department of Politics and International Relations, University of Oxford, and Fellow in Politics at St Edmund Hall, Oxford. She is the author of *Traditions of War: Occupation, Resistance and the Law* (Oxford: Oxford University Press, 2005) and has written numerous articles on the philosophy and ethics of war, the laws of war, European political history and theory, and Palestinian history and politics. She is currently completing a book on the Young Europe movement in the 1830s, and what their struggles for liberty reveal about republican theory and practice.

Mark Philp is University Lecturer in Political Theory in the Department of Politics and International Relations, University of Oxford, and Fellow and Tutor in Politics at Oriel College, Oxford. He has published widely on late eighteenth-century British political thought and social movements, including books and editions of William Godwin and Thomas Paine, and on contemporary political theory. His most recent book, *Political Conduct*, was published by Harvard University Press in 2007. He is currently leading a team preparing a digital scholarly edition of Godwin's Diary, and is working on the development of democratic thinking in the early nineteenth century.

Marc Stears is University Lecturer in Political Theory in the Department of Politics and International Relations, University of Oxford, and Fellow in Politics at University

College, Oxford. He is the author of *Progressives, Pluralists and the Problems of the State* (Oxford: Oxford University Press, 2002), and of numerous articles in political theory, the history of political thought, and American political development. He is currently completing a book on radical democratic theory in the twentieth-century United States entitled *Democracy's Demands: Deliberation, Agonism and the American Radical Tradition*.

Adam Swift is CUF Lecturer in Political Theory in the Department of Politics and International Relations, University of Oxford, and Fellow in Politics and Sociology at Balliol College, Oxford. He is co-author of *Liberals and Communitarians*, second edition (Oxford: Blackwell, 2006) and *Against the Odds? Social Class and Social Justice in Industrial Societies* (Oxford: Oxford University Press, 1997), and author of *Political Philosophy: A Beginners' Guide for Students and Politicians*, second edition (Cambridge: Polity Press, 2006) and *How Not to Be a Hypocrite: School Choice for the Morally Perplexed Parent* (London: Routledge, 2003). He is currently working, with Harry Brighouse, to develop a liberal egalitarian theory of the family.

Stuart White is Tutorial Fellow in Politics at Jesus College, Oxford and Director of the Public Policy Unit in the Department of Politics and International Relations, University of Oxford. His research interests focus on the theory and practice of egalitarianism and, in particular, on exploring ideas, institutions, and currents of egalitarian thought that combine a critical approach to capitalism and authoritarian forms of socialism. He is a co-editor of *The Ethics of Stakeholding* (Basingstoke: Palgrave, 2003) and *The Citizen's Stake: Exploring the Future of Universal Asset Policies* (Bristol: Policy Press, 2006); editor of *New Labour: The Progressive Future?* (Basingstoke: Palgrave, 2001); and the author of *The Civic Minimum* (Oxford: Oxford University Press, 2003) and *Equality* (Cambridge: Polity Press, 2006).

Introduction

David Leopold and Marc Stears

1

Political theorists are often silent on questions of method and approach. While scholars in other branches of political and social sciences expend great energy debating the right way to conduct research—arguing about the appropriate place of quantification, the nature of survey design, the ethical acceptability of particular investigative approaches, and the like—political theorists generally spend little time addressing questions of 'how' and 'why' in their work. Instead, they dive straight into their analysis, turning immediately to the task at hand; arguing, for instance, about the meaning and value of particular key concepts such as liberty, justice, and rights. The books that political theorists write thus rarely include much explicit reflection on method, even though such reflection is a standard expectation in other areas; even less frequently do they produce works explicitly concerned with research methods, although the shelves of libraries are crowded with such texts from related disciplines.[1]

Of course, there are some sub-fields within political theory which are not characterized by such unwillingness. Methodological discussion is widespread, for example, in the work of the 'Cambridge School' of historians of political thought, such as Quentin Skinner, John Dunn, and Geoffrey Hawthorn, all of whom have produced nuanced analyses of the how and why of political theoretic research.[2] Such discussions are also commonplace among followers of Leo Strauss or Eric Voeglein, who frequently suggest

---

[1] There are, of course, some exceptions to this rule, including Terence Ball, *Reappraising Political Theory* (Oxford: Oxford University Press, 1995); Terence Ball and Richard Bellamy (edited), *The Cambridge History of Twentieth Century Political Thought* (Cambridge: Cambridge University Press, 2003); Gerald Gaus and Chandaran Kukathas, *Handbook of Political Theory* (London: Sage, 2004); Keith Topper, *The Disorder of Political Inquiry* (Cambridge, MA: Harvard University Press, 2005); Andrew Vincent, *The Nature of Political Theory* (Oxford: Oxford University Press, 2004); and Stephen K. White and J. Donald Moon (edited), *What is Political Theory?* (London: Sage, 2004).

[2] See, e.g., John Dunn, *The History of Political Theory and Other Essays* (Cambridge: Cambridge University Press, 1996); Geoffrey Hawthorn, *Plausible Worlds: Possibility and Understanding in History and the Social Sciences* (Cambridge: Cambridge University Press, 1991); and Quentin Skinner, *Visions of Politics*, volume 1: *Regarding Method* (Cambridge: Cambridge University Press, 2002). For overviews and analyses of this work, see James Tully, *Meaning and Context: Quentin Skinner and his Critics* (Cambridge: Polity, 1988).

that the normative conclusions of liberal political theorists are misguided, largely because the latter have failed to challenge their implicit methodological assumptions sufficiently carefully.[3] Nonetheless, the vast majority of students beginning advanced research in political theory in the United States and Britain still embark on their studies without any significant training in, and reflection on, the research methods that they will have to employ if they are to produce high quality work of their own. This reluctance to talk about method is perplexing. After all, the choice is not between having a method and not having one, but rather between deciding to think about that method or simply carrying on unreflectively. It is odd that so many political theorists take the latter option while at the same time priding themselves on both their analytical rigour and their ability to challenge widely held assumptions.[4] More worryingly, those who are new to the field are frequently unclear as to what it is that political theorists actually *do* and are puzzled by the apparent unwillingness of scholars to reveal and interrogate the assumptions that shape their day-to-day practice.

It was in order to address these concerns that our colleague Michael Freeden initiated a graduate-level course in research methods in political theory in the Department of Politics and International Relations at the University of Oxford, a course for which responsibility more recently fell on us. Its aim was to enable those beginning advanced work in political theory to question their assumptions about what such work might entail, and to encourage them to think seriously about how it should best be conducted. While designing a relevant programme of study to meet these aims, it quickly became apparent that even within a single department such as ours there was little agreement about what methods and approaches are best suited to the tasks of political theory today. Some colleagues conducted historical work, often using primary sources hidden away in archives; others analysed questions formally, employing methods borrowed from economics and game theory; still others combined techniques from analytical philosophy with those from empirical social science. Moreover, there was significant disagreement as to the proper object of study in political theory. Some felt that it lay in scrutinizing the meaning and value of key terms in our contemporary political vocabulary; others argued for the need to make concrete recommendations for public policy; others emphasized the importance of recovering lost traditions of thought and comparing them with the established norms of today.

---

[3] For an introduction to these arguments, see Catherine Zuckert and Michael Zuckert, *The Truth about Leo Strauss: Political Philosophy and American Democracy* (Chicago: Chicago University Press, 2006) and Barry Cooper, *Eric Voeglein and the Foundations of Modern Political Science* (Columbia, MO: Missouri University Press, 1999).

[4] See Vincent, *Nature of Political Theory*, pp. 1–3.

Such diversity provided a daunting challenge, making it impossible to capture the essence of the practice of political theory in any single explanatory framework. However, it also offered a great opportunity. It became evident that the study of methods and approaches in political theory was not only vocationally useful for those beginning research, but might also reveal crucial insights into the nature, point, and purpose of the discipline itself. Debates about practical 'methods' in political theory thus developed into arguments about overall 'approach'; the task of reconsidering daily practices led on to thinking more critically about the very foundations of the subject itself, its rationale and epistemological and metaethical underpinnings. Far from being a distraction from the task of conducting 'substantive' research, such methodological conversations added significantly to our appreciation of the character and value of our work.

This book is a continuation of the conversations that began as a result of that initiative. Its aim is not to promote any single way of conducting research in political theory, nor to suggest that any single set of methodological guidelines can protect students from error and shepherd them towards the 'truth'. Instead, it presents a range of alternatives, with each chapter championing or interrogating a particular perspective. Contributors outline the merits and difficulties of particular approaches, and describe some of the day-to-day tasks involved in their pursuit. Taken together, these chapters provide a snapshot of some of the many ways in which political theory is conducted today. Our hope is that readers will thereby have the opportunity to reflect on a wide range of approaches, to consider the relevance of these approaches for their own work, and to reshape their understandings and expectations of political theory accordingly.

Despite our commitment to plurality, not every method and approach is covered here. For instance, there are no chapter-length discussions of Leo Strauss and his followers, the proponents of Natural Law theory, or particular variants of post-structuralism. Such absences are partly because what follows reflects a discussion taking place in just one particular centre of political theory at one particular time. In addition, we doubt that it is possible to survey the vast multiplicity of available methods and approaches in political theory adequately in a single volume of this sort. We hope that these absences are not taken in the wrong spirit; what follows is intended as an invitation to others to debate, and not an effort to provide the conclusive word on questions of method. Our aim is rather to aid understanding and to stimulate argument by examining assumptions that all too often remain obscure in political theory today, to enable both senior scholars and those newer to the field to see the hidden workings of the discipline, to re-evaluate the practical tools of analysis employed, and to think again about why the research they do matters.

2

Each of the chapters in this volume has been written so that it can be read as a stand-alone piece. Students may wish to pick their way through the collection selectively, paying closest attention to the chapters which cover issues that are pertinent to their own work and choosing those pieces which help them most in their own reflections on questions of method and approach. However, there are some striking common themes which enable a broader narrative to emerge. Perhaps the most important of these larger themes is the question of the complex relationship between political theory and related disciplines. Most of the chapters trace some aspect of those contested connections, examining issues of both subject matter and practical approach. No consent or agreement is sought between the various arguments presented, as one of the key purposes of the collection is to illustrate variety. Nonetheless, close attention to this theme does provide one pathway through the chapters that follow.

Daniel McDermott opens this volume by outlining the approach often called 'analytical political philosophy'. McDermott portrays political theory as a *complement to*, rather than a branch of, the social sciences. Whereas social scientists are concerned with empirical facts about human behaviour and institutions, McDermott insists that political theorists are properly concerned with moral 'oughts'. As such, political theory should be thought of as a branch of moral philosophy. More precisely, political theory should be thought of as the branch of moral philosophy that deals with the rules of morality as applied to states. Such theory is said to be truly 'analytical' when its reflection on these issues takes the same approach, broadly speaking, as the natural and social sciences (even though its subject matter remains distinct). Although this may seem an unlikely comparison, McDermott employs a series of plausible analogies in order to make his case, concentrating especially on the development and testing of theories in both political theory and the natural sciences. In pursuing his argument, McDermott contends that the primary purpose of political theory is the pursuit of the 'truth' in matters of political morality. He roundly rejects the widespread view that analytical political theorists should aim to derive their principles from an existing consensus or agreement, or from a hypothetical agreement among 'reasonable' people.

In the second chapter, David Miller further examines the relationship between claims of 'fact' and claims of 'value' in the enterprise of political theory. He sets out to demonstrate that the political principles of political theory are in some important ways dependent on underlying 'facts' of political and social life. The task of the political theorist is thus, in Miller's view, to investigate both the principles and the facts that underpin them. This is not strictly incompatible with McDermott's position, but Miller diverges from McDermott in his insistence that the relevant facts include facts about the deeply held commitments and beliefs of members of a society or kind of society. The status of our political principles, he claims, is at least partially dependent on widely held beliefs about those principles. Miller draws out two practical implications of his argument for those engaging in their own research in political theory: first, that political theorists should always attempt to be clear and appropriately modest about the scope of their principles, avoiding, for example, any confusion of the particular with the universal; second, that political theorists should ensure that arguments they make about core political principles respect beliefs about those principles that are held by the public at large.

One implication of Miller's view is that political theorists need to become aware of the arguments of those in the empirical social sciences. This theme is taken up further by Adam Swift and Stuart White in Chapter 3. Swift and White interrogate the relationship between political theorists and the world of 'real politics'; the world of politicians and other policymakers. They note that all policy choices and political positions presuppose, more or less explicitly, the kind of principled or normative commitments which form the subject matter of political theory, and they suggest that the insights of political theorists may well be helpful in the policymaking process. They also note, however, that there are some circumstances in which the insights of political theory are of more limited purchase in the world of real politics, and in which the expertise of others becomes important. Swift and White overcome this difficulty by calling for a 'division of labour' between political theorists, empirical social scientists, and practitioners of politics. They think that the role of political theorists, in this context, is best described as 'democratic under-labouring'; theorists should understand their role as contributing to, and not short-circuiting, the democratic process. In order to play that role effectively, political theorists need to be alert to the differences between ideal and non-ideal theory, make efforts to understand the social scientific evidence, show tolerance for the particular characteristics of real politics and of real politicians, and avoid unnecessary abstruseness and complexity.

Chapter 4 pursues the relationship between political theory and the social sciences from a somewhat different angle. Iwao Hirose asks whether the formal theoretical methods more often associated with economics and social choice theory might have a role to play in political theory. Formal theory, he explains, uses mathematical and logical symbols to model political behaviour and phenomena. When used well, Hirose maintains, such models can offer an alternative and illuminating point of view for political theorists, helping them to see old issues in a new light, in particular by elucidating their form or structure. He seeks to persuade the reader of this by considering a number of issues in political theory from a formal perspective. In one example, Hirose shows how formal methods might be used to illuminate a current debate in egalitarian political theory: the argument between Derek Parfit and the advocates of so-called 'telic egalitarianism'. Hirose demonstrates that a formal modelling of the claims of 'telic egalitarianism' helps us to understand better the ways in which the theory's advocates could respond to Parfit's critique. This example and others in Hirose's chapter are designed to illustrate his argument that formal theory can reinforce normative political theory. Formal and informal approaches to theory are not mutually exclusive, Hirose insists, but should be seen as partners in a potentially fruitful collaboration.

In Chapter 5, Lois McNay develops the connections between research in political theory and other branches of political and social enquiry. However, her concern could not be more different from Hirose's. Rather than trying to connect political theory with mathematical modelling, she emphasizes the importance of the relationship between political theory and 'critical social theory' of the sort practised, for example, by Jürgen Habermas. McNay demonstrates that the contested connections between these two approaches are at the heart of contemporary debates about the politics of recognition. Theorists of recognition maintain that we need to think of individuals as constitutively situated within a specific social context—rather than, for example, as abstract ends in themselves—in order to think meaningfully about desirable political arrangements. McNay examines this argumentative thread as it is developed in the work of both Habermas and John Rawls. She shows how one aspect of Habermas' critique of Rawls can be applied to his own work, and concludes that neither author actually succeeds in integrating claims in political theory with sophisticated understandings of the prevailing social order. In short, the account of personhood presupposed both by Rawls' theory of justice and by Habermas' communicative ethics appears insubstantial, crucially lacking in determinate social content. Normative political theory, of both a Rawlsian and a Habermasian variant, is to be sharply criticized for its inadequately examined sociological assumptions. In making such a claim, McNay is not encouraging us to abandon political theory in favour of social theory, but is rather trying to get us to take seriously the possibility of a constructive dialogue between the two.

The relationship between mainstream analytical approaches and seemingly radical alternatives also provides the subject matter of Chapter 6. Here, David Leopold takes a sceptical but not dismissive look at another proposed alternative to mainstream analytical methods. He structures his discussion around a contrast between 'extravagant' and 'modest' accounts of dialectic found within the Marxist tradition. He examines exemplars of these two contrasting accounts taken from either end of the twentieth century, with the writings of the Hungarian Marxist Georg Lukács and the work of the Analytical Marxist school illustrating the extravagant and modest possibilities, respectively. Leopold's chapter ranges widely but develops three main claims.

First, talk about dialectic is often horribly confused. Not least, the term gets used of a huge variety of very different things. Second, some accounts of dialectic are more clear and persuasive than others. Few modern readers will swallow Hegel's account of the world as an organic structure, analogous to a human subject, but perhaps equally few would deny the possibility that it might be suggestive or illuminating to ascribe a dialectical pattern to certain processes in nature, society, or consciousness. Third, dialectical talk can often be translated into more analytical language. Leopold is sceptical about the suggestion that dialectic makes sense as a methodological alternative to analytical approaches (provided that the latter are characterized fairly). In particular, defending the idea of dialectic need not offer support for those who insist on the existence of a radical gulf between 'dialectical' and 'analytical' reasoning.

At this point, this volume turns away from the relationship between political theory and social theory and moves instead to one of the most controversial questions in the study of political theory today: the relationship between political theory and history. Mark Philp begins this discussion in Chapter 7, asking whether political theorists have distinctive reasons for being interested in history in general and the history of political thought in particular. Political theory and history intersect, he maintains, not only in that contemporary political theory is shaped by its past but also in that the past is one field on which theorists can draw for insights and evidence. Philp cautions us, however, to remember that historical approaches do not and should not displace the distinctive concerns of political theory. In particular, he rejects what he sees as the relativizing of truth in many historical studies of conceptual change. As political theorists, he argues, our interest in the past should be subordinated to our disciplinary concern with perennial questions in political theory, including understanding the character of political rule, the conditions for social order, the parameters of political possibility, and the analysis of the values we should pursue within those possibilities.

In Chapter 8, Sudhir Hazareesingh and Karma Nabulsi approach the relation between history and political theory from a very different angle. They insist on the centrality of historical methods to successful work in political theory, and consider the ways in which archival documents of various kinds can illuminate political questions, especially when those sources are understood as part of a political tradition. A political tradition should be understood as a distinct and stable body of thought which serves as the principal basis for argument and theorized action by individuals, groups, and states. Political traditions constitute a way in which a coherent body of political thought and practice is passed from one generation to another. Hazareesingh and Nabulsi use a series of examples from the republican tradition, broadly construed, to illustrate the potential of this interpretative framework. One of these examples concerns Rousseau who, in the *Social Contract*, is often said to have appealed to a distinction between combatants and civilians. However, careful attention to the political tradition on which he drew, and to which he contributed, reveals Rousseau rather as a promoter of republican war which incorporates citizen involvement in defence. Political traditions, on this account, form the active site of, and not simply the passive backdrop to, political theorizing. In tracing some developing threads in this tradition of war, the authors emphasize the importance not just of focusing on practical and theoretical activity but also of broadening our notion of sources beyond 'classic' texts, to include pamphlets, proclamations, parliamentary and other debates, film, song, and even ceremony and ritual. These sources, they conclude, act as a corrective to the 'tyranny of the present', the parochial and false notion that present-day challenges are unique. The authors see the history of ideas and political theory as 'interdependent' realms, and maintain that theorizing without sensitive historical understanding is necessarily impoverished.

Having surveyed the relationship between political theory and history, moral philosophy, social science, public opinion, practical politics, formal modelling, and social theory, the final two chapters in this volume ask whether there is anything distinctive about the idea of a *political* theory, as opposed to any other sort of theory. They begin by noting that a surprising number of (otherwise dissimilar) accounts insist that political theory does *not* have a distinctive subject matter, that it is really just ethics, law, economics, social theory, or something else. The variety of contenders for the role of substitute is striking, and the resulting methodological implications can vary considerably. There is a similar diversity among those supporting the contrasting view of the political as a distinct realm which resists reduction to some other sphere. Elizabeth Frazer and Michael Freeden give us two different ways of negotiating these crucial disputes.

In Chapter 9, Elizabeth Frazer reminds us that the scope and value of 'politics' is itself a fiercely contested issue. She shows how 'politics' and its various cognates get used in a wide variety of different senses, and with positive, negative, and neutral evaluative connotations. Frazer distinguishes, in particular, between those who identify the distinctive character of politics with 'means' and those who identify it with 'ends'. Her discussion ranges widely over views of politics which can be labelled 'Machiavellian', 'Weberian', 'Platonic', 'Aristotelian', and 'Arendtian'. Politics here gets associated variously with domination or conflict, with harmony, with the city state, and with cooperative endeavour. Among the issues raised are the precise boundary between state and society, and whether and how that boundary might map onto the division between the political and other areas of life. Given this breadth of issues, and the variety of positions taken on those issues, there is scarcely room in one chapter to clarify, still less resolve, all of the questions raised. Frazer's ambition here is rather to convey a sense of the scale, complexity, and import of these disputes about the subject matter of politics.

This theme is taken up further in Chapter 10, the final chapter in this volume, by Michael Freeden. He insists on the centrality of what he calls the study of 'actual political thinking': the language, subtleties, and structure of ordinary manifestations of political thought. The study of actual political thinking has two constituent parts, which Freeden calls thinking *in* a political manner and thinking *about* politics. The former refers to 'thought-practices' deemed to be political (such as ranking priorities or justifying power); the latter refers to the various ideological configurations which shape our thinking about politics. He insists that since both aspects of political thinking are structured conceptually and expressed linguistically, 'finality' as regards meaning is unobtainable. Political theorists consequently need to develop tools and approaches which cope with the indeterminacy and vagueness of language, and in doing so draw from other disciplines, such as hermeneutics. Our thinking *about* politics is organized through ideologies: structured clusters of concepts in which one conception of a concept is selected, or decontested, by being placed in a particular relationship with other surrounding concepts. As Hazareesingh and Nabulsi also maintained, students of ideologies should not limit their sources to the familiar 'canonical' texts, but extend them to include other political writings, parliamentary debates, newspaper editorials, popular literature including pamphlets and belles-lettres, everyday conversation, and even visual and aural displays, such as ceremony and architecture. Freeden contends that drawing on these broader, non-elitist, spheres of political thinking can help 'democratize' the study of political thought. He concludes by reflecting on some ways in which the study of actual political thinking (whose most developed aspect is the study of ideologies) could be combined with political philosophy and the history of political thought, and some ways in which the various practitioners of these disciplines might learn from each other.

3

This emphasis on plurality—of method and of subject matter—is an appropriate place for this volume to end. If there is one overall conclusion to emerge from the chapters here, it is that political theory is an exceptionally wide-ranging and open-ended branch of scholarly enquiry, within which there is very little in the way of settled agreement with regard to questions of method and approach. Such open-endedness provides those new to the field with great opportunities. They can make their way in research without needing to stay within a rigid methodological paradigm and they are, accordingly, far freer to experiment than their colleagues in some cognate disciplines. However, this open-endedness can also present serious challenges. It can be very difficult to make one's way into a new field of study without a clear understanding of the expectations of its practitioners and a secure sense of how successful research is conducted within it. Our goal here is not to suggest that there is only one right way to conduct research in political theory, but rather to introduce readers to some of the methods and approaches that currently inform the work of leading scholars in the field. If this volume helps new practitioners to negotiate their way around the discipline, without dampening their willingness to explore and innovate, it will have succeeded in its aims.

1 Analytical political philosophy[1]

Daniel McDermott

1

Analytical political philosophy is a complement to social science. Whereas social scientists aim to determine the empirical facts about human behaviour and institutions, political philosophers aim to determine what *ought* to be done in light of that information. How should states be organized? What kinds of projects should they pursue? Are there some actions that are impermissible? No set of empirical facts can dictate the answers to these kinds of questions. You could pile up a mountain of data about the differences between, say, democracies and dictatorships, but without the normative element that is the political philosopher's concern, nothing would follow about which form of government ought to be implemented.

What distinguishes the enterprise as *analytical*? This label is often applied to draw a contrast with other styles of philosophy, such as Continental and Eastern. It is also typically associated with certain features, such as clarity, systematic rigour, narrowness of focus, and an emphasis on the importance of reason. There are a number of different ways to characterize it, but probably the best is that analytical political philosophy is an approach to gaining knowledge that falls into the same broad category as science.

This claim may sound like an extravagant conceit. Many scientists, I'm sure, would argue that they are engaged in a very different kind of endeavour. There is no denying that there are differences, but at the basic level the two disciplines have a great deal in common. That, in any case, is the idea I develop here. Building on my primitive understanding of how things work in science, I illustrate some of the methods of analytical political philosophy by way of comparison. This is not meant to be an exhaustive survey of methods, nor is it meant to be impartial. While many political philosophers do go about their business in the way I describe, much of what follows is controversial,

[1] For helpful criticisms of earlier drafts of this chapter, I thank Mark Philp, Jonathan Quong, and Adam Swift.

and throughout this chapter I take a stand on how I think political philosophy should be done.

2

Political philosophers traffic in 'oughts'—*moral* oughts. The discipline is thus a branch, or subset, of moral philosophy. Taking the citizen–state relationship as the target of their investigations, political philosophers try to figure out the implications of the requirements of morality for this relationship, a particular instance of the more general problem with which moral philosophers are concerned.

Suppose, then, that we wanted to investigate a problem of political philosophy. There is some institutional arrangement, or some type of state action, that is controversial, and we want to figure out what morality has to say about the issue. That may seem like a daunting task. Where would one even begin such a project?

The method is, in the first instance, straightforward: start with what we think we know and use that as a basis to investigate what we don't know. What do we think we know? Most sane adults are in possession of a complex package of beliefs about the content of morality, beliefs such as, for example, that we shouldn't commit theft, rape, and murder, that we should fulfil promises and help the needy, and that states shouldn't punish the innocent or engage in racial discrimination. If I were to try to plot my beliefs in relation to the set of all the oughts, the picture might look something like this:

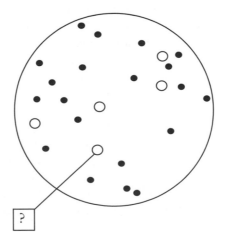

Each of the solid points represents a particular belief about what ought to be done in which I am reasonably confident. Each open circle represents a moral question to which I do not know the answer, or I am unsure about, or that is so controversial that I'm willing to suspend judgement. The target of the investigation, the problem I hope to solve, is the circle that is singled out: should my state do A or –A?

The role of a normative theory is to help solve this kind of problem by providing better understanding of the requirements of morality. Theories are composed of elements—such as principles, rules, goals, rights, and duties—and those elements serve to illuminate the connections and relationships between the oughts. Ideally, a theory would capture everything, providing a complete picture of morality. No theory is perfect, however, and so the best we can hope for is a partial picture, one that will include significant gaps. Furthermore, it is likely that some of the beliefs with which we started will have to be abandoned in order to accommodate favoured principles, a move that should yield benefits such as greater consistency, coherence, and understanding. The actual process by which one develops and tailors a theory in relation to its target is complicated, but if all goes well, a pattern should emerge from which we can infer a solution to our problem –A.[2]

Consider, for example, one of the most important problems in political philosophy—the legitimacy problem. States make demands of us, such as that we pay taxes, and they back these demands up with the threat of force. *Should* they be doing this? Are they committing any injustice by acting this way? What if I were to make similar demands of you, forcing you to give me money at the point of a gun? That would obviously be unjust, so why believe that things are any different when states engage in this kind of behaviour? Anarchists will respond that there is no difference, and that what these institutions should do is stop perpetrating such injustices. This is not a terribly popular view, but political philosophers have taken it very seriously, for it is essentially the position of the sceptic about legitimate political authority. In response, they have developed a number of competing theories of state legitimacy, each of which purports to account for how states come to hold the right to make demands of their citizens.

The most well known of these theories is consent theory, which holds that state legitimacy is grounded in the consent of the governed. Why take this theory seriously? The theory gains much of its strength from the fact that, across a wide range of arenas, the voluntary choices of individuals trigger transfers of rights. If, as part of a theory, we were to identify the connection between those particular cases—such as the choice to promise, to make a contract, to consent to sex, and so on—then we might call this the principle of voluntary transfer (V):

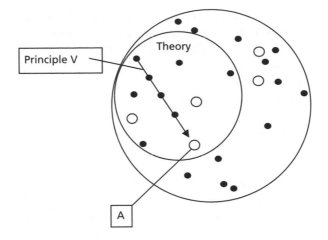

Consent theory applies this principle to the citizen–state relationship: it is the citizens' choice to consent that puts a state in a position of authority over them. So, if a particular state does in fact meet the conditions necessary for gaining valid consent, then the consent theorist will conclude (*contra* the anarchist) that the institution is legitimate (A), a conclusion that draws its strength from its consistency with all those other oughts.

That is obviously an oversimplification of both consent theory and the political philosopher's method. At this level, however, the method is not much different from the one employed by scientists. Confronted with a scientific problem, some feature of the natural world that they don't understand, scientists start with what they think they know, and they use that as a basis to gain insights about what they do not know. If we were to map a scientific theory, it would look identical to the one above, only the solid points would now represent my beliefs about the physical data, the 'is's' rather than the 'oughts'. The role of the scientific theory is to provide a better understanding of the empirical facts, identifying connections and relationships between them that are spelled out in terms of laws, principles, and so on. If all goes well, the theory will yield a pattern, suggesting a solution to the particular problem (A), just as with the normative theory.

At this point, some will object that I'm overlooking an important disanalogy between these two enterprises. Whereas scientists build their theories around the facts, there are no facts on the other side. Political philosophers merely deal in 'intuitions', which makes whatever theories they develop fundamentally different.

It is true that political philosophers sometimes talk as if intuitions were the subject of their investigations. Political philosophy, according to this view, is a type of intuition-ology, a project whose goal is to shed light upon the philosopher's intuitions about political arrangements. Why anyone should care about the outcome of this kind of onanistic enterprise is not clear, but what is clear is that this way of thinking is confused. Intuitions are not the subject in political philosophy. The oughts are the subject, and an ought is not an intuition.

Intuition is an intellectual faculty that human beings employ to make judgements. The mechanics of human judgement are still largely a mystery, but what we do know is that many of the conclusions we reach are not the product of conscious calculations. Instead, they are the result of a gut feeling in response to the available evidence, a reaction that we call an 'intuition'. I may, for example, have an intuition that there is a mistake in a mathematical proof, even though I haven't taken the time to work through it to identify the error. Or I may have an intuition that if I try to jump ten feet in the air, I will fail. Or I may have an intuition that it is wrong for states to outlaw unpopular religions. The strength and reliability of intuitions can vary significantly, but the important point is that is all of these intuitions are directed outward: they are intuitions *about something*, about the facts, whether mathematical, physical, or moral.

Another way of putting this is that political philosophers rely upon intuitions when trying to determine what the rules of morality require, but those intuitions are not *themselves* the rules of morality.

It is easy to see why some might think that moral intuitions are fundamentally different from those about the physical world. Moral truths cannot be seen, touched, or located in space, and so, the thinking goes, if the principles are not 'out there' somewhere, then they must be 'in here' somewhere, a part of my internal make-up. But would anyone say a similar thing about mathematical truths? Such truths cannot be seen, touched, or located, but they obviously have nothing to do with me or what's inside my head. It won't change anything for the political philosopher to switch the focus of the discussion to 'our' intuitions, as a group or a political community, and cast the problem as one of bringing 'harmony' to these diverse intuitions. Leaving aside the fact that, in practice, when a political philosopher mentions 'our' intuitions that invariably means 'my' intuitions, the problem is that an intuition without a target is nonsense. As for harmonizing intuitions across a political community, harmonizing nothing with nothing will yield you exactly nothing.

This leads to a deeper, and more interesting, version of the objection to the political philosopher's project: there simply are no moral facts, ever. The theories political philosophers develop really are theories about nothing, like those medieval theologians developed about the number of angels that could fit on the head of a pin.

This is a genuine worry, but it is the kind of *metaethical* worry that is none of the political philosopher's business. In philosophy, as in most intellectual endeavours, progress depends in part upon a successful division of labour. All of biology, for example, is ultimately physics, but that does not mean biologists should become physicists. Nor should they allow worries about the origins of the universe to distract them from their projects. To make any progress, biologists must be prepared to leave all sorts of important problems for others to solve—and the same holds true for political philosophers.

My claim that political philosophers should set aside worries about whether there are moral facts is controversial, and I may be in the minority here, but consider an example that illustrates my point. Imagine that you and I wanted to play chess, but that we didn't know the rules of the game. The board and the pieces are in front of us, and we face the *normative* problem of determining how they should and should not be moved. How could we solve this problem? Well, we could consult books, or talk to experts, or watch other people play, but suppose that I were to suggest that our first step should be to tackle some metaethical issues. Before we can know what the rules of chess require, wouldn't we first need to know what a rule is? Then there is the problem of determining whether, and how, rules give us reasons. And besides, what is a reason anyway? These are interesting questions, but focusing on them, rather than on our normative problem, would almost certainly be a waste of time. There is no need to get distracted by metaethical worries to figure out the rules of chess, in other words, as should be clear from the fact that many people do learn how to play the game without ever studying ethics.

None of this should be taken to mean that metaethics has no relevance to what goes on in political philosophy, because the outcome of metaethical investigations could well have profound implications for particular normative theories. The point, instead, is that to do political philosophy successfully one must recognize, and truly accept, that it is essentially a normative enterprise. The concern, in other words, is to identify the *content* of the rules of morality as applied to states, a project that can and should proceed without getting bogged down with worries about the nature and origins of those rules. Just as we should assume that there are such things as the rules of chess if we want to figure out how to play the game, so too should political philosophers make assumptions to get their project going, one of which is that there are such things as moral facts.[3]

Of course, because these are assumptions, any theory based upon them will remain vulnerable to failure if they turn out to be false. But then, scientists are in exactly the same position. All scientific theories rest on undefended

---

[3] I suspect that this holds true even for non-cognitivists, who do not believe that moral claims can be true or false, but merely reflect the pro and con attitudes of those who make them. Supposing that one can, as a non-cognitivist, develop a political theory, then this project is unlikely to be helped by constantly reminding oneself that it is a non-cognitivist theory. Instead, to make any progress, the non-cognitivist would have to frame the theory using the same kind of normative language that the rest of us use when making claims about which projects states should and should not pursue.

assumptions, often extremely sensible assumptions, but assumptions nevertheless.

Nature, scientists assume, is orderly, which leads geologists and palaeontologists to build theories about things that happened in the distant past based upon regularities they witness today, and which leads astronomers to build theories about what is going on in the far corners of the universe based upon what they observe occurring locally. The centrality of *observation* in science raises further difficulties, as scientists assume that the evidence of their senses in some way reliably corresponds to what's going on in the external world. But maybe it doesn't. Maybe all that we see before us is an illusion—maybe we're living in the Matrix. Scientists can't *prove* that their assumptions about any of these matters are true—these really are assumptions—and so their theories could fail if they turn out to be false. This possibility won't cause them to lose much sleep, however, nor should the possibility that there are no moral facts cause political philosophers to lose much sleep. Success in any intellectual endeavour requires the confidence to make assumptions, along with the wisdom to tell the good from the bad.

3

Political philosophers certainly develop theories, and perhaps there is a crude similarity between these theories and scientific theories, but, sceptics will be quick to point out, there is still a major difference between the two enterprises: normative theories cannot be *tested*. Whereas scientists have tests to keep them honest, determining whether their theories succeed or fail, political philosophers face no such threat, leaving them free to build castles in the sky without any real fear of failure.

There is a grain of truth in this objection. There is no laboratory experiment we could conduct, nor any physical data we could gather, to test the principles upon which normative theories rest. Nevertheless, the claim that such theories cannot be tested at all is false. The assumption animating the objection is that 'test' is synonymous with '*empirical* test', but that is a narrow and naive understanding of what a test is. Because the subject matter of scientific theories is the physical world, they should be subjected to empirical tests. There are other disciplines, however, whose subject matter is such that the appropriate way to test their theories is by conducting non-empirical tests.

At this point, a sceptic could make two very silly claims in response. First, that there are no truths apart from those that can be empirically tested. Second, while there may be truths that cannot be empirically tested, those truths not are worth pursuing.

Both of these claims are tenets of scientism, a quasi-religious faith in the power of science that, like all religious faith, serves to protect its adherents from having to think about uncomfortable questions. None of us, not even scientists, would get very far in life relying only on beliefs that can be empirically tested. The truths of mathematics and logic, for example, cannot be empirically tested. Nor can the truths of etiquette and grammar. Do you think it would be rude for me to throw a drink in my host's face at a dinner party? Is this sentence grammatically correct English: 'Sally the shopping buy'? The answers to such questions cannot be tested empirically, but that doesn't mean there is no truth of the matter. Nor does it mean that such questions are not important. Of course we should care about being polite and writing well, and so we have good reason to investigate these issues.

Scientists do not hold a monopoly on truth, but can non-scientific claims really be tested? Though it may sound strange, this is a process we engage in all the time. Theories are composed of elements, such as principles or rules, and those elements can be tested by considering their implications, running them against particular cases or against other elements. Suppose, for example, that I were to claim that it is a rule of English grammar that all verbs take the letters 'ed' to form the past tense, as in she talk*ed*, she walk*ed*, and she jump*ed*. Is that correct? Obviously not. And the way to determine this would be to subject my rule to some tests, considering verbs such as *bought*, *saw*, and *went*, cases where the rule is flatly incompatible with the data.

Political philosophers employ different kinds of tests for their theories, but the basic idea is the same. Consider again consent theory. As I presented it, this theory faces a major problem: citizens in modern societies apparently do not consent to the authority of their states. Recognizing this problem, consent theorists have modified the theory, aiming to ground states' rights over citizens not in the act of *express* consent, but in the act of *tacit* consent. The idea is that there are things that citizens do in their daily lives that have the same moral effect as saying the words 'I consent', acts such as using the roads, owning property, or even continuing to reside in a territory.[4] So long as the individual has the option to leave, the theory holds, then the choice to remain is a sign of consent to the authority of the governing institution. Many have found this theory to be convincing, but it has been subjected to a number of devastating tests. David Hume put forward a particularly good case, asking us to imagine a person who has been taken by force onto a ship and who is then, once far out at sea, given this choice: submit to the authority of the ship's master, or else get off the ship. Would this individual's decision to remain be a genuine sign of consent? Hume didn't think so, and he argued that this person's situation is not significantly different from the one faced by many citizens, since the alternative to continued residence in their native countries

---

[4] John Locke, the most important consent theorist, claimed that such actions are signs of tacit consent. See John Locke, in Peter Laslett (edited), *Two Treatises of Government* (Cambridge: Cambridge University Press, 1960).

would be a life without family, friends, and most of what they value in life, a fate almost as bad as walking the plank.

Does this test provide sufficient basis to reject consent theory? Not for some consent theorists, who have responded by claiming that there are important differences between the rule of a just, democratic state and that of a tyrannical master on a ship, and it is only in the former situation that the theory of tacit consent applies. One way to test this position would be to consider more particular cases, but another is to re-examine the principle upon which the theory rests. Recall that consent theory, in its original form, drew its strength from its consistency with the larger pattern of oughts, all those other cases where a *voluntary* choice leads to a transfer of rights. In the revised version, however, the element of voluntarism is cast aside, for it now seems that people can 'consent' even if they are unaware that they are doing so, and even if the costs of not consenting would be disastrous.[5] The defect with tacit consent theory is thus not merely a minor inability to handle a troublesome case—it is that this version is inconsistent with the very principle that made consent theory plausible in the first place.

Consent theory has been one of the most influential theories in political philosophy. It is also a theory that demonstrates that political theories can be tested—and that they can fail. For other theories, it won't be so clear how to test them, or whether they pass or fail, but such difficulties (which scientists must face as well) pose no threat to the claim that such theories can be tested.

The sceptic might respond at this point that these kinds of normative 'tests' involve a circularity that renders them meaningless. The philosopher's method, as I've sketched it, is to build a theory based on his normative beliefs—the 'oughts' as he sees them. And then, when it comes time to test that theory, what does he test it against? More of his normative beliefs. Doesn't that seem like cheating?

Perhaps it is, but if so, then scientists are guilty of exactly the same offence. Scientists build theories based on their beliefs about the empirical world, beliefs that are ultimately grounded in the evidence of their senses. When it comes time to test those theories, what do they test them against? More of their empirical beliefs. The evidence they gather, the experiments they conduct, all of it is based on the evidence of their senses, the only connection creatures like us have with the external world. Thus, a scientific theory, just like a normative theory, will eventually end up in a perfect circle.

Circles, perfect or otherwise, are deeply unsatisfying. When confronted with one, the natural urge is to try to break out, to find stronger support for the theory by going to a 'deeper' level. In moral and political philosophy, this has often led to a search from some kind of empirical grounding for moral

---

[5] See A. John Simmons, *Moral Principles and Political Obligations* (Princeton: Princeton University Press, 1979), chapters 3–4.

principles. That may sound like a sensible move, but suppose I were to attempt something similar with a physical theory, looking for a way out of the circle by finding the *moral* grounds for the laws of nature. This kind of thing is not unheard of ('Galileo must be incorrect', I proclaim, 'because the idea that the Earth is not the centre of the universe is evil'), but it is obviously pretty foolish. Attempting to ground the moral in the physical certainly seems less foolish, and plenty of smart people have thought it a project worth pursuing, but for what it's worth, I think this is mostly driven by an inability to accept that the normative and the empirical are just different kinds of things. To hope for the day when we identify the physical grounds for particular moral principles is like hoping for the day when scientists identify the physical grounds for the rules of English grammar, the day when we can finally understand the truth of, say, the rule of subject–verb agreement right down to the level of protons and electrons.

4

One of the reasons tests play such an important role in science is that they are an excellent way of settling disputes. I have a theory, you are sceptical of my claims, and so we conduct some tests. If all goes well, then the outcome of these tests should settle the matter, demonstrating to the satisfaction of both of us whether my claims are correct.

Is that the way things work in political philosophy? Political philosophers may have similar aspirations, but their tests, it seems, rarely settle things. No matter how sensible a normative theory may appear, we can be sure that people will disagree about it, and we can also be sure that they will continue to disagree regardless of the outcomes of any tests.

Imagine, for example, that a neighbour and I are having a dispute over the practice of cannibalism. He believes that it is morally permissible to kill and eat anyone who sets foot on his lawn, and he is outraged that our state might interfere with him. I disagree. Brimming with confidence after years of studying philosophy, I prepare to undermine his position with a few simple tests. First, I make an appeal to *rights*, pointing out that the practice conflicts with the right to life. He responds by agreeing that there is such a right, but says that it is forfeited when someone commits the crime of trespassing. I then take a different route, claiming that it would be *unfair* to take a person's life away for this offence. He says that there is nothing unfair about this, because he'd be vulnerable to exactly the same treatment if he stepped on anyone else's lawn. Next, I make an appeal to human *dignity*, arguing that it is disrespectful to treat other persons as food. He agrees that we should respect other persons, but claims that anyone foolish enough to set foot on his lawn doesn't deserve respect. I try a few other routes, and he makes some concessions along the way (he accepts, for example, that mentally retarded trespassers shouldn't be eaten, though he hedges by pointing out that such people should have been killed at birth). On the main issue, however, every strategy I try fails, and it becomes clear that he and I will never agree about cannibalism.

What conclusion should I draw from this encounter? Stay off my neighbour's lawn, obviously. There are some, however, who believe that this kind of disagreement, and the inability of any tests to resolve it, shows that normative theories are fundamentally different from scientific theories. Indeed, some will go so far as to infer that there is no truth of the matter in this domain, just differing opinions.

Let's *test* that idea by changing the example a bit, so that my neighbour is no longer a cannibal, but something far worse. Suppose, now, that he is a *creationist*, and that we are having an argument about human origins. He believes that humans were deliberately created by an intelligent superbeing, while I believe that they are merely the outcome of a natural process that is accounted for by the theory of evolution. Our debate proceeds in a similar fashion. I claim that all species of animals on this planet, including human beings, have evolved over time from a common ancestor, and he responds by claiming that God created all of them at once. I then point to the fossil record, arguing that it shows a pattern of progressive development, with simpler life forms at lower layers and more complex forms at higher layers. He claims that they were all there from the beginning, but that they died out at different rates. I ask why we never see any human skeletons at the bottom layers, and he plays his trump card: God has hidden those fossils to test our faith. The debate continues along these lines until, again, we reach a point where it becomes clear that we will never agree about evolution.

What conclusion should I draw from this encounter? Well, I certainly wouldn't infer from the fact of our disagreement that there is no truth of the matter about human origins, just differing opinions. Nor would I allow this disagreement to undermine my confidence in scientific methods and tests. What I'd conclude, instead, is that my neighbour is a bonehead.

That is not because I can *prove* he is wrong, because I cannot. The creationist's theory gives a central role to an all-knowing, all-powerful magical creature. I cannot prove that this creature does not exist, nor can I prove that it didn't do all of the things the creationist claims. (Nor can I prove that fairies and leprechauns do not exist.) The disagreement between us, then, is every bit as intractable as any moral disagreement.

The idea that there is some radical difference between scientific and normative theories is based on the mistaken belief that in science facts are sufficient to settle disputes. The truth is that facts are never enough, because the success of a theory, whether in science or philosophy, ultimately rests on the uncertain terrain of individual judgement. We develop theories that seem to capture the truth, those theories are subjected to some tests, and then, once the evidence is in, it comes time to make an evaluation. Is the theory correct? Do the reasons in favour of accepting it outweigh those against it? At that point, all we have to rely on is an intuitive judgement that the theory *looks* right.

This may seem like an overly pessimistic view. Can't we at least point to the logical errors in creationist theories? And wouldn't those errors provide us with a decisive basis to conclude that their theories fail?

There is no doubt that creationists commit all sorts of errors, but there is a deeper issue here about the *limits* of theory that cannot be dodged. The dispute between creationists and evolutionists is not over competing arguments, which can be proven to succeed or fail, but over competing theories. Darwin and his defenders have certainly made many arguments in defence of the theory of evolution, but the theory itself is not an argument. A theory is a package of ideas, or elements, put together in order to explain or illuminate some phenomenon. Assembling a theory can be a very messy process, as it will involve the fitting and weighting of elements in relation to each other and the evidence. Good theories, unlike good arguments, can include problems, even inconsistencies. An invalid argument, like an invalid mathematical proof, is garbage, but a theory that has problems is not, simply for that reason, a failure. All good scientific theories have gaps, pieces that don't fit together, even contradictory elements. That's why scientists are still in business, attempting to work out those problems. Indeed, it is often such problems that set scientists onto the path to major discovery.

At the same time, however, those problems can serve as the basis for disagreement, because any particular problem with a theory could, in the end, turn out to be a fatal flaw. A good theory will be so powerful that only boneheads will reject it, but whether one accepts or rejects a theory still comes down to a value judgement—a judgement that the theory does a *better* job than its competitors. Neither scientific theories nor normative theories can ever give us anything stronger than that, and so we must resign ourselves to living with creationists, flat-earthers, astrologists, communitarians, and lots of other crackpots without any hope of ever proving them wrong.

All this talk of theory and its limits, I'm sure, will leave some philosophers cold. Do philosophers really develop theories in this sense? One obvious example is John Rawls' *theory* of justice. Rawls deploys plenty of arguments in his book, but theory itself is not an argument: it is a complex set of components put together to shed light on the structure and content of justice. Rawls is not a special case. I use the word 'theory' loosely to describe an intellectual tool that enables us to gain understanding that goes beyond observation and intuition alone. A theory need not be elaborate, nor Rawlsian, nor must its proponents endorse the method of 'reflective equilibrium'. What is crucial is that developing a theory is a process of organizing ideas in order to solve a problem, a process that is very different from making an argument, which taken by itself is sterile, a dead end.

5

No one can be compelled, as a matter of logic, to accept a theory, but that does not mean that all theories stand as equals. So far, I've been emphasizing the similarities between science and political philosophy, but I do think there is a genuine, and important, difference between the two enterprises: we can generally be more *confident* about the truth of scientific theories.

But why should that be the case? If both types of theories aim to account for facts, if there really is a truth of the matter, why should one be stronger than the other?

There are at least two reasons. First, the empirical judgements upon which scientific theories rest are usually more reliable. Human brains are machines that make many different types of judgements—about maths, language, etiquette, self-interest, morality, and physics—but the reliability of these judgements varies. That may be because in some areas the subject matter is fuzzier or more complex, or because our intellectual equipment is not as well suited to the tasks, or because of some combination of these factors. Whatever the case, I believe that my empirical judgements are generally far more reliable than my normative judgements. For example, I am extremely confident about what will happen if I hurl a piece of glass against a concrete wall, and that is due to my long history of being correct about such matters. My moral judgements, in contrast, inspire much less confidence, because I've so often been wrong about these things. Of course, we've all met people with unshakeable confidence in their moral judgements, people who think they never make moral errors—and such people are unbearable. For the rest of us, uncertainty is the near-constant companion of moral judgements, which translates into a relatively low level of confidence for any theories based upon those judgements.

This does not mean that all empirical judgements, simply because of their empirical content, necessarily occupy a superior position. Many of my beliefs about physics, for example, are based on little more than my confidence in the authority of experts. I guess I believe what scientists say about quantum mechanics is true, but that is not because I understand it in any meaningful sense. Or suppose, for example, that we were told by an omniscient god that one of the following beliefs is false: (*a*) the US landed men on the moon; (*b*) torturing small children for fun is morally wrong. I happen to think that both of those are true, but if I had to abandon one as false, it's not obvious to me that it should be (*b*). I wasn't at the moon landing: it is possible that, as some conspiracy theorists allege, the whole thing was faked, and so maybe this is the belief I should abandon. Whatever the case, I certainly wouldn't reject (*b*) simply because of its moral content.

The second reason to be more confident about scientific theories is that they typically command greater agreement. One way to gain confidence about a theory is to subject it to public scrutiny. I think that I've solved some problem, but I could be wrong, and so I turn to others to get their response. Does my theory succeed? Have I made any errors? If others look at my work and agree with my results, then that won't be sufficient to guarantee its success, but it would give me reason to be more confident about it. How much agreement theories tend to generate varies across disciplines, but nowhere is the level of agreement higher than in science. Most of us see the physical world in the same way, and so we get the same results from the same tests, leading to an extremely high level of agreement—and hence confidence—about the success of scientific theories.

Normative theories, in contrast, are usually much more controversial. Part of this is due to the fact that self-interest distorts moral judgements, but even among honest, well-intentioned people, there will always be significant moral and political disagreement. It is important, again, not to overstate the difference with science. From the outside it may seem like scientists form a harmonious community, with individual scientists unveiling new theories to the happy applause of their colleagues, when the truth is that scientists often disagree profoundly about methods and results, leading to disputes as bitter as any you'll find in a humanities department. Nevertheless, that all takes place against a background of agreement whose range and depth far outstrips that of any other discipline.

Taken together, these two factors account for much of the difference in confidence between science and political philosophy, but that difference is still, in the end, a matter of degree. The world isn't always the way our senses tell us, and scientists, fallible human beings like the rest of us, often incorporate empirical mistakes into their theories, mistakes it may take years, or centuries, to discover. No matter how obviously true it may seem now, any theory could ultimately turn out to be false, whether in science or philosophy.

6

The fact of normative disagreement is a source of profound discomfort for some political philosophers. It is this discomfort that provokes them to search for moral principles capable of commanding widespread agreement. The hope is that once such principles are identified, a political theory can then be built upon them that will generate *consensus* (or as at least as close to consensus as one could hope for).

Consensus may sound like a good thing, but it is a terrible idea for political philosophers to frame their projects around meeting this goal. Perhaps there are some principles so uncontroversial that almost no one would disagree with them, but to build a theory upon those principles, simply because they are widely accepted, would almost certainly distort the enquiry. Imagine a biologist taking a similar approach, developing a theory based only upon assumptions capable of commanding widespread agreement, even from creationists. However carefully he proceeded from there, the fact that the theory was constrained to stay within the boundaries set by creationist beliefs would inevitably cause it to veer wildly away from the truth.

The mistake here, obviously, is that the biologist should not be aiming to develop a theory with which no one could disagree. The goal, instead, should be to pursue the truth, wherever that leads, even if it turns out to be unacceptable to religious fanatics, even if lots of other scientists end up disagreeing.

Is political philosophy different? One feature that might seem to set it apart is the practical nature of its subject matter. Political philosophers are concerned with what *ought* to be done, with action rather than simply ideas, and unless a political theory is able to generate support, then the political philosopher's prescriptions will have no hope of being implemented.

This objection confuses political philosophy with politics. Political philosophy is not about getting things done—it is about discovering the truth. As part of this, political philosophers should aggressively defend their theories, but the motive for doing this should not be to gather support for some political project, but to put those theories to the test, to see whether they survive public scrutiny. That is radically different from the motive for engaging in politics, where the problem isn't a worry that *I* might be wrong, but that all those other people out there don't see the truth.

I'm not saying that political philosophers should not engage in politics. What I'm saying is that converting one's political opponents is not a philosophical problem. Nor is convincing creationists to accept the theory of evolution a biological problem. Figuring out how viruses inject their DNA into host cells is a biological problem. This line may be a bit more difficult to identify in political philosophy, but the point is that political philosophy should not be conceived of merely as a rarefied extension of battles occurring in the political arena. The political philosopher who sees himself as a man of the left or the right, and his challenge to be one of providing intellectual ammunition for his side, is no different from a creationist who sets out to get a Ph.D. in biology in order to better equip himself to defend the Bible against assaults from evolutionists.

Most political philosophers (I like to believe) avoid this trap and conduct honest, open-minded investigations of political problems. There is, however, a more serious reason to think that political philosophers face a justificatory worry that scientists do not. Political philosophy is concerned with identifying the moral grounds of legitimate state action, all of which, ultimately, is based upon *coercion*. (If you don't believe that, then just keep saying 'no' in response to your state's demands, and sooner or later a policeman will come knocking at your door, gun in hand.) It is this fact, some believe, that raises the justificatory bar dramatically. We cannot do such things to other persons, so the thinking goes, unless this treatment has been justified *to* them.

This line of thought has been very influential (in a number of different forms), but it's not entirely clear to me what the issue is. Of course, if I'm going to coerce other persons, or if I'm going to endorse state coercion, then I should worry about whether doing this is justified. But what, exactly, is added to the mix by claiming that such actions must be justified *to* those who are coerced? How is that different from justified *simpliciter*?

To say that an action is justified is to say that some standard has been met, that in light of the available evidence the conclusion that we ought to act is warranted. Perhaps, then, the idea is that the correct standard of justification is that those being coerced must *in fact* accept that treating them this way is justified. If so, then we can give up on the project of justification right now, because there is no possibility that all of the individuals states coerce are going to accept that this treatment is justified. There are rapists who really believe that women are a resource for their enjoyment, and there is no way to convince them otherwise. And so, if the use of force against such people is ever justified, then a justification of coercion must be able to stand even if those being subjected to it disagree.

Maybe the way to avoid this problem is to set our sights a bit lower and only worry about justifying coercion to *reasonable* people, which might entitle us to exclude chronic troublemakers, such as rapists and cannibals. Even this won't be enough, however, because if we're talking about a modern state, which may govern many millions of individuals, then it won't be possible to gain actual agreement from all of those who are coerced.

The next move is to say that we should not worry about whether reasonable people have in fact accepted the justification offered, but whether they *could* accept it (or, alternatively, whether they could not reject it). What does this mean? Well, it can't mean that these individuals really would, if given the chance, accept the justification, because they won't. It is a fact of life that no matter how sensible a proposal, some reasonable people will disagree with it. What the claim must mean, then, is that reasonable people *should* accept the justification. But once cast in that form, then all that is really being said is that the justification is a good one: the reasons in favour of coercion outweigh those against it, and so reasonable people should accept that this treatment is justified.[6]

Is that any different from justification *simpliciter*? Consider the comparison with justification in science. The scientist develops a theory, and if the reasons in favour of it are strong enough, then others *should* accept it. The theory of evolution, I believe, succeeds in this sense. Of course, there are lots of people in

---

[6] For further arguments along these lines, see Joseph Raz, 'Facing Diversity: The Case of Epistemic Abstinence', *Philosophy & Public Affairs*, 19/1 (1990), pp. 3–46.

Kansas who won't accept this theory, and it is at this point that some scientists play a game similar to the one played by political philosophers who attempt to cast those who disagree with them out of the community of the reasonable. Rather than calling creationists 'unreasonable', what these scientists will say is that the creationists are not 'doing science'. In so far as that is shorthand for an attack on the kinds of methods by which creationists come to hold their beliefs, then it is a perfectly legitimate criticism. For some, however, dismissing an alternative view as 'unscientific' is merely an attempt to define away a problem, as if we are entitled to assume that any belief arrived at unscientifically must therefore be false, a view that is as arrogant as it preposterous. The real problem with creationists isn't that they are unscientific—it's that they are mistaken. They hold false beliefs, for bad reasons, and once we've done the hard work of identifying the substantive defects in their theories, to then attach epithets such as 'unscientific' or 'unreasonable' is an empty exercise in name-calling.

And the same holds true in the domain of political philosophy. I firmly believe, for example, that the practice of circumcising young girls is unjust, and I also believe that my state is justified in outlawing this practice. When confronted with those who disagree with me—intelligent, rational parents who passionately believe that doing such things to their daughters is morally right—my claim would not be that these people are unreasonable (though they might well be), but that they are mistaken.

Is that enough to conclude that coercion against those who engage in this practice is justified? Not necessarily. Perhaps coercion will only be justified if it is approved by a particular type of institution, using certain kinds of procedures (say, a majority vote), acting for particular types of reasons, and there are lots of other conditions we might wish to add. Liberal political philosophy is, to a large degree, a spelling out of those conditions: it is a project aimed at identifying the kinds of constraints that must be placed upon political institutions in order for their coercive actions to be legitimate. But no matter how many conditions we add to the standard of justification for coercion, this won't make the justificatory problem raised by intractable normative disagreement go away. In the end, after the debates, after the vote has been taken, and after any other conditions have been satisfied, some individuals will *still* disagree, bitterly, leaving us exactly where we started: facing the choice of whether to coerce people who do not accept that this treatment is justified.

What then? Who makes the final decision about justification? You do. I can't compel you to accept a justification of coercion any more than I can compel you to accept the theory of evolution. Justification always comes down to individual judgement, as it is individuals who must decide whether to act—to vote one way or another, to support this or that political party, to comply with a state's demands or to resist.

7

Investigating the complex relationship between politics and morality raises many serious challenges, and in this chapter I have barely touched upon the rich array of methods analytical political philosophers have developed to meet those challenges. There is one point I'd like to make in conclusion, though, a final comparison between political philosophy and science.

Critics of analytical political philosophy sometimes complain that it is too dry and technical, that it is so myopically obsessed with trivial details that it loses sight of what is interesting and important about politics. Some of those who make this complaint flatter themselves into thinking that they have deep methodological objections to the analytical project, when the only real problem they have is that the 'method', when rigorously applied, doesn't deliver the substantive conclusions to which they are already committed. But still, the worry remains. Has something gone wrong with analytical political philosophy?

I don't think so, and I take comfort in the fact that contemporary scientists often hear similar complaints about their projects, which may seem narrow and overly technical when compared to those of great scientists in past. Scientists have a perfectly good response to such attacks, which is that this specialization is a by-product of the success of the scientific enterprise. Given the amount of scientific knowledge that has been accumulated, it can take many years for a very intelligent person to even begin to understand what is going on in science, much less make a contribution. Good scientists are keenly aware of the limits of their abilities, and it this awareness that leads them to tackle what may seem like minor technical projects. I wouldn't dare suggest that the amount of progress made in political philosophy is comparable to that made in science, but I do believe (perhaps naively) that there has been significant progress. I also believe that political philosophers should approach their tasks with the same sense of humility as scientists, and that they should be happy to make a successful contribution, however small and unsexy it may seem, to the overall project of increasing human knowledge.

2 Political philosophy for Earthlings[1]

David Miller

1

The question that I want to pursue in this chapter concerns the relationship between political philosophy as a normative enterprise whose purpose is to identify and justify principles intended to guide us politically, and what we can call the facts of political life—everything that we know about human beings and human societies, either through common sense or through the more formal methods of the social sciences. How, if at all, do the principles of political philosophy *depend* on those facts, in the sense that if the world changes in certain ways, or we make new discoveries about it, our political concepts and principles should change too? This question has several dimensions to it. We can treat it as a question about the formal structure of political theories: given that such theories often include descriptive or explanatory claims about human nature, or about how societies or governments function, as well as normative claims about how we ought to organize our collective life, what precisely is the relationship between the two kinds of claim? If the empirical claims are shown to be false, does that mean that the normative claims must be abandoned too, or can they survive without such support? But our question also bears directly on a more practical issue: how should we, as scholars, go about doing political philosophy? Ought we to be spending considerable amounts of our time immersing ourselves in the literature of history and the social sciences, in order that the empirical claims we make are as well grounded as possible, or should we be focusing our attention more narrowly on conceptual and normative questions—trying to decide, for example, what liberty means or whether liberty and equality are compatible—without

[1] This chapter began life as a lecture delivered to a conference on 'Political Philosophy and Empirical Research', Department of Philosophy, University College London. I thank Jo Wolff for inviting me, and the participants for their questions and comments. Since then it has undergone extensive revision, and I have received many helpful suggestions along the way, not least from the editors of this book, David Leopold and Marc Stears. My greatest debt, however, is to Jerry Cohen, who provided very extensive critical comments on an essay with whose main thesis he profoundly disagrees, in the forlorn hope that I might change my mind.

concerning ourselves too much, at this stage at least, about aspects of the real world that might bear on the conclusions we reach? And finally, there is a third issue, which concerns the purpose or point of engaging in political philosophy in the first place. How far should we intend our theories to have a practical impact, that is to say contain ideas that people engaged in real-world politics can take up and act upon when drafting legislation or making public policy? Is political philosophy to be understood as a purely speculative activity that aims to delineate the ideal state or the ideal society, or should it aim to engage with the political issues that arise in contemporary societies, in circumstances that are usually far from ideal?

The question I am asking, in other words, embraces not only 'What is political theory (how are its component parts related)?' but also 'How, and why, should we go about doing it?' There is one answer to that question that has proved attractive not only to philosophers but also to social and political scientists of a positivist cast of mind, because it allows for a mutually convenient division of labour between them. The answer runs as follows. The basic principles of political philosophy are to be established without reference to empirical questions. By rational reflection or in some other way we decide upon fundamental principles of liberty, justice, democracy, and so forth. These principles are universally valid and hold regardless of circumstances. But in order to *apply* these basic principles and come up with some practical rules for ordering society, we have to bring in factual evidence about the kind of society in which the principles are going to be applied. Empirical evidence about the society will determine, for example, how far each of the basic principles can be implemented—there may be empirical barriers to the full realization of our favoured principle of justice, say. General facts about the society may also determine which institutions we will select as the best embodiment of a given principle—for instance which political institutions will best achieve or approximate our ideal of democracy in a particular society. Or in cases where we regard the basic principles not as holding unconditionally but as standing in trade-off relationships to one another—some amount of liberty may be sacrificed in order to achieve greater equality, say—empirical evidence will be needed to tell us what the optimal mix of values will be for the society we are considering. To put the point more formally, philosophical reflection will establish the shape of our indifference curves between, say, different quantities of liberty and equality; social scientific investigation will reveal the shape of the feasibility curve in any given place and time—the set of feasible social states providing greater or lesser degrees of liberty and equality in combination. Once the shapes of the curves are known, it is then just a matter of identifying the point at which the feasibility curve touches the indifference curve furthest from the origin and recommending this as the optimum.

To paint the picture a bit more colourfully, and to explain my title, we might imagine the well-intentioned inhabitants of a spaceship—the Starship

Enterprise let's say—deciding, while still in outer space, on the principles they will attempt to apply to each of the life forms that they discover on their voyage of planetary exploration. Having established the basic principles, they then examine each new planet, looking at its physical composition, the kind of creatures who exist on it, their level of social organization, and so forth, and work out which principles to try to implement when they beam down on to the planet's surface. The basic principles are always the same, but the secondary or applied principles will vary according to the general facts of life on a particular planet.

It is this Starship Enterprise view of political philosophy that I mean to challenge in what follows. The Starship Enterprise view draws a line between political philosophy proper, which involves defining concepts and setting out principles in an entirely fact-free way, and applied political theory, which takes these basic concepts and principles and, in the light of empirical evidence, proposes a more concrete set of rules to govern the arrangements of a particular society, or a particular group of societies. In contrast, I want to argue that even the basic concepts and principles of political theory are fact-dependent: their validity depends on the truth of some general empirical propositions about human beings and human societies, such that if these propositions were shown to be false, the concepts and principles in question would have to be modified or abandoned. In other words, I am advocating political philosophy for Earthlings—political philosophy that is sensitive not only to general facts about the human condition but also to facts of a more specific kind, facts about particular societies, or types of societies. Whatever Captain Kirk and his crew are doing in outer space, it is not political philosophy—unless, of course, the principles they come up with to guide their interventions depend on tacit assumptions drawn from their human experience (even Mr Spock, we should recall, is only half Vulcan and his human half frequently rescues him when pure logic runs out).

2

Why, one might ask, should anyone wish to deny that the concepts and principles of political philosophy are fact-dependent? Perhaps life is made easier for the political philosopher if she does not have to worry at all about empirical questions while formulating her basic principles, but that alone does not seem sufficient justification. A more compelling reason is that by allowing empirical claims to influence the way these principles are formulated, we run the risk that our political philosophy becomes too conservative, adapting itself to aspects of human existence that may be contingent, and therefore potentially alterable. Consider, for example, John Rawls' well-known theory of social justice, which openly proclaims that 'the fundamental principles of justice quite properly depend upon the natural facts about men in society' or that 'there is no objection to resting the choice of first principles upon the general facts of economics and psychology'.[2] Among the facts that Rawls appeals to in defending his principles are the fact that people may need to be given economic incentives if they are to use their talents in the most socially productive way, and the fact that people do not agree, and cannot be brought to agree, about what is of ultimate value in life. Treated as empirical claims about how things are in contemporary liberal societies, both of these seem highly plausible. Yet they are not 'facts' in the sense in which the laws of physics are facts—societies in which neither fact obtains are not only conceivable but may actually have existed in other times and places. Rawls' critics therefore claim that by making 'the fundamental principles of justice' depend upon such facts, he is committing a serious error. He is confusing political philosophy proper with applied political theory, which takes the fundamental principles and, in combination with the relevant facts, derives lower-level principles to regulate the institutions and practices of a particular society. He is wrong to call these applied principles 'principles of justice': they are better described as, for example, 'principles of regulation'. As one critic has put the charge, 'it is a fundamental error of *A Theory of Justice* that it identifies the first principles of justice with the principles that we should adopt to regulate society'.[3]

It is important, however, to distinguish two versions of this challenge to Rawls. The first, less radical, version does not fault Rawls simply for making his fundamental principles of justice fact-dependent, but criticizes the particular set of facts that he chooses to invoke—claiming, for instance, that the 'general facts of economics and psychology' that he relies upon in defending his principles obtain only in certain contemporary societies (capitalist market societies, for example), and are not, therefore, facts about the human condition as such. Reliance on such facts distorts the theory and makes it ideological rather than philosophical: justice comes to mirror too closely prevailing institutions and practices, rather than serving to assess them critically. The second, more radical, version challenges the idea that fundamental principles of justice should be fact-dependent in any sense. This is the challenge that Cohen mounts in the article cited above, and I shall explore it next, before coming back later in the chapter to look at different ways in which principles in political philosophy might be fact-dependent, and consider how far this fact-dependence is acceptable.

Let's begin, then, with the radical thesis that the task of political philosophy is to elaborate fundamental, fact-independent principles. Cohen defends this thesis indirectly, by calling upon those who take the opposite view—that the

---

[2] John Rawls, *A Theory of Justice* (Cambridge, MA: Harvard University Press, 1971), pp. 158–9.

[3] G. A. Cohen, 'Facts and Principles', *Philosophy & Public Affairs*, 31/3 (2003), p. 241.

fundamental principles of political philosophy depend on facts—to explain the nature of this dependence. His claim is that where a political principle is said to be fact-dependent, there must be a further, fact-independent, principle that explains how the facts in question support the first principle. Or as he puts it, 'principles that reflect facts must, in order to reflect facts, reflect principles that don't reflect facts'.[4] In other words, if we have a fact-sensitive principle, one whose truth depends on the facts being the way they are claimed to be, then in order to understand *how* the principle reflects or responds to the facts, we have to appeal to another principle that isn't fact-sensitive, or at least isn't sensitive to those same facts. There could be a hierarchy of principles, Cohen thinks, where principles at each successive level respond to different facts, but eventually we must reach a supreme principle that is wholly fact-insensitive.

For example, Cohen says, if principle P—'we should keep our promises'—is sensitive to fact F—'only when promises are kept can promisees successfully pursue their projects'—that must be because it also reflects another principle such as P1—'we should help people to pursue their projects'.[5] P1 is not sensitive to fact F; its truth does not depend on whether F holds or not. It might be fully fact-insensitive, or it might turn out to depend on a different fact F1, in which case there will be a further principle P2 which explains why P1 holds given F1. Eventually we will reach a fact-insensitive principle Pn.

Why, in order to explain the sensitivity of P to F, do we need to invoke another normative principle such as P1? Cohen describes the relation of F to P as one of 'grounding'. The fact that people can only pursue their projects successfully when promises made to them are kept grounds the principle that we ought to keep our promises. And he further says that there must be some explanation as to why F grounds P. Someone who asks why the fact that people can only pursue projects if promises are kept supports the principle that promises should be kept is entitled to an answer. And the explanation, Cohen suggests, must be some further principle such as P1. To defend this suggestion he issues a challenge: 'provide an example in which a credible explanation of why some F supports some P invokes or implies no such more ultimate principle'.[6]

If we are to rise to this challenge, we need to look more closely at the relationship of 'grounding' on which Cohen's argument relies. What might it mean for a fact to ground or to support a principle, or for a principle to reflect a fact? In the examples that Cohen uses, facts ground principles by virtue of being premises in a relationship of logical entailment. If we combine F—'only when promises are kept can promisees successfully pursue their projects'—with P1—'we should help people to pursue their projects'—then P—'we should keep our promises'—follows necessarily. So although Cohen does not say explicitly what form the grounding relationship must take, his

---

[4] Ibid. 214.   [5] Ibid. 216.   [6] Ibid. 218.

implicit idea of what it means for A to ground B is that when A is combined with one or more other premises, A will entail B. Now if A is a fact and B is a principle, then to set up a relationship of entailment what we need is a further premise that will combine with A to yield B, and only another principle can fit that bill. To vary the example, if our principle P is 'eating people alive is wrong', and this is said to reflect fact F 'it's agony to be eaten alive', then what we need to create a relationship of entailment is the principle P1 'it's wrong to cause people agony'.

But should we understand 'grounding' or 'support' in such a narrow way? Let's step back for a moment from the facts/principles question and consider two other ways in which one proposition might be said to ground another. The first of these we might call 'evidential grounding', where a fact supports a conclusion, not by entailing it, but just by providing evidence that makes it likely to hold. So 'that is a small bird with an orange breast and a white wing-bar' grounds 'that is a chaffinch' because, given the context (we are sitting in an English garden), a bird meeting the former description is very likely indeed to be a chaffinch, even though there is no entailment (there exist other birds fitting the description that are not chaffinches). So here we can explain why A grounds B without converting the grounding relationship into one of entailment. The second kind of grounding we might call 'presuppositional grounding', where although A doesn't entail B, A's being true is a necessary condition of B's being true.[7] Thus we might say that 'Fred is a pig' grounds 'Fred is a readily available source of pork chops'. Fred's being a pig doesn't entail that he is available for conversion into chops—he might be a pet pig or a diseased pig—but being a pig is certainly a precondition for that fate. Or to take a different case, 'Radcliffe is a woman' grounds, in this presuppositional sense, 'Radcliffe is entitled to enter for the women's marathon'—the former does not entail the latter, since there may be other qualifying conditions, but unless the premise holds, the conclusion cannot.

As I have indicated, the examples used to explain these two forms of grounding are not examples of facts grounding principles. We have yet to see whether facts can ground principles in either the evidential or the presuppositional sense. Their purpose is to show that grounding need not mean entailment. Recall that Cohen's requirement of a grounding relationship is that it should be possible to *explain* how A grounds B. That requirement is met in the cases I have cited. I can explain how the fact that a bird is small with an orange breast, etc., grounds the claim that it is a chaffinch. But the explanation won't convert the grounding into an entailment. To insist that an

---

[7] I should add, to avoid possible misunderstanding, 'without at the same time being a necessary condition of B's being true'. Thus although Fred's being a pig is a presupposition of Fred's being a thin pig, this is not a case of presuppositional *grounding* in the sense used here, since the same fact is also a presupposition of Fred's being a fat pig.

explanation of how F grounds P doesn't count as such unless it shows how F (along with other premises) *entails* P is to beg the question at stake.

So can we find cases in which facts ground principles without the help of fact-insensitive principles? Consider a putative case of presuppositional grounding, involving a principle of liberty, such as Rawls' principle of greatest equal liberty or Mill's principle of liberty to perform self-regarding actions. Assume that the principle asserts the intrinsic value of liberty, within the designated limits—it is intrinsically valuable for humans to enjoy liberty of thought and action provided they do not infringe the equal liberty of others, or harm others' interests, as the case may be. Now consider how this principle may reflect a very general fact about human beings, namely their capacity, in normal cases, to make self-conscious choices as to how to live. This fact differentiates humans from the rest of the animal kingdom, and explains why liberty is intrinsically valuable for humans but not for other animals. So what we can call, for short, the fact of human self-consciousness grounds the principle of liberty. The relationship between the fact and the principle appears to be one of presupposition: if the fact were not to hold—if human beings were no more capable of self-conscious choice than other animals— then the principle would not apply.

How might Cohen respond to this example? He is committed to claiming that if the principle of liberty is fact-dependent in this way, there must be a fact-independent principle that explains the grounding relationship. Which principle might be a plausible candidate for this role? It may be tempting to suggest a principle such as the following: 'Creatures who are capable of self-conscious choice ought to enjoy the greatest equal liberty, etc.'. But this principle does not explain the grounding relationship, it merely restates it in more general form. It is equivalent to the conditional principle: 'If a crea-ture is capable of self-conscious choice, then it ought to enjoy the greatest equal liberty, etc.'. Clearly anyone who was puzzled by the alleged grounding relationship—who could not see why the truth or validity of the proposed liberty principle depended on the fact of human self-consciousness—would not be enlightened if they were presented with the conditional principle just stated. Cohen's thesis that fact-sensitive principles must reflect fact-insensitive principles becomes trivial if we include among the fact-insensitive principles conditional principles of the form 'if F, then P'. For the thesis *not* to be trivial, the ultimate fact-insensitive principles that ground fact-sensitive principles must be unconditional in form.[8]

So where else might we look for a principle that explains the grounding relationship between human self-consciousness and liberty? We might observe

---

[8] Cohen does not always seem alive to the danger of trivializing his argument by allowing condi-tional principles to count as fact-independent. For instance, on p. 225 of 'Facts and Principles', he treats the principle 'If a being is liable to pain, you ought not to cause it pain' as fact-independent.

that human beings, because of their capacity for self-conscious choice, often strongly desire to have the greatest possible freedom of thought and action, and so the underlying, fact-insensitive, principle in the case is that, *ceteris paribus*, people should be allowed to have what they strongly desire. However the effect of this move is to convert liberty from being something of intrinsic value to being something of instrumental value only. People should have maximum liberty because that is conducive to satisfying their desires. Many of Cohen's examples of fact-insensitive principles take such a utilitarian or quasi-utilitarian form—the explanation for why a fact supports a principle is that it reveals why following the principle satisfies human wants or avoids human pain. But we need not go down this route. We can hold that liberty is of intrinsic value independently of whether it satisfies people's desires. And this belief can be conditional on the fact of human self-consciousness, in the sense that if it proved to be the case that humans lacked the capacity for self-conscious choice, we would abandon the principle.

But, Cohen might argue, if we pass up on fact-independent principles such as the one proposed in the previous paragraph, we are left with no way of explaining how a fact grounds a fact-dependent principle. *How* does the fact of human self-consciousness support the liberty principle, if we refuse to tell a story about the satisfaction of human desires, or something similar? Remember the challenge: 'to provide an example in which a credible explanation of why some F supports some P invokes or implies no such more ultimate principle'. In responding to the challenge, it is important to underline once again that we do not have to show that F can conclusively justify P, alone or in combination with other premises—that by invoking F we are presenting a knock-down argument that anyone currently opposed to P would be compelled to accept. If we took that as our model, we would have fallen back into the entailment view of grounding. What we have to explain is simply the role played by F in supporting P—in the present instance why, if F did not obtain, we would have no reason to assert P. Imagine, then, somebody who is disposed to accept the liberty principle, but who cannot see the relevance to it of the fact of human self-consciousness. Such a person must presumably think that, other things being equal, the liberty principle should also apply to certain animals. Explaining to this person the relevance of F would involve pointing out how a cow, say, would not experience choice as valuable—would not be able to imagine being in a field other than the one she was currently in, and therefore would not be deprived, in a morally relevant way, by being denied a choice of fields. This is just to remind our interlocutor of some very familiar facts of human experience, and to show how it is those facts that bring principles like the liberty principle into play—if the facts were otherwise there would simply be no reason to propose such a principle.

Consider now a second example, which will prove to be instructively different from the first. This is Hume's depiction of the circumstances of justice, which plays an essential part in his account what justice is and why it is valuable. Hume argues that principles of justice apply only because of certain contingent features of the human condition, namely that resources are scarce relative to human desires, that human benevolence is limited, and that external goods can be readily transferred from person to person. In the absence of these features, there would be no need to have principles of justice to regulate the distribution of resources: 'if men were supplied with every thing in the same abundance, or if *every one* had the same affection and tender regard for *every one* as for himself; justice and injustice would be equally unknown among mankind'.[9]

Now admittedly Hume himself goes on to give a somewhat utilitarian account of the relationship between the cited facts about the human condition and the principles of justice he proposes. This would fit with Cohen's view about how facts ground principles, with utility playing the role of fact-insensitive principle. But it is not essential to Hume's argument that we should interpret it in this way. We can read him simply as saying that notions of justice, and the more specific principles that he proposes to regulate the allocation of external goods, arise as a response to the features of the human condition he has identified. Such facts ground justice in a presuppositional sense. If we imagine, as Hume does, a golden age in which 'the rivers flow'd with wine and milk: The oaks yielded honey' and so forth, then justice would have no place: we would find instead 'much nobler virtues, and more valuable blessings'.[10]

So interpreted, Hume's account of the circumstances of justice does not fully determine the content of our normative theory of justice. The account tells us that we need principles of justice, understood as principles that assign resources to people in such a way that I know what is mine and what is not, by virtue of facts about the human condition. How those principles should be specified is a further question. One possibility considered and rejected by Hume is an equal division of resources. To defeat this possibility Hume invokes further facts about the human condition, such as differences in 'art, care, and industry' which 'will immediately break that equality'.[11] The circumstances of justice taken by themselves show only why a division of property is necessary, and why therefore we understand and value justice as the virtue that upholds that division. If the facts were different, justice would have no point: we could still invent and apply principles that assigned rivers and oaks to particular people, but, of course, we wouldn't, because it would appear senseless by

    [9] David Hume, *A Treatise of Human Nature*, edited by L. A. Selby-Bigge, revised by P. H. Nidditch (Oxford: Clarendon Press, 1978), p. 495.

    [10] Ibid. 494–5.

    [11] David Hume, 'An Enquiry Concerning the Principles of Morals', in *Enquiries Concerning Human Understanding and Concerning the Principles of Morals*, edited by L. A. Selby-Bigge, revised by P. H. Nidditch (Oxford: Clarendon Press, 1975), p. 194.

virtue of the abundance of what was being assigned. In such circumstances the 'cautious, jealous virtue of justice would never once have been dreamed of'.[12]

Cohen would no doubt claim here that to explain how the facts ground the principles of justice, we need to make explicit certain steps that are only implicit in Hume's argument. So reconstructed, the argument might take the following form:

> F: Resources are scarce and readily transferable, while human benevolence is limited.
>
> F1: Given F, humans will suffer if we do not assign resources using principles of justice.
>
> P1: We should not allow human beings to suffer.
>
> Therefore:
>
> P: We should assign resources using principles of justice.

In this reconstruction, P1 serves as a fact-insensitive principle which, in conjunction with F1, explains how F grounds P. I have not denied that such a reconstruction is possible, nor have I denied that it may capture Hume's own intentions. But I do want to deny that we need to reconstruct the argument in this way in order to understand how F can ground P—always provided, of course, that we do not equate grounding with entailment. My counterclaim is that we can see directly how a principle depends on the truth of certain claims about the human condition without having to explain this dependency in utilitarian or quasi-utilitarian terms. It is pointless to apply principles of distributive justice in circumstances of abundance like Hume's golden age, just as it is pointless to apply principles of liberty to creatures who lack the capacity for self-conscious choice. Facts ground principles, in these cases, by indicating that circumstances are such as to make principles of a particular kind relevant. Or to make the same point from the other side, principles reflect facts because by applying a principle of a certain kind—justice or liberty, say— we presuppose, usually tacitly, that the context in which we apply it displays certain empirical features.

3

In the previous section I offered a general defence of the claim that political principles are characteristically fact-dependent. In advocating political philosophy for Earthlings, I suggested that the political principles we adopt—principles of liberty and justice, for instance—are grounded in certain

---

[12] Ibid. 184

familiar, though nonetheless important, facts about the human condition, such as that each human being forms a separate centre of consciousness, that human bodies are vulnerable to pain and disease, that there are at least two human sexes, and so forth—facts, let it be noted, that the crew of the Enterprise could not assume would hold for each form of life they might encounter. Earlier on, however, I noted that attacks on fact-dependency might take a more radical or less radical form. The more radical position is the one taken up by Cohen, and discussed in the previous section, which holds that the ultimate principles of political philosophy are fully fact-insensitive.[13] I shall not discuss this position any further. The less radical view, by contrast, aims to draw a line between what we might call universal features of the human condition, on the one hand, and facts about particular societies, or types of society, and their inhabitants, on the other. On this view, it is acceptable for basic political principles to depend on facts of the first kind, but not for them to depend on what may prove to be merely contingent features of particular societies. Fact-dependence of the second kind, it is argued, makes political philosophy too conservative—too reluctant to subject our current political arrangements and social practices to critical appraisal.

Someone who took this position might want to draw a line between the two examples that I discussed in Section 2. Making our principles of liberty depend upon the fact of human self-consciousness is not problematic, because the fact invoked here qualifies as a rock bottom fact about human beings: we cannot envisage human beings (other than those who are mentally damaged, comatose, etc.) who do not have that feature. By contrast, making our principles of justice depend on facts such as the scarcity of resources relative to human desires, or limited human benevolence, *is* problematic, because we can envisage circumstances in which resources become abundant or in which people are altruistically motivated. Our most basic principles should apply to these circumstances too, and then we will derive secondary principles that take into account the contingencies of particular societies. So the question that now arises is: if we abandon the attempt to find basic principles that are independent of *all* facts about the human condition, how far should we allow the fact-dependence of principles to go?

Answering this question will require us to take a stand on the issue that I signalled at the beginning of this chapter, the issue namely of the underlying purpose of political philosophy. To help answer it, I want to return to the

[13] Cohen does not say explicitly that the fact-insensitive principles that he claims explain how facts ground political principles are themselves political; nevertheless his quarrel with Rawls is a quarrel about what should be regarded as fundamental principles of *justice*, normally understood as a political idea; and on pp. 242–3 of 'Facts and Principles' he presents his thesis as a thesis about the nature of political philosophy. For a fuller discussion of Cohen's conception of political philosophy, see Marc Stears, 'The Vocation of Political Theory: Principles, Empirical Inquiry and the Politics of Opportunity', *European Journal of Political Theory*, 4/4 (2005), pp. 325–50.

example of Rawls' theory of justice, which is heavily fact-dependent in two quite different ways. First, the theory openly rests on a number of assumptions about the subject matter of justice, using that phrase in its broadest sense. For instance, it assumes that the concept of justice (or at least the concept of *social* justice) applies within the boundaries of a self-contained community whose members are held together by common sentiments; that the members of such a community nevertheless hold an irreducibly plural set of beliefs about the good life; that there exists a basic structure of social and political institutions capable of being regulated by principles of justice and determining, to a large extent, the different life-chances of individuals; that we can identify a set of primary goods—income, wealth, employment opportunities, and so forth— that serve as all-purpose means to individual ends; that the production and distribution of such goods occurs primarily through some form of market economy; that children are raised in families rather than communally; and so forth. We do not have to join the crew of the Enterprise to see just how contingent these assumptions are: we need only to look back through human history to find societies in which none of these conditions holds.[14] The principles Rawls proposes only make sense at all if we take for granted many of the features of a modern, technologically advanced, liberal society.[15]

Rawls himself would have no problem with this dependence on contingent facts, as I shall illustrate in a moment. But now consider a second way in which his theory is fact-dependent: it depends on facts about people's beliefs or judgements about justice. Rawls relies on the existence of a 'public political culture' made up of commonly accepted beliefs from which the ideas that go into the theory of justice can be drawn. This makes it possible for the theory to achieve what he calls 'full reflective equilibrium', where not only has each individual person reconciled his or her pre-theoretical judgements about justice with the principles laid out in the theory, but each member of the political community arrives at the same public conception of justice as every other.[16] In other words, he assumes two things: first that people's judgements of justice will converge, when they go through the testing and refining process that culminates in a reflective equilibrium for each person taken separately; and second, that what they will converge *on* is the Rawlsian theory of justice, or at least a liberal theory of justice that is a close cousin of that theory.

It is not fanciful, I think, to regard these two kinds of fact-dependence as corresponding roughly to the two forms of grounding that I identified in the

---

[14] With the possible exception of the first—although even here we can say that by no means all human communities have taken the form assumed by Rawls, which is more or less that of the modern nation-state.

[15] For further reflection on, and justification of, the fact-dependence of Rawls' theory of justice, see Joshua Cohen's very illuminating paper 'Taking People as They Are?', *Philosophy & Public Affairs*, 30/4 (2002), pp. 363–86.

[16] See John Rawls, *Justice as Fairness: A Restatement* (Cambridge, MA: Harvard University Press, 2001), p. 31.

previous section of this chapter. Facts of the first kind ground the theory in a presuppositional sense: unless they held true of the society to which the principles of justice are to be applied, principles of the kind that Rawls proposes would be irrelevant. The facts do not determine the content of the principles—they do not, for example, require that equality of some kind must feature in the set—but they do determine what the theory must be *about*. Facts of the second kind ground the theory in an evidential sense: the theory must respond in the right kind of way to the considered judgements of justice that people are disposed to endorse before they encounter it. I do not want to say that the evidential grounding takes exactly the same form here as it does in a case where the proposition to be grounded is empirical; nevertheless I find in Rawls a tendency to treat pre-theoretical judgements of justice as somewhat akin to the raw data that might serve to ground a scientific theory.[17] So in consequence not only the subject matter but also the content of the theory of justice comes to depend on certain facts that are external to it.

Rawls, as I noted, willingly embraces both forms of fact-dependence, and the reason he does so is that he holds a certain view about the aim of political philosophy, which in his later books he describes as the delineation of a 'realistic utopia'.[18] The meaning of this phrase is not self-evident. According to Rawls, 'political philosophy is realistically utopian when it extends what are ordinarily thought to be the limits of practicable political possibility and, in so doing, reconciles us to our political and social condition.'[19] The two halves of this sentence might seem to contradict each other. How can a theory that aims to stretch the limits of political possibility at the same time have a reconciling purpose, since reconciliation appears precisely to mean accepting, not struggling against, things as they are? But Rawls' idea, I believe, is that by extending the limits of political possibility—exploring different ways in which societies might be reordered in the name of greater justice—we shall also come to a better understanding of the limits of the reshaping, and therefore become reconciled to those aspects of our condition that cannot be changed. Thus, we can try to discover the terms on which people whose conceptions of the good life are radically divergent can better live together in a single political community, but we can also learn not to hope or wish for a society in which everyone adheres to the same conception.

---

[17] For instance, 'one thinks of the moral theorist as an observer, so to speak, who seeks to set out the structure of other people's moral conceptions and attitudes.' John Rawls, 'The Independence of Moral Theory', *Collected Papers*, edited by Samuel Freeman (Cambridge, MA: Harvard University Press, 1999), p. 288. For discussion of this and other passages in which Rawls addresses questions of method, see Thomas Scanlon, 'Rawls on Justification', in Samuel Freeman (edited), *The Cambridge Companion to Rawls* (Cambridge: Cambridge University Press, 2003). Scanlon cautions against attributing to Rawls too close an analogy between moral and scientific theory.

[18] See John Rawls, *The Law of Peoples* (Cambridge, MA: Harvard University Press, 1999), section 1 and Rawls, *Justice as Fairness*, sections 1 and 4.

[19] Rawls, *The Law of Peoples*, p. 11.

The next question that we face is how the limits of political possibility are to be established. Rawls acknowledges the significance of the question without really providing an answer:

I recognize that there are questions about how the limits of the practically possible are discerned and what the conditions of our social world in fact are. The problem here is that the limits of the possible are not given by the actual, for we can to a greater or lesser extent change political and social institutions and much else. Hence we have to rely on conjecture and speculation, arguing as best we can that the social world we envision is feasible and might actually exist, if not now then at some future time under happier circumstances.[20]

Nor does Rawls get us much further when he says that a realistic conception of justice 'must rely on the actual laws of nature and achieve the kind of stability those laws allow'. This is too weak a constraint if all that it means is that such a conception should not violate the laws of physics or biology by, for example, requiring people to levitate or become immune to disease. But it is arguably at least too strong a constraint if 'the actual laws of nature' are to include propositions about human behaviour in contemporary societies, for instance the proposition that people need material incentives to be productive, or that by the free exercise of reason they will reach different conclusions over moral, religious, and other such questions.

I believe in fact that the notion of practical possibility that Rawls relies upon has an inescapable normative element. The limits of political possibility are set not just by physical and sociological laws, but by implicit assumptions about what, for us, would count as a tolerable or intolerable outcome. This can perhaps best be illustrated by considering what Rawls has to say about the family as a social institution. Rawls accepts that the existence of the family, and the formative influence that it exercises upon children, is a powerful barrier to fair equality of opportunity—or to be more precise, that because the existence of the family is taken for granted, the definition of fair equality of opportunity must be narrowed to accommodate it.[21] In his later and more extensive discussions, Rawls makes it clear that he does not require or presuppose any particular family structure—he is in favour of greater equality between men and women, he doesn't rule out same-sex marriage, etc.—but he nonetheless continues to assume that children will continue to be raised in small family units, and therefore, as a matter of fact, to enjoy the very

---

[20] Ibid. 12.
[21] Rawls, *A Theory of Justice*, section 46. Fair equality of opportunity is said to require equal prospects only for those 'similarly endowed and motivated', so if the effect of family upbringing is only on endowment and motivation, there is no inconsistency between the family and equality of opportunity so defined. I have discussed the ambiguities of Rawls' idea of equal opportunity more fully in 'Equality of Opportunity and the Family', in Rob Reich and Debra Satz (edited), *Toward a Humanist Justice: The Work of Susan Moller Okin* (Oxford: Oxford University Press, forthcoming).

significant advantages and disadvantages that result from this.[22] Why does he assume this? Presumably because he believes that, for us, the freedom to form family units and to raise children within them is fundamental—we would find an imposed regime of collective childrearing, say, intolerable. He says at one point:

We wouldn't want political principles of justice to apply directly to the internal life of the family. It is hardly sensible that as parents we be required to treat our children in accordance with political principles. Here those principles are out of place.[23]

'We wouldn't want' in this passage is a characteristically Rawlsian piece of understatement. What Rawls really means is that having political principles of justice applied to the internal life of families would be wholly unacceptable to us. Proposals to reform the family so that women are treated more fairly within it (by, for example, being entitled to a share of their husbands' income on divorce) remain within the bounds of feasibility, whereas proposals to get rid of the family altogether and replace it with some other institution for raising children step beyond those bounds—not because they break some natural law (Rawls cannot be unaware that there are alternative ways of raising children that human societies have followed[24]), but because in liberal societies people are fundamentally committed to family life in some form.

We can conclude from this example that for Rawls the limits of political possibility are set not just by physical laws, but by the range of outcomes that we—people in modern liberal societies—would regard as fundamentally unacceptable. This, then, is a fact of a different kind to which the theory of justice must respond. A proposed principle will be ruled out if implementing it would produce consequences that step beyond these limits in one or another direction. A principle whose implementation requires the abolition of the family would be one example. A principle whose implementation requires that everyone should adhere to the same religion would be another.

An obvious objection to this way of construing normative feasibility is that it makes the limits of the possible depend upon beliefs and attitudes that may be widely and firmly held in contemporary societies, but are clearly not unchangeable. Abolishing the family may be unthinkable for us, but in other societies different arrangements have been accepted without difficulty. Here we need to return to our central question about the aim of political philosophy, to see what can be said in defence of the view that it should be realistically utopian in Rawls' sense.

---

[22] See Rawls, *Justice as Fairness*, section 50 and Rawls, 'The Idea of Public Reason Revisited', section 5, in Rawls, *The Law of Peoples*.

[23] Rawls, *Justice as Fairness*, p. 165.

[24] For comments on this aspect of Rawls' thinking, see section 2 of Martha Nussbaum, 'Rawls and Feminism', in Freeman (edited), *The Cambridge Companion to Rawls*.

I start from the assumption that political philosophy is a branch of practical reason—it is thought whose final aim is to guide action, as opposed to having a merely speculative purpose. The question that then arises is whose action it is intended to guide. There is no simple answer to this question. Political philosophy might be written to guide the actions of political rulers, as it was in the so-called 'mirrors for princes' tradition in medieval political thought. It might be written to direct legislators and administrators, as (at least arguably) was older utilitarian political philosophy. But in Rawls' view (and in mine), political philosophy in democratic societies should be aimed at citizens generally, setting out principles that they might follow when supporting or changing their institutions and practices. That this is Rawls' conception is suggested by a tantalizingly brief remark near the end of *The Law of Peoples*: 'By showing how the social world may realize the features of a realistic utopia, political philosophy provides a long-term goal of political endeavour, and in working toward it gives meaning to what we can do today'.[25]

What this implies is that the principles political philosophers propose must be principles that citizens can act upon, not in the sense that they can fully implement them here and now, but in the sense that their present actions can be guided by the longer-term goal of realizing the principles in question. But if they are action-guiding in this way, they cannot contravene the deeply held commitments of present-day citizens such as those described above. People cannot reasonably be expected to act politically on principles which if realized would have outcomes that they regard as wholly unacceptable.[26] It might be said in reply that a political philosopher could recommend the principles without drawing attention to the abhorrent outcomes: by acting on these principles, people's sense of what is acceptable and what isn't would change over time. If, for example, they accepted the arguments in favour of (really fair) equality of opportunity and supported policies that brought it closer to fruition, such as extensive preschool education for children, they would come to regard the family as less valuable and would finally be happy to see it disappear. But even if that causal prediction were accurate, it would cast the political philosopher in a very different role from the one envisaged (I believe) by Rawls. It would require political philosophy to be less than fully open with its addressees, concealing from sight some of the known consequences of the principles it puts forward. What one might call such a neo-Leninist view of political philosophy is certainly possible, but it seems to me very unattractive by comparison to the more democratic view implicit in Rawls, where political philosophy aims to proceed by modes of reasoning that are accessible to all

---

[25] Rawls, *The Law of Peoples*, p. 128.

[26] See also here the thoughtful discussion in Thomas Nagel, 'What Makes a Political Theory Utopian?', *Social Research*, 56/4 (1989), pp. 903–20.

citizens, and to develop principles that cohere with their most basic political beliefs.

4

If the claims I have made in this chapter about the fact-dependence of political principles are accepted, what does this imply about how we should go about doing political philosophy? There are two primary implications that I want to draw out by way of conclusion.

The first of these is that we need to be self-conscious about the status of the principles we put forward to govern our political life. As I have argued, these principles will not in general hold unconditionally. They will have factual presuppositions. But these presuppositions can be of different kinds. In some cases the facts that ground the principles will simply be general features of the human condition, of the kind that I sought to illustrate in the case of the principle of liberty. So long as we are doing political philosophy for Earthlings and not for Martians, etc., we can take these facts for granted, and need not speculate about what we should think were they not to obtain. But in other cases the presuppositions will be more limited in scope, in the sense that they hold true in some human societies but not in others, and then we need to be clear about exactly what we are taking for granted when we assert the principles in question. Many of the principles that feature prominently in contemporary political philosophy—democracy, equality, or social justice, for example—fall into this category. These are principles that apply only in societies of a certain kind, each principle having specific presuppositions— presuppositions that we may be able to identify by tracing when and how the principle established itself in political debate.[27]

Paying attention to the factual presuppositions of our principles in this way would help us avoid two serious errors. Most obviously, we will no longer be tempted to dismiss political thinkers living in societies where the presuppositions don't hold as simply blinkered or benighted. We won't, for example, believe that medieval political philosophers who failed to take the idea of democracy seriously were just making a mistake or were unable to see beyond the limits of their own time. In feudal Europe, valid arguments could be made about better or worse forms of government, but democracy was not on the agenda because its presuppositions were not fulfilled. So we will be saved from a certain kind of intellectual arrogance. But more importantly, we will not be tempted to apply the principles in question outside of their proper

---

[27] In the case of the idea of social justice, I sketched an account of this sort in *Principles of Social Justice* (Cambridge, MA: Harvard University Press, 1999), chapter 1.

context. We will not, for example, prescribe that governments everywhere should be constituted democratically, on the grounds that democracy is the only legitimate principle for allocating political authority. Nor will we assume that principles of social justice that apply within societies of a certain kind can be abstracted from that context and applied elsewhere—to the world as a whole, for example. Where the presuppositions no longer obtain, the principle ceases to apply.

The first implication of the fact-dependence of political principles is, then, a certain modesty in the way that we apply these principles across time and space. The second implication concerns the conditions under which a political theory becomes feasible, if we assume, following Rawls, that the aim of such a theory is to delineate a 'realistic utopia'. Feasibility is important, but we need to be clear about what it means. The feasibility condition I want to endorse must be distinguished from two other kinds of feasibility:

(a) What we can call 'political feasibility', feasibility of the kind that concerns practical politicians.[28] In this sense, whether a proposal is feasible depends on whether it can command sufficient political support to be adopted, and this will depend, among other things, on the range of interests that might be affected if the proposal were implemented. For example an environmental policy that required doubling the price of petrol to cut down on car use would be politically infeasible if adopting it would provoke mass protest and civil disobedience and condemn the party that brought it in to electoral defeat.

(b) What we can call 'technical feasibility', that is whether a proposal contravenes physical laws or rock bottom social or psychological laws. In this sense, a proposal that required all citizens to have advanced mathematical skills or to be able to recall every transaction they had made over the last twelve months would not be feasible. On the other hand, it would be technically feasible for contemporary Britain, say, to be reorganized politically along the lines of North Korea: since North Korea exists, its form of social organization clearly breaks no sociological or other law, and a political theory that recommended such a regime could not be dismissed on grounds of technical feasibility.

As will be apparent, the feasibility constraint we need falls somewhere between political and technical feasibility. A political philosophy that presents itself to any given society as realistically utopian must contain principles that members of that society could be brought to accept by reasoned discussion, which means that the principles cannot have implications that those citizens would

---

[28] For a fuller discussion of political feasibility, and of the relationship between the political theorist and the practical politician, see Adam Swift and Stuart White, 'Political Theory, Social Science, and Real Politics', Chapter 3, this volume.

find abhorrent. This doesn't mean that the principles must be accepted immediately they are laid out. They may be unfamiliar, or they may be resisted simply because they impose sacrifices that many citizens are initially unwilling to make. Political philosophy *should* be in the business of changing political attitudes, of showing people what their convictions mean when applied consistently to political questions. It should not be constrained merely by political feasibility in the above sense. But at the same time it implies more than technical feasibility, because many technically feasible proposals would fail the requirement that they be reasonably acceptable to present-day citizens.

If they are to satisfy this feasibility condition, political philosophers must also be social scientists, or at least be prepared to learn from social scientists. They need to discover what it would mean, empirically, to implement their principles, and they need to discover whether the ensuing consequences are acceptable, in the light of the fundamental beliefs of their fellow citizens. They also, therefore, need to explore the structure of those beliefs, to find out which are fundamental, and which are open to change in the light of evidence and argument. There is no need to capitulate in the face of 'raw' public opinion as it is captured by snapshot polls, but there is every reason to pay attention to the judgements that emerge from deliberative settings in which participants search for agreement on questions of public policy by considering the evidence and arguments for and against particular proposals.

5

I began this chapter by presenting a certain conception of the nature and role of political philosophy that I characterized as the view from the Starship Enterprise. On this view, political philosophy proceeds by first developing a set of basic principles that are fact-independent—and these are the principles that specify what we really mean by justice, liberty, democracy, and so forth—and then by applying these principles to the circumstances of a particular society, or set of societies, derives some secondary principles that if we follow Cohen are best described as principles of regulation. By disputing Cohen's claim that all fact-dependent principles require ultimate fact-independent principles to explain how they are grounded in fact, I sought to show that we are not compelled by simple logic to adopt the Starship Enterprise view. This left it an open question, however, how far we should go in allowing our political principles to be fact-dependent. Drawing on Rawls' conception of the aim of political philosophy, I argued that our choice of principles can properly depend not only on general facts about the human condition but also on more specific facts about a particular society, or group of societies. If political philosophy aims to give practical guidance to citizens, it must propose principles that it is feasible for them to act on, where feasibility in turn depends not just on physical and sociological laws, but on what, empirically, they would regard as an unacceptable outcome.

If these arguments are valid, then political philosophy is only for the locals, on whichever planet they happen to be. The crew of the Enterprise should not try to engage in it while still in outer space. No doubt there are rules they should follow, such as 'Don't fire your photon torpedoes without first of all finding out what's going on down there'. More positively, they should act on the maxim: first understand the form of life on this planet, then try to discover what are the appropriate principles to implement when you beam down. But these principles won't be derivative from some fact-independent super-principles. And the maxim itself, although it may guide the way that Captain Kirk and his team behave, isn't a political principle but a meta-principle, a guide for arriving at valid political principles for each planet to which they boldly go.

3 Political theory, social science, and real politics

Adam Swift and Stuart White

1

Political theory students are often also interested in real politics—the kind that they read about in the newspapers and that get debated at election times. Sometimes they study political theory *because* they are interested in real politics. Many are then disappointed. What they are asked to read is disappointingly abstract, utopian or apparently irrelevant; it can be hard to connect debates as conducted by political theorists with policy issues or political choices in the real world. This chapter will try to ease the frustration, partly by exploring how best to make those connections, partly by urging reconciliation to the inevitability of disconnection. Political theory, as we understand it, occupies a very specific place in the political and policymaking process. That space is crucial and fundamental, but it is also modest and limited.

It is limited in two ways. On the one hand, normative theorizing at the level of abstract principle typically does not yield policy prescriptions on its own. Only by combining value judgements with relevant and appropriately detailed empirical social science can one ordinarily work out what policies should be urged in any particular context. On the other hand, the political theorist and the politician have quite different vocations. In democratic polities, politicians need to win elections. To do that they must operate strategically, working within the bounds of political feasibility, bounds that are in large part set by public opinion.

These two limitations are closely connected. The constraints constituted by the bounds of public acceptability, and hence of political feasibility, are simply a subset of the empirical context, knowledge of which depends on social-scientific investigation. A wise politician will consult opinion pollsters and the findings of focus groups just as she will formulate her political programme by attending to the best available empirical evidence. Still, we will discuss the modesty that must be urged vis-à-vis social science and the real world of electoral politics separately, since the latter throws up rather distinctive considerations. In both cases, too, our exhortation to modesty will be accompanied by the less humble suggestion that political theory has something important to offer. We will urge a collaborative division of labour, in which the political theorist has a fundamental, but precise, role to play.

2

The significance of political theory for public policy is fairly straightforward. There can be no value-free assessment of policy proposals. When politicians say that they are not interested in ideology, but care only about 'what works', it is always appropriate to ask 'works to achieve what?'. Sometimes the values that policies are trying to realize are so commonsensical as not to require much, or indeed any, explicit discussion. In some contexts it can be taken for granted that 'what works' is shorthand for 'what works to achieve goal X', and goal X is so uncontroversially A Good Thing that nothing more needs to be said. Sometimes, however, a goal that has seemed uncontroversial is thrown into question, and the weighting of values implicitly being appealed to by advocates of the policies that promote it is suddenly exposed.

For many years, for example, economic growth was regarded as so obviously desirable that it had became a kind of unspoken über-goal. Not the only one, of course. Some trade-offs between it and other goods were always acknowledged, and its more sophisticated advocates, often under pressure from political theorists, recognized that attention had to be paid not only to the total amount of economic output but also to its distribution. But recently, as we have become more concerned about the environment, and sensitive to the way in which ever bigger per capita GDPs don't seem to have made people much happier, it has no longer become possible to argue for a policy simply by appeal to its beneficial impact on economic growth.[1] There has, in effect, been a re-evaluation of 'what matters'—one that nicely reveals the value claims that inevitably underlie arguments for, and against, *any* policy. Like Moliere's Monsieur Jourdain, who discovered late in the day that he had been speaking prose all his life, anybody who argues for any policy is taking a normative position, whether she realizes it or not.

On the other hand, if people who work at the level of policy ought to take seriously their role as closet political theorists, political theorists are surely going to have some interest in the policy implications of their theorizing. True,

---

[1] For an accessible introduction to this topic, see Richard Layard, *Happiness: Lessons from a New Science* (Harmondsworth: Penguin, 2006), pp. 29–54.

there is no conceptual incoherence in a particular individual's conceiving her intellectual task as being at such a level of philosophical abstraction that she does not see it as part of *her* project to think through or work out those implications. But unlike other branches of philosophy, such as epistemology or metaphysics, political theory is typically—and in our view rightly—conceived as a practical discipline, as being concerned with what we should *do*. The moral principles and values that theorists interrogate, however abstractly and at whatever remove from the empirical contexts of particular societies, are intended as principles and values to guide political action. Since we act politically in part by enacting policy, it would be odd for a political theorist to evince no interest in the policies implied by her theorizing—even if she leaves it to others to work out what those implications are.[2]

Our aim in this chapter is to explore the relationship between political theory and public policy more fully, identifying some of the potential problems and giving examples of where that relationship works well. We hope thereby to encourage the reader to pursue the connections, but a note of caution is appropriate. Not only is the role of political theory in the realm of 'real politics' always modest and specific, sometimes its practical significance is so limited as simply not to repay study at the graduate level. There are many policy issues where the research that needs doing is not really at the level of values and principles at all, simply because the values and principles are indeed as straightforward as they seem. In those cases, what we need to know is indeed 'what works'.

Some students are drawn to political theory because they feel strongly about a particular issue: the environment, poverty, racism, the violation of human rights, and so on. They judge that something is seriously wrong with the society, or world, they live in, and want their academic work to be about the things they care about, the problems that they regard as morally urgent. This desire to integrate one's sense of what matters with one's academic research is natural. Certainly our own has been motivated by it. But neither of us would claim that our academic work has been devoted to those issues that we regard as the *most* morally serious in the world today. What is morally urgent, and what repays serious attention by the political theorist, do not necessarily coincide. Putting it bluntly, and perhaps somewhat paradoxically, what is wrong about the most serious wrongs in the world is often so obvious that there is little of normative interest to say about them.

---

[2] We do not act politically *only* by enacting government policy. Some theorists are concerned not with the issue of what policies should be pursued by the state, acting as our collective political agent, but rather with that of what individuals should do given the policies that in fact exist. This seems to us an area to which political theorists could profitably devote more attention but we will not discuss it further here. For examples of this kind of work, see G. A. Cohen, *If You're an Egalitarian, How Come You're So Rich* (Cambridge, MA: Harvard University Press, 2000), chapter 10, and Adam Swift, *How Not to Be a Hypocrite: School Choice for the Morally Perplexed Parent* (London: Routledge, 2003).

An anecdote may illustrate the point. Swift was approached by a would-be graduate student who wanted to work on sex trafficking. She was outraged by the data she had come across about the number of women being brought to the UK from Eastern Europe to work in the sex industry. Rightly sensing that her anger was moral, she thought that political theory was the proper discipline within which to research and write about sex trafficking and what might be done to end it. His response was that although he agreed entirely about the awfulness of sex trafficking and thought it an important (albeit also difficult and dangerous) subject for a graduate research project, he didn't see that there would be much political theory in it. It would not take long for her to articulate the values at stake, and there are unlikely to be many theorists offering arguments defending the practice. Of course, there are related issues that do indeed warrant serious theoretical attention. Whether people should be free voluntarily to sell sexual services to others is an interesting question that does raise deep questions—about the proper role of the state in limiting voluntary exchanges between individuals, about the extent to which a state's policies may legitimately reflect controversial judgements about how its citizens should live their lives. But what's wrong with sex trafficking has little to do with these more subtle or complex issues, and somebody really concerned to engage with and try to do something about it does not need to engage with political theory at graduate level to do that. A similar point applies across a whole range of issues.

However, just as one doesn't need to study political theory in any great depth to see how imperfectly the world realizes the values and principles argued over in such detail by political theorists, so the most fascinating theoretical issues often have little immediate or concrete significance for policy. To some, this can make political theory seem 'academic' in the pejorative sense, a fruitless exercise in navel-gazing, intellectual masturbation, fiddling with interesting but useless ideas in a way that not only yields no practical benefit but is positively harmful in drawing valuable energy and attention away from the things that really matter. From this perspective, futility, or worse, comes in two guises.

On the one hand, some political theory simply operates at a different level of abstraction from the political choices actually on the agenda for a particular polity at a particular time. Some theorists are interested less in evaluating policy options than in questioning the basic assumptions that govern the way policies are discussed and decided in systems like our own. One tradition in political thought, with roots in ancient Greece, holds that political philosophy must grow out of ethics: We first answer the question 'What is the good life?', and then go on to consider questions like 'What is the good society?' or 'What is the just state?'. Another perspective holds that since people inevitably, and reasonably, disagree about the answer to the first question, we should seek, as citizens, to justify government policy and shared institutions to one another in more 'ecumenical' terms than by appeal to our preferred theories of the good life. The first perspective implies that it is legitimate for political parties to justify their programmes by invoking values that appeal to controversial—in Rawls' terms 'comprehensive'—doctrines about how people should live their lives, while the second holds that those seeking to harness the coercive power of the state should invoke only values that are in some sense justifiable to all those whom they seek to govern. A great deal of work in contemporary political philosophy is concerned with exploring the relative merits of these two rival perspectives and, as part of this exercise, with trying to identify more precisely just what kind of reasons it is legitimate to invoke in public deliberation over policy.[3] At stake here are some fundamental questions about the proper use of state power, about how politics should be done, but, like many other basic questions concerning the rules of the political game (rather than the moves to make within it), they rarely arise in an explicit way in politics as currently practised.

On the other hand, even where theorizing is not of this 'meta' or 'framework' kind but does engage with issues up for decision within the existing framework, it often happens that theorists are disagreeing not so much about *what* should be done but about *why*, precisely, we should be doing it. Should we be trying to abolish child poverty because: (*a*) it is unfair for some children's life-chances to be much worse than others'; (*b*) no child should be brought up in conditions that give her a quality of life below a decent minimum; (*c*) social justice requires that we seek to maximize the well-being of the least advantaged members of our society; (*d*) the worse off someone is the more important it is to improve their position; (*e*) the poorer somebody is the greater the return, in terms of utility or well-being, from any given amount of extra resources; or (*f*) all children should be raised in ways that will enable them to take their place as full members of their political community? Political theorists are currently arguing about which of these principles is the pertinent one, and, of course, there are practical issues where they do come apart, yielding different implications. But, to the campaigner, outraged by the extent to which wealthy societies tolerate current levels of child poverty, their arguing about the detail is likely to seem rather like Nero's fiddling while Rome burns. The same applies to a host of other issues—perhaps most obviously environmental justice and global poverty. Here too, it can seem that, whatever the finer points at stake in their theoretical disputes, there must be sufficient common ground for theorists to suspend their disagreements and agree on some obvious wrongs that need to be addressed as a matter of urgency.

---

[3] Much of the contemporary debate around this issue is in response to John Rawls' later work. See John Rawls, *Political Liberalism*, second edition (New York: Columbia University Press, 1996), which defends a version of the second perspective.

We will defend these modes of theorizing later. For now, the point is simply to warn the reader that, although all policy choices and political positions implicitly presuppose normative commitments, sometimes those commitments are fairly unproblematic, while, on the other hand, not all political theorizing yields immediately relevant practical pay-offs.

3

We have talked about a division of labour. We have said that political theory makes a specific yet crucial contribution to our political life, that its role is both modest and fundamental. These formulations may seem self-contradictory. So how exactly do we conceive the role of the political theorist?

For us, the political theorist is essentially a democratic underlabourer.[4] Trained in particular skills—the making of careful distinctions, an understanding of how to assess and examine arguments about values, arguments for and against political principles—the political theorist is specially equipped to help her fellow citizens make their political choices. She can help them understand better what is at stake and can offer them a perspective from which to assess and evaluate their would-be leaders' political rhetoric. These are hugely important tasks. While it may be naive to expect a philosophically acute citizenry—or even philosophically acute politicians—some raising of the quality of political argument, at all stages in the policymaking process, is not unrealistic. And the political theorist is the person trained to contribute to that enterprise.[5]

But she can do more than this. Not confined to this clarificatory role, she can offer arguments and justifications of her own, seeking to persuade her readers about which values (or, more likely, which *conceptions* of those values, or which *balance* between competing values) are the right ones for them to be pursuing in their policy choices. This last role remains underlabouring, despite being substantively normative, precisely because the arguments she makes are, indeed, *offered*. It is for her fellow citizens to decide whether they want to accept them.

We stress this underlabouring aspect of our enterprise because there is a tendency in some quarters to regard the political theorist as seeking to

---

[4] See Stuart White, *The Civic Minimum: On the Rights and Obligations of Economic Citizenship* (Oxford: Oxford University Press, 2003), chapter 2.

[5] For our own attempts in this direction, see Adam Swift, *Political Philosophy: A Beginners' Guide for Students and Politicians*, second edition (Cambridge: Polity Press, 2006) and Stuart White, *Equality* (Cambridge: Polity Press, 2006). Some of the material towards the end of this chapter is reproduced, with slight revision, from the former.

supplant or short circuit the democratic process, not to contribute to it.[6] On this, caricatured, view, theorists are would-be philosopher kings, impatient of the moral myopia of their fellow citizens, contemptuous of popular opinion, and disappointed not to find themselves in the utopian polity outlined in Plato's *Republic*, a polity where an intellectual elite is trained from birth to rule over the ignorant masses. Of course, many political theorists *are* impatient and sometimes perhaps even contemptuous. We do tend to think that we have correctly identified the principles that should be put into practice in our politics, and we are quite ready to criticize and condemn as mistaken those who disagree with us. But no contemporary political theorist that we know of believes that their expertise puts them in a position legitimately to put their *ex hypothesi* correct principles into practice, bypassing the democratic decision-making process. On the contrary, their own theorizing—not now about *what* decisions should be made, but about *how* they should be made—tells them that there is a crucial distinction between correctness and legitimacy. Their theories are resources, offered as contributions to a democratic debate about how authority should be exercised, not alternatives to it. As John Rawls puts it: '. . . citizens, must after all, have some ideas of right and justice in their thought and some basis for their reasoning. And students of philosophy take part in formulating these ideas but always as citizens among others.'[7] Indeed such contributions are not merely consistent with democratic legitimacy, but arguably essential to it. If what matters for legitimacy is not only that in some real sense the people rule, but that they rule in a way that is informed by political values such as justice, then the contribution of political theorists to public debate, as we have described it above, can potentially increase democratic legitimacy.

To be sure, sometimes political theorists' expertise leads them to be given a special advisory role in the higher reaches of government. (William Galston's position in the Clinton administration comes to mind here.)[8] Think-tanks

---

[6] This issue lies at the heart of the debate between Jürgen Habermas and John Rawls about the relationship between substantive theorizing about social justice and democratic politics. See Jürgen Habermas, 'Reconciliation Through the Public Use of Reason: Remarks on John Rawls's Political Liberalism', *The Journal of Philosophy*, 92/3 (1995), pp. 109–31, and John Rawls, 'Reply to Habermas', in Rawls, *Political Liberalism*, second edition, pp. 372–434. For helpful discussion of this debate, see Joshua Cohen, 'For a Democratic Society', in Samuel Freeman (edited), *The Cambridge Companion to Rawls* (Cambridge: Cambridge University Press, 2003), pp. 86–138, especially pp. 111–28. As Rawls and Cohen point out, Rawls' theorizing about justice, including the thought-experiment of asking what principles of justice people would choose in a hypothetical 'original position', is not offered as a substitute for democratic decision-making, but as a resource to assist democratic decision-making. How far it is used to inform democratic decision-making depends entirely on how far citizens in fact are persuaded of the theory's merits.

[7] Rawls, 'Reply to Habermas', in Rawls, *Political Liberalism*, second edition, p. 427.

[8] Galston's experiences in the White House have informed his subsequent work as a political theorist. See William Galston, *Liberal Pluralism* (Cambridge: Cambridge University Press, 2002) and *The Practice of Liberal Pluralism* (Cambridge: Cambridge University Press, 2004). For an entertaining and insightful personal account of the involvement of political theorists in the Clinton White House,

will often invite political theorists to contribute a philosophical perspective to their seminars on policy issues or to write papers that help to clarify the normative issues and principles that underpin their more empirically oriented research.[9] So it would not be quite honest to suggest that, as a profession, they have no special access or input to political practice. But even here their voice is just one among many. And, of course, however much they may have influenced the policy proposals that emerge, those proposals are themselves no more than fed into the democratic process. In this respect, then, they are like other professionals—transport analysts, economists, scientists, and so on—who lend their expertise where it is asked for. So this is one way in which the contribution of the political theorist is modest, or at least more modest than is sometimes alleged. Whatever her conclusions, and however confident she is of their truth, they have no special authority in the democratic arena.

4

The arguments political theorists offer, then, are best understood as contributions to the democratic process. This hardly counts as modesty; it is no more than a standard view about how political decisions may legitimately be made. Humility is more appropriate when theorists get into the business of evaluating and recommending policies. However good they may be at conceptual analysis and assessing the validity of one another's arguments, or, more substantively, at defending particular normative principles or endorsing particular conceptions of contested concepts, they must recognize that values and principles nearly always yield concrete policy prescriptions only when combined with empirical facts about the particular situations to which they might be applied.[10] Where political theorists do want to assess and recommend policy options, they need to be willing to engage with, and able to understand, the relevant social-scientific evidence.

see Benjamin R. Barber, *The Truth of Power: Intellectual Affairs in the Clinton White House* (New York: Norton, 2001).

[9] See, e.g., David Miller, 'What is Social Justice?', in Nick Pearce and Will Paxton (edited), *Social Justice: Building a Fairer Britain* (London: Institute for Public Policy Research, 2005), pp. 3–20; and Stuart White, 'A Social Democratic Framework for Benefit Conditionality', in Kate Stanley and Liane Asta Lohde with Stuart White (edited), *Sanctions and Sweeteners: Rights and Responsibilities in the Benefits System* (London: Institute for Public Policy Research, 2004), pp. 9–24.

[10] We say 'nearly always' because some normative principles imply some policies directly, as it were, without the mediation of empirical claims about their likely effects. For some theorists, e.g., it is *always* wrong to torture, and the policy of 'no torturing' does not depend on anything we might need social scientists to tell us about. Even in that case, however, there will be some participants in the debate who will adopt a more consequentialist perspective, thinking it relevant to assess the likely effects of such a policy (e.g., the likely reliability of the information elicited by torture). It is very rare in politics for issues to be considered solely in non-consequentialist terms.

Consider, for example, the normative debate around welfare-to-work policies. In a stimulating paper on this subject, Jonathan Wolff argues that such policies are ethically undesirable because (or primarily because) of the problem of 'shameful revelation'.[11] When welfare benefits are made conditional on a test of willingness to work, then the unemployed can only establish their entitlement to benefits by showing that they have looked for employment but failed to get it. Repeated showings of this kind are shameful and damage the self-respect of the unemployed. For this reason, Wolff argues, it is more desirable to have unconditional welfare benefits.

While Wolff is pointing to something that is potentially important, we need to be clear that he has no more than alerted us to a possible mechanism by which welfare-to-work policies might have adverse effects on the self-respect of welfare recipients. One can tell other plausible stories according to which the impact on self-respect is a positive one (for example, perhaps welfare-to-work policies help some individuals overcome weakness-of-will problems, enabling them to act more consistently on the norms that they themselves endorse). The only way to assess the relative importance of the various ways in which welfare-to-work policies might impact on self-respect is by doing, or looking to, empirical research. Wolff's article criticizing welfare-to-work policies does not cite a single empirical study of the psychological impact of welfare-to-work schemes on welfare recipients. Clearly, this limits the force of his critique.

A particular danger that arises when political theorists engage with public policy is that they are not sufficiently attentive to the specifics of policy design or to the particular circumstances in which the policy is being introduced. In making evaluations and offering prescriptions, they may be inclined to overgeneralize with respect to a given type of policy or with respect to the situations in which a given policy is introduced.

Wolff's argument illustrates the risk of overgeneralization. He appeals to the idea that some people may be unable to find a job, despite real effort to do so, and that this fact, when revealed through the job search requirements of the welfare system, is shameful. But what if the specific welfare-to-work policy under scrutiny contains measures to address the problem of unemployability, starting with drug rehabilitation schemes and working up to help with vocational training? Wolff acknowledges this possibility in a footnote, writing that while measures designed to increase employability 'may be the ideal solution in certain cases ... it is at best unclear how generally effective remedial training can be.'[12] However, absent any direct reference to relevant empirical research, there remains a risk of overgeneralization here. Are the 'certain cases' in which

---

[11] Jonathan Wolff, 'Fairness, Respect and the Egalitarian Ethos', *Philosophy & Public Affairs*, 27/2 (1998), pp. 97–122.
[12] Ibid. 117, n. 24.

remedial policies work a small minority, the vast majority, or something in between? Until we know this, it is hard to say whether Wolff's basic argument is one that can be reasonably applied to welfare-to-work schemes in general, or whether it falls down in the case of some welfare-to-work policies which take the obstacles to employability seriously.[13]

The risk of overgeneralization across contexts is something that Harry Brighouse has emphasized in his detailed exploration of social justice and school choice programmes.[14] Proposals for 'choice' are central to the contemporary politics of the welfare state. Proponents argue that choice mechanisms in education and health care provide a way of increasing efficiency in the delivery of public services and meeting the demands of less deferential, more demanding clienteles. But critics worry that choice mechanisms will increase inequality of service provision. Brighouse's analysis, which is deeply informed by relevant empirical literatures, shows that it is very unwise to try to generalize about the effects of choice on equality. In the circumstances of some US cities, given the background pattern of educational provision, some choice-based programmes have been good for equality, or else have been good for other values without making things worse in terms of equality. However, this does not mean we can simply conclude that 'choice' is a good or acceptable thing from an egalitarian point of view. For if the policies that seem to have worked quite well in the US context were just transplanted to Britain, the difference in background institutions means that they might have quite different effects. There might be choice-based options that would work in British circumstances. But these have to be designed very specifically and carefully in light of Britain's own circumstances.

One aspect of the sensitivity-to-context concern is particularly important: the need to keep in mind the difference between ideal and non-ideal theory. There is a crucial distinction between policies that would be justified in an ideal, perhaps ideally just, society and those policies that are justified here and now, in societies that are a long way from the ideal. Again, welfare-to-work policies provide a nice example. On a view of social justice like that set out by John Rawls, it is plausible to argue that welfare-to-work policies would be permissible, perhaps even required, in a just society. For, as Rawls says, in a just society 'each is to do their part in society's co-operative labour.'[15] But it would clearly be mistaken to transfer this judgement uncritically from discussion of

---

[13] Of course, even if a welfare-to-work scheme succeeds in raising the employability of the vast majority of previously unemployable individuals, it may not do this for every initially unemployable person, and the few who are left unemployed might still experience shameful revelation. But whether this would still constitute a decisive objection to the welfare-to-work scheme would depend on the weight we give to the positive impact the scheme has on the employability and self-respect of other initially unemployable citizens. Once we get into the empirical complexity of the policy's effects, ethical evaluation of the policy also becomes more complex.

[14] Harry Brighouse, *School Choice and Social Justice* (New York: Oxford University Press, 2000).

[15] John Rawls, *Justice as Fairness* (Cambridge, MA: Harvard University Press, 2001), p. 179.

the just society to discussion of policy here and now. To the extent that Rawls accepts the case for what Lawrence Mead calls 'work enforcement', he accepts it for a society that satisfies the principles of fair equality of opportunity and the difference principle. But it is unlikely that, say, contemporary British or US society satisfies these principles. Almost certainly, empirical research would show that these societies fall far short of them. Moreover, enforcing work through the welfare system could quite conceivably (again, we need the evidence) consolidate the unjust disadvantage suffered by those who have been disadvantaged by society's failure to satisfy the demands of fair equality of opportunity and the difference principle. Hence, for us, here and now, work enforcement might well be unjust even though it would be permissible or even required in a just society.[16]

It is easy to come up with further examples of policies that would be justified in some, better, circumstances but might only make matters worse if they were implemented here and now. Opponents of selective education in Britain urge the case for comprehensive secondary schools, but while parents with money are able to buy their way into the catchment areas of the best schools there is a case for selection by ability. If schools are not to be genuine microcosms of the wider society, then educational segregation by ability might be a lesser evil than segregation by mortgage. Advocates of greater political equality might favour more direct decision-making by the people as a whole, with a lesser role for elected legislators. But while citizens have very unequal resources with which to pursue their political goals, and very unequal levels of political engagement, it may be that the interests of all members of the population are better respected by representatives elected every few years than by greater reliance on popular participation. Perhaps in a perfectly just society there would be a case for denying the vote to convicted criminals—it is not implausible that those who break the law should forfeit their right to make it. But anybody who knows the demographics of crime and the recent huge expansion in incarceration of young black men must doubt the justice of such a policy in the US today.

Much academic work in political theory today—including much that disputes his substantive positions—operates in a Rawlsian paradigm. Rawls saw his work as operating at the level of ideal theory, assuming just background conditions and that citizens would fully comply with the demands that justice makes of them. Rawls knows that non-ideal theory matters too. 'Obviously the problems of partial compliance theory are the pressing and urgent matters. These are the things that we are faced with in everyday life'. But he continues:

---

[16] Stuart White, *The Civic Minimum*; and Stuart White, 'Is Conditionality Illiberal?', in Lawrence Mead and Christopher Beem (edited), *Welfare Reform and Political Theory* (New York: Russell Sage Foundation, 2005), pp. 82–109.

The reason for beginning with ideal theory is that it provides, I believe, the only basis for the systematic grasp of these more pressing problems ... At least I shall assume that a deeper understanding can be gained in no other way, and that the nature and aims of a perfectly just society is the fundamental part of a theory of justice.[17]

Rawls, then, explicitly contrasts the 'pressing and urgent' with the 'systematic', 'deeper', and 'fundamental', and urges attention to the latter. For some, however, this methodological commitment is very problematic. According to Charles W. Mills, ideal theory 'is in crucial respects obfuscatory, and can indeed be thought of as in part *ideological*, in the pejorative sense of a set of group ideas that reflect, and contribute to perpetuating, illicit group privilege'. For Mills, 'the abstractions of ideal theory are not innocent'. By simply ignoring the actual 'structures of oppression and exclusion that characterize the social and political order', ideal theory has effectively served to 'rationalize the status quo'.[18]

This is not the place to debate the merits and demerits of ideal and non-ideal theory. Our 'division of labour' perspective suggests that there is a place for both. If all political theorists blithely ignored existing injustice in favour of ever-finer-specification of the perfectly just, then that would indeed be a problem, and the discipline could fairly be accused of complacency and 'obfuscation'. Perhaps, under Rawls' influence, the balance did swing a bit too far in the ideal direction, but more recently there has been a clear trend towards applied political theory. What matters, for current purposes, is that theorists are clear about the level at which they are operating and, where the work they are doing is indeed fundamental or abstract, they are realistic about its implications for policy here and now. Matters would be easier if the long-term vision could be achieved smoothly, as it were, by a set of incremental steps each of which brought us unambiguously closer to the goal. In practice, however, there is sometimes an opposition between the sort of policy we think applicable in the ideal scenario and that we think most just, on balance, here and now.[19] Going for the latter might in fact involve moving in some ways further from the sort of policies we think would apply in better circumstances. On this view, then, political theorists who want their work helpfully to engage with existing contexts need to develop what economists call theories of the second best. As Geoffrey Brennan and Philip Pettit put it: 'The second-best option is often not the intuitively closest to the first-best'.[20]

[17] John Rawls, *A Theory of Justice* (Cambridge, MA: Harvard University Press, 1971), p. 9.

[18] Charles W. Mills, '"Ideal Theory" as Ideology', *Hypatia*, 20/3 (2005), pp. 165–84, 166, 184, emphasis in original.

[19] The discussion above suggests that welfare-to-work policy might be a case in point: although arguably permitted or required in a just society, it may be that one way to make our far from ideally just society incrementally more just would be to relax work conditions in welfare.

[20] Geoffrey Brennan and Philip Pettit, 'The Feasibility Issue', in Frank Jackson and Michael Smith (edited), *Companion to Contemporary Philosophy* (New York: Oxford University Press, 2006), pp. 258–79, 261.

Sometimes reading social science, or engaging directly in empirical research of one's own, can change the focus for political theorists, bringing to their attention perspectives and insights that might otherwise go unseen and untheorized. Thus, for example, it was mainly by reading empirical studies on social mobility that Swift became interested in the difficult issue of what precisely parents should be allowed to do to promote their children's interests. The finding that patterns of social fluidity were rather similar across rather different kinds of society, and studies of the processes generating social stratification (understood as a tendency for there to be an association between parents' and children's positions in the distribution of social goods), suggested that a key causal factor generating markedly unequal life-chances between children—quite apart from prejudice or discrimination, direct transmissions of wealth or property, and inequality in access to human-capital-developing private education, which an egalitarian might more readily reject as morally impermissible—were intra-familial interactions of an informal kind (such as the reading of bedtime stories). Since few egalitarians are so keen on equality that they would advocate attempts to prevent behaviour that constitutes the internal life of the family, this prompted a research programme attempting to identify the proper limits of parental partiality, which in turn requires us to think about the fundamental issue of what families are for, morally speaking.[21]

But this kind of empirically informed political theorizing illustrates another point too. Just as political theory must be informed by social science to lead to effective policy, political theory also has a good deal to offer to the social sciences. Having reflected on normative issues, clarified concepts, carefully worked out what values we should be aiming to realize, the political theorist is often in a good position to help social scientists make sure that the empirical phenomena they are investigating are the right ones—the ones that really matter. For although social scientists rightly aim at to be 'value-free' in the way they conduct their empirical research, not allowing their moral views or ideological biases to influence their findings, few would deny that their research is motivated, one way or another, by moral beliefs of one kind or another. Rarely is their interest in describing and explaining the phenomena they seek to describe and explain simply that of acquiring knowledge for its own sake—as, say, a mathematician might value mathematical discovery just to have increased the sum of human understanding. More than this, look carefully at what they do—the way concepts are constructed, the particular things they choose to observe or measure—and one will usually find a host of more specific, often unconscious, assumptions about what precisely is interesting or significant about their work. By being explicit and specific about these

---

[21] Adam Swift, 'Justice, Luck and the Family: Normative Aspects of the Intergenerational Transmission of Advantage', in Samuel Bowles, Herbert Gintis, and Melissa Osborne-Groves (edited), *Unequal Chances: Family Background and Economic Success* (New York: Russell Sage Foundation, 2005), pp. 256–76.

normative assumptions, the political theorist can help to make sure that the focus is in the right place.

Social mobility again provides a nice example. Mobility research is among the most technically sophisticated areas of investigation in sociology, with experts squabbling over precisely how the data should be modelled and which statistical techniques are most appropriate to their analysis. Most sociologists are interested in mobility because of a concern for equality of opportunity. They sense, rightly, that there is something unfair about the inequalities in life-chances, as between children born into different social classes or positions in the income distribution, that their empirical researches uncover. But for most sociologists that normative interest remains rather vague and diffuse. They are not nearly as careful and precise in their analysis of why social mobility matters, or what is morally significant about it, as they are in their attempts to measure it. Here there is room for useful clarification of the normative issues that underlie sociologists' own fundamental interest in their research and, perhaps, scope for an attempt to reorient mobility research in directions likely to shed more light on those issues.[22] In our view, one of the most useful roles for political theorists to play, a particularly helpful contribution to the intellectual and practical division of labour, is that of using their conceptual skills and sensitivity to morally significant distinctions to help social scientists ensure that they are focusing their empirical investigations on the right—the normatively relevant—phenomena.

One area of empirical research where political theorists are particularly well placed to contribute is that of popular beliefs about and attitudes to normative issues. Because they are well versed in the different positions that can be taken on value questions, in the reasons people are likely to have for endorsing the positions that they do, and in the way that different normative concepts (for example, justice, equality, rights, duties...) relate to one another, political theorists are potentially valuable allies of the social scientist trying to find out 'what the people think'. On the one hand, they can help to make more subtle and precise, or better focused on the issues under investigation, the questions that make up the standard research instrument, the questionnaire.[23] On the other hand, conventional opinion polling may yield an overly conservative reading of where the public stands, one that fails to factor in the extent to which a process of public argument over, say, a controversial initiative might shift existing, pre-reflective attitudes. Here the political theorist can use her

[22] Gordon Marshall, Stephen Roberts and Adam Swift, *Against the Odds? Social Class and Social Justice in Industrial Societies* (Oxford: Oxford University Press, 1997); Adam Swift, 'Class Analysis from a Normative Perspective', *British Journal of Sociology*, 51/4 (2000), pp. 663–79; and Adam Swift, 'Would Perfect Mobility Be Perfect?', *European Sociological Review*, 20/1 (2004), pp. 1–11.

[23] For somewhat salutary reflections on his attempt to contribute in this way to the International Social Justice Project, which investigated popular attitudes to social justice in 13 countries, see Adam Swift, 'Public Opinion and Political Philosophy: The Relation between Social-Scientific and Normative Analyses of Distributive Justice', *Ethical Theory and Moral Practice*, 2/4 (1999), pp. 337–63.

expertise to help design and run deliberative polls, or deliberative workshops, which attempt to assess how exposure to relevant evidence and arguments might change people's views and allow the exploration of more considered judgements and attitudes.[24]

Political theorists disagree about the normative significance of 'what the people think', so it may be helpful to clarify our suggestion here. We are not urging attention to public opinion, not even to post-reflective public opinion, because it has any claim to superior insight. True, if public opinion is consistently and substantially out of line with a theorist's position, that may give her grounds for thinking again about her views. And certainly— as we are about to emphasize—it matters hugely in practical terms whether a theorist's arguments gel with the fellow citizens to whom they are offered. But, for us, 'what the people think' is in no sense constitutive of 'the right thing to think' about normative issues. It is, rather, a constraint on the feasibility set— a constraint on the political outcomes that may legitimately be achieved. The theorist is under no injunction to tailor her views on fundamental normative issues to fit the empirical findings that her expertise can help to discover.[25] Indeed, we think this would be to abandon her distinctive role. To act properly as a democratic underlabourer, the political theorist must work out her ideas independently, following her reasoning where it leads, and not simply mirror back to society what most people already think.

5

Public opinion, and the contribution that political theorists can make to its investigation, is an appropriate topic with which to shift our focus from the interface between the political theorist and the social scientist to that between the theorist and the politician. For just as the theorist cannot translate her principles into policy without factoring in evidence supplied by social science, so the theorist is only going to be a useful guide to the practising politician if she is willing to accept the constraints within which contemporary politics operates. Prominent among these, and importantly determining the political feasibility set, is public opinion itself—what the electorate is willing to vote for.

---

[24] For a no less salutary example of this, focused on the issue of inheritance tax and the idea of a 'citizens' inheritance', see Miranda Lewis and Stuart White, 'Inheritance Tax: What Do the People Think? Lessons from Deliberative Workshops', in Will Paxton and Stuart White with Dominic Maxwell (edited), *The Citizen's Stake: Exploring the Future of Universal Asset Policies* (Bristol: Policy Press, 2006), pp. 15–35.

[25] For differing views on this issue, and a case study on the topic of justice-as-desert, see David Miller, *Principles of Social Justice* (Cambridge, MA: Harvard University Press, 1999); and Adam Swift, 'Social Justice: Why Does It Matter What the People Think?', in Daniel Bell and Avner de-Shalit (edited), *Forms of Justice* (Lanham: Rowman and Littlefield, 2003), pp. 13–28.

While the political theorist can happily stick to her guns, as it were, continuing to argue for positions with which few of her fellow citizens agree, politicians who do the same are committing electoral suicide. So if she wants to have any influence on what (non-suicidal) politicians do, the theorist must show what we might think of as a qualified tolerance of the 'princely' vocation.

It is easy to see why political theorists might be intolerant of that vocation. Politicians fudge, evade, and are reluctant to say 'I don't know' or 'I've changed my mind'. Their interest in abstract ideas—'community' or 'social justice' or 'freedom'—or intellectual traditions—'liberalism' or 'social democracy'— is typically short term and strategic. Relying on them rhetorically, for their feel-good factor and useful branding, politicians usually aren't interested in what they actually mean and, when they are, want only inoffensive, innocuous versions. Their concern to stay 'on message'—sticking to the party line for fear of provoking newspaper headlines—prevents that honesty and freedom of thought without which serious discussion is impossible. They concentrate on the defects in opponents' arguments, ignoring—if they can—the bits most likely to lead to intellectual progress. Obsessed with sound bites and simple messages, they won't follow ideas to the point where they get complicated or controversial. Reluctant to accept that they cannot be all things to all voters, they shy away from the hard choices they talk about, preferring convenient fudge to the honest acknowledgement that all good things do not go together.

Politicians use concepts in vague, imprecise ways. They sometimes like it when it's unclear what words mean, because then they can gloss over disagreements and appear to be on everybody's side. They are reluctant to admit that the policies they advocate, though justified overall, will make some people worse off than the policies of their opponents. They are preoccupied with rhetoric and spin, rather than with content or substance; what matters is how things sound, how they play with the electorate, not what they really mean. Sometimes they are slippery—deliberately using weasel words to paper over the cracks in their arguments, avoiding the difficult questions by talking about something else, typically reverting to a favoured mantra ('opportunity for the many not the few', 'there will be no return to the old boom and bust', etc.). Sometimes they just slide around: lacking sufficient precision or clarity, not having thought carefully or specifically enough about the issue under discussion, they shift from one point to another without realizing it. Quite different phenomena—slipperiness is a kind of dishonesty while sliding around is an intellectual failing—they are often combined. Amorphous concepts are favoured because they leave plenty of room for manoeuvre. 'Community' is a prime example.

Political theorists, by contrast, hate it when things are unclear and will harass one another until vagueness is dispelled. They accept the necessity of difficult choices, or of concluding that policies may be justified that make some people worse off—perhaps much worse off—than they might otherwise be.

They understand that intellectual progress is achieved not by easy repetitious exposure of the weak bits of their opponents' arguments but by painful and productive engagement with cogent criticism. Being committed to the pursuit of truth, they are happy (well, prepared) to change their minds, and to admit to changing their minds, when somebody shows them they were wrong. They don't claim to have all the answers. Although apparently and self-indulgently obsessed with words, close inspection reveals the opposite: 'conceptual analysis' is just the only way to get at what people mean when they say things. Once we know the content, the words used drop out as irrelevant.

This last point is important. What should matter to the normative political theorist are not concepts but propositions. It is propositions that are true or false and can be judged in such terms. Concepts are important because they are the terms within which propositions are framed. We don't know what the proposition *is* until we have understood how the person using it understands the concepts used. So we need to engage in conceptual analysis, but we have no interest in claiming one use of a concept better or worse than another. Political theorists want to get beyond concepts to assess the propositions framed in their terms. Politicians like concepts that sound good, however meaningless—or rife with multiple meanings—they may be.

The last few paragraphs have presented the political theorist in rather heroic terms, nobly pursuing arguments where they may lead. The politician, by contrast, appears a grubby figure, steeped in confusion or dishonesty (or both). Of course there is a quite different way of presenting the two vocations. From this alternative perspective, theorists' clarity and purity are in fact irresponsible self-indulgence. The honourable course is to be willing to get one's hands dirty, for that is the price paid by those who attempt to change things through politics. Certainly the theorist tempted to look down on the practising politician must accept that politicians operate in an environment that imposes constraints far more demanding than those faced by political philosophers. The competitive and confrontational nature of today's electoral politics means that any admission of ignorance, change of mind, or acknowledgement that one's opponents might have got something right will be seized on as incompetence, a 'U-turn' or evidence of weakness. The need to win votes, and to present one's party as the representative of the country as a whole, makes it dangerous to concede that one is prepared to make anybody worse off than they might otherwise be. The slightest slip will be spun and exaggerated in the media. Unlike political theorists, politicians have to get elected. This restricts their options. In terms of form, there must be a simple message, one that will immediately make sense to the public. Hence their preoccupation with sound bites, slogans, and the continual search for the 'Big Idea' to lend a simplifying rhetorical unity to their position. In terms of content, they must not be too far removed from current public opinion. Hence their preoccupation with focus groups and the median voter.

Modesty for the theorist here consists in reconciliation to these hard truths about contemporary democratic politics. Since the political theorist does not want to set herself up as a philosopher king, she must accept that the only legitimate way for anybody's views about principles or policy to be put into practice is through the dirty and messy business of politics. Of course, she can criticize the dirtier and messier aspects of that business. She can detest the media's interest in personality rather than politics, or politicians' preoccupation with spin and news management, and she can argue for a better, more principled, way of doing democracy itself. But if she wants to operate at the level of policy—to propose practical measures that would make things better, albeit far from perfect, here and now—then there is no alternative to a sober engagement with the realities of contemporary politics, and, perhaps, a more sympathetic attitude to those who struggle with them on a daily basis.

But reconciliation should not obscure the crucial role that the political theorist has still to play. It may be true that politics is not a wholly rational activity, that the careful exposition of clear arguments will simply triumph over emotion and prejudice. There is always going to be a place for rhetoric, and there may well be good strategic reasons for politicians to pander to the confusions and false beliefs of those whose votes they seek. Given the way in which their words are misrepresented by opponents and amplified in the media, some evasion and fudging are doubtless justified. Party unity may indeed be essential for political success, and that will imply some reluctance to say what one really thinks. If that is how to get elected and make the world a better place than it would otherwise have been, these strategic reasons may also be moral reasons. So sliding and slipperiness are not always bad. But reasons for saying vague or mistaken things are not reasons for holding vague or mistaken beliefs. When it comes to *thinking*, clarity, precision, and truth have to be better than the alternatives. Even if political strategy requires politicians not to be too pure or precise in the positions they present to voters, that is no reason for them to be unclear about what they really believe, about what values they expect such a strategy to realize, and why they endorse those values. Indeed, a clear sense of the normative principles that underlie a political position—a clear understanding of what that position really is— helps politicians deal with unexpected events and provides a unity to their various policy proposals in ways that can themselves bring electoral advantage. Voters can sense when politicians are trimming or politically opportunistic. The pragmatic and strategic pursuit of carefully thought through goals is one thing. Flailing around without a moral compass is quite another. Political theorists can help provide one.

Nor, finally, should the political theorist entirely reconcile herself to the constraints that define the feasibility set confronting today's politicians. We have already suggested that she can criticize the way that politics is conducted, urging reform of the more blatant unfairnesses in current ways of doing democracy. The idea, of course, is that the urging of reform is part of the process whereby reform is brought about. That applies across the full range of political issues—what policies we should pursue as well as our ways of deciding them. Politicians are indeed subject to short-term electoral constraints, but those constraints are in large part constituted by the values and attitudes of the democratic public. It is precisely those values and attitudes that political theorists can seek to change. That change will not happen immediately—it took over 100 years for the arguments of Mill's *On Liberty* to find their way into liberal legislation on homosexuality in the UK. But it will not happen at all unless it is argued for.

Again, then, our exhortation to modesty must be tempered by a proper sense of the fundamentally important task of political theory. Yes, it would be helpful for theorists to develop a philosophically informed approach that takes social science and feasibility sets more seriously, a middle ground between unworldly utopianism and grubby electoral politics. We should indeed think hard about how to tailor our proposals to the realities we seek to improve. But we must be clear about what exactly is being tailored and why. Theorists should not allow political constraints, or the results of social science, to corrupt their reflection on ultimate principles. What social justice requires of us or what it would mean to take equality of opportunity or community seriously are questions that cannot be answered by considering how much of them can be achieved, or how much it makes political sense to argue for, here and now.

We must steer clear of what psychologists call 'adaptive preference formation' or what in this context we might call 'value creep': allowing one's sense of what is of ultimate value to be dictated by one's perception of what is politically feasible in the near term.[26] Those who focus too much on 'the kind or amount of justice it is realistic to pursue here and now' are in danger of believing their own rhetoric. They start with an assessment of what is politically feasible in the short run. From this they work out a policy agenda. They then fit an account of ultimate values around this policy agenda. A good deal of theorizing around New Labour's 'Third Way' seems to us to proceed in this kind of way.[27] This makes political theory hostage to public opinion, and thereby fails to respect the political theorist's own vocation. Politicians can be relied on to dilute the truth if feasibility constraints and electoral considerations require it. The political theorist's task is to prevent that truth from slipping out of sight altogether, not simply to accommodate public opinion but, as we implied earlier, to change, and improve, it.

[26] On the risk of adaptive preference formation in political theory, see G. A. Cohen, 'The Future of a Disillusion', in G. A. Cohen, *Self-Ownership, Freedom and Equality* (Cambridge: Cambridge University Press, 1995), pp. 245–65.

[27] See Anthony Giddens, *Where Now for New Labour?* (Cambridge: Polity, 2002). See, e.g., the discussion of equality at pp. 38–43 in which considerations of principle and political feasibility seem unduly entangled.

6

For us, the political theorist is making a vital yet distinctive contribution to a collaborative division of labour. She clarifies concepts, interrogates claims about how the political community should organize its collective affairs (including claims about what should count as that community's 'collective affairs'), and argues for particular principles (or conceptions of values, or balances of competing values). It is, typically, only when combined with empirical knowledge, of the kind generated by social science, that her analysis and justification of fundamental principles implies particular policies. And the practical skills of the democratic politician—sensing what is and is not politically feasible at any time, building coalitions behind political programmes, communicating those programmes to the public—are needed for those policies to be put into practice. So the theorist should be modest in her understanding of her role, while simultaneously insisting that hers is a crucially important part of the process—and one that, in the long run, changes both the data that social scientists investigate and the feasibility sets within which politicians operate.

If one accepts that doing politics well involves different tasks with different expertises, then the division of labour has to be the right model. Those who are skilled in conceptual analysis and nice moral distinctions cannot realistically be the same people as those who know how best to research complex empirical phenomena. And neither of them can also be the people who can stir a nation to political action—even to the voting booth—through fine speeches and political leadership. One develops true mastery of any of those activities only by experience and practice, so to deny a division of labour model risks encouraging jacks of all trades who are masters of none. This decidedly does not mean that those engaged in any of these activities can and should remain unaware of what others are doing. Quite the contrary. We hope that the examples discussed in this chapter illustrate the kind of work that can be done by theorists who take the trouble to come to terms with relevant social science. But it does mean that one needs to keep very clear precisely what kind of contribution one is seeking to make—what level one is operating on at any given time. For theorists, we have suggested, this is most true where the ideal/non-ideal distinction rears its challenging head.

According to Bernard Williams:

Philosophers often say that the point of their efforts is to make the unclear clearer. But they may make the clear unclear: they may cause plain truths to disappear into difficult cases, sensible concepts to dissolve into complex definitions, and so on. To some extent philosophers do this. Still more, they may seem to do it, and even to seem to do it can be a political disservice.[28]

---

[28] Bernard Williams, 'Human Rights and Relativism', in Geoffrey Hawthorn (edited), *In the Beginning Was the Deed* (Princeton University Press, 2005), pp. 62–74, 64.

While we defend the kind of careful clarification that philosophers go in for, we also accept that there are ways in which it risks making things more obscure. So the division-of-labour approach has one clear implication for political theorists. We are not doing our job if the fruits of our research remain inaccessible, often simply unintelligible, to those outside the charmed circle of academic political theory. We are not suggesting that all political theorists should do popularizing or user-friendly work. Much of the really important foundational work in political theory is of necessity difficult and complex, and there is no more reason why it should be susceptible to understanding by the untrained citizen than is the discourse of contemporary science. But unless some of us engage in the project of translation—from abstruse, sometimes technical, books and journal articles into modes that our fellow citizens, or even our politicians, can make sense of—our discipline will not be playing the vital role of which it is capable.

4 Why be formal?

Iwao Hirose

1

Formal analysis in political theory is concerned with the form, as distinguished from the matter, of political behaviour and phenomena. It reduces political behaviour and phenomena to a model represented by mathematical and logical symbols, and elucidates its structure rather than its meaning. Decision theorists and economists have developed formal analysis of individual choices and complex economic phenomena. The results of this are political analysis involving public choice, game theoretic models of politics, spatial models of party competition and legislative behaviour, and deductive modelling of political phenomena. Formal methods can also be used when we analyse normative political theories. For example, game theory helps us to look at much-discussed theories of justice in a new light.[1]

Some political philosophers believe that formal analysis is shallow. They maintain that the subject matter of political theory is irreducibly complex, and that formal analysis is not meaningful because it reduces political phenomena to simplified models. I disagree. Formal analysis is not supposed to explain every political problem. It merely offers a new perspective to issues in political theory. In this chapter I hope to show how formal analysis sheds a new light on normative political theories.

This chapter is not intended to survey the extensive literature of formal analysis in political theory, nor is it intended as a general introduction to formal theory. Rather, it focuses on some aspects of formal analysis in order to elucidate how it can be used in studying normative political theory. No technical background is assumed. This chapter is organized as follows. Section 2 explains why we use the formal methods in normative political theory, and introduces the very basic notion of binary relations. Section 3 introduces Arrow's impossibility theorem in social choice theory as an example of formal analysis that has many far-reaching implications for normative political theory, and offers an account of how an axiomatic analysis is conducted. Section 4 considers Derek Parfit's 'levelling down' objection to a version of

---

[1] A good example is Jean Hampton, *Hobbes and the Social Contract Tradition* (Cambridge: Cambridge University Press, 1988).

egalitarianism, and shows that relatively straightforward mathematics can be useful in the analysis of one of the central issues in contemporary political philosophy. Section 5 presents two fundamental problems of the consistency requirements that are usually assumed in the formal and deductive model in normative political theory.

2

Why do we use formal methods to analyse political theory? At the beginning of this chapter, I said that formal analysis elucidates the structure of a theory. Let me explain. Consider axiomatic analysis, which is a standard approach in formal analysis. Axiomatic analysis starts with a set of abstract conditions (axioms), each of which is believed to be true, and reaches a conclusion (theorem) that is proved to be logically true from that set of conditions through the process of reasoning (proof) alone. If you believe that every individual axiom is true, you would believe that the theorem is also true in so far as the process of reasoning is valid. If you find the theorem hard to believe, you may well want to revise one or more axioms you initially believed to be true, and prove another theorem. Axioms are seen as the basic properties of a theory, and we can see in them the basic features that a theory is made of. For example, utilitarianism is informally defined as the principle that it is right to maximize individuals' aggregate welfare. In axiomatic analysis, utilitarianism is characterized in various ways, depending on the set of axioms we assume. There are several ways to break down utilitarianism into a set of basic properties (putting that another way: we can *axiomatize* utilitarianism in multiple ways).[2] By examining the different characterizations, we can understand the structure of utilitarianism from each different standpoint. This can then be useful when we consider the nature of utilitarianism.

It would be helpful to start with some basic formal notions that are used in almost all formal analysis. Let us start by defining *binary relations*. A binary relation is used to represent a relation between two alternatives, for example, 'Liz is at least as tall as Tiffany', 'Scotland is at least as beautiful as England', and so on. To talk about a binary relation, we must specify (*a*) a set of alternatives we are to compare and (*b*) in which term we are to compare the relevant alternatives (it does not make sense to say 'Liz is greener than England'). When I say 'Liz is taller than Tiffany', I rank a set of people in terms of their height. In microeconomics, the relevant set is usually a set of bundles of goods and services, and we define a person's preference relation over the set of bundles

[2] For example, see John C. Harsanyi, 'Cardinal Welfare, Individualistic Ethics, and Interpersonal Comparisons of Utility', *Journal of Political Economy*, 63/4 (1955), pp. 309–21; and Eric S. Maskin, 'A Theorem on Utilitarianism', *Review of Economic Studies*, 45/1 (1978), pp. 93–6.

of goods and services. In social choice theory, a binary relation is defined as a preference relation over a set of states of affairs (a state of affairs is a complete description of the world). A binary relation on X is written as xRy for any ordered pair $(x, y) \in X \times X$. Read this as 'x is at least as R as y' (for example, 'Liz is at least as tall as Tiffany', which means either 'Liz is just as tall as Tiffany' or 'Liz is strictly taller than Tiffany'). The symmetric part of R, I (for example, 'Liz is just as tall as Tiffany') is defined as xIy if xRy and yRx (if 'Liz is at least as tall as Tiffany' and if 'Tiffany is at least as tall as Liz', this implies that 'Liz is just as tall as Tiffany'). The asymmetric part of R, P (for example, 'Liz is strictly taller than Tiffany') is defined as xPy if xRy and not yRx (if 'Liz is at least as tall as Tiffany' and if 'Tiffany is *not* at least as tall as Liz', this implies that 'Liz is strictly taller than Tiffany').

There are some properties of binary relations that are relevant. A binary relation R is *reflexive* on X if for all $x \in X$, xRx. It is *transitive* if for all x, y, $z \in X$, xRy and yRz, then xRz. It is *complete* on X if for all $x, y \in X$, either xRy or yRx (i.e., we can rank every pair of alternatives in the relevant set). If a binary relation R is reflexive, transitive, and complete, it is a *complete weak ordering*. If a binary relation R is reflexive and transitive but not complete, it is a *partial weak ordering*. In economics, a binary relation is usually taken to be a *weak preference relation* of an individual. For each $i \in N := \{1, 2, \ldots, n\}$, $xR_i y$ denotes the individual i's preference on X, where $xR_i y$ holds if i strictly prefers x to y or i is indifferent between x and y. Needless to say, a person's preference relation is concerned with her mental states. A binary relation R can be a relation of non-mental states. For example, R can be a *betterness relation*. That is, $xR_i y$ means that x is at least as good for the individual i as y.[3]

Formal analysis must be consistent. There must be no inconsistency or contradiction. Formal analysis in political theory is built upon the assumption that individual preference orderings are consistent. There are different sorts of consistency requirements. Suppose that you strictly prefer x to y, and that you strictly prefer y to x simultaneously. Your preference is contradictory. Formally, you are not allowed to have contradicting preferences simultaneously. The consistency requirement, that is the requirement of non-contradiction, tells us that there is something wrong in your mind, and probably that you should revise your preferences. Suppose now that you strictly prefer x to y and y to z, but you strictly prefer z to x, in which case your preferences violate transitivity. Transitivity tells you there is again something wrong in your mental states. Some people would find that these two consistency requirements are quite different in the sense that transitivity is more demanding than non-contradiction. Once your strict preference of x over y is recognized, then

---

[3] For the betterness-based moral and political theory, and its difference from the preference-based one, see John Broome, *Weighing Goods* (Oxford: Blackwell, 1991).

your strict preference of y over x does not make sense. Thus, people would agree that you should comply with the requirement of non-contradiction. On the other hand, some people would find transitivity to be less clear-cut. We sometimes happen to have an intransitive preference, and we would not be strongly inclined to comply with transitivity. There is a difference in the degree of demandingness between various consistency requirements.

Consistency constrains the preferences of individuals. Why do we expect individuals to put on such a straightjacket? There are three reasons for imposing consistency requirements. First, consistency helps us to *predict* individuals' choices and behaviour. Many works in formal theory rely on the specific view of consistency formalized in what is called *revealed preference theory*. Given some observation of a person's choices, consistency requirements made in rational choice theory tell us what she will choose when faced with a choice between different alternatives. When it is observed that you strictly prefer x to y and y to z, from transitivity, it is predicted that you would strictly prefer x to z, even if your preference regarding x and z is not yet observed.

Second, consistency requirements help us to *explain* why an individual behaves in a certain way. A person has various considerations and motivations, and acts with or without deliberation, but a certain systematic structure may underlie a series of her choices and behaviour. This structure would be explained by consistency requirements. Again, if you strictly prefer x to y and y to z and if you happen to prefer x to z, we can explain that you strictly prefer x to z because of transitivity.

Third (and most controversially), consistency requirements are *normative*. On this view, there is a normative reason to meet consistency requirements, that is, we *ought* to have a consistent preference ordering. If you have, for example, an intransitive preference, then you commit a normative failure. If a person's preference satisfies consistency requirements, she would be seen to be acting wisely and sensibly. Otherwise, she would be seen as unwise. There might be some advantage in being seen as wise and sensible. I shall come back to this point later.

3

To give some idea about how formal analysis proceeds, I shall start by presenting a rough sketch of Kenneth Arrow's *impossibility theorem*, which has been extensively discussed in political theory.[4] To introduce Arrow's impossibility

---

[4] Kenneth J. Arrow, *Social Choice and Individual Values* (New York: Wiley, 1951). For a comprehensive survey of the literature of social choice and welfare, see Amartya K. Sen, 'Social Choice Theory',

theorem, it would be helpful to present *Condorcet's voting paradox*, as Arrow's impossibility theorem is seen as a generalization of this paradox. Suppose that there are three voters (i, j, and k), and three alternatives (x, y, and z). Suppose further these three individuals have the following strict preference ordering over x, y, and z:

i: $xP_i yP_i z$

j: $yP_j zP_j x$

k: $zP_k xP_k y$

Apply the simple majority rule to the binary comparison of alternatives. When we compare x and y, xPy, because $xP_i y$ and $xP_k y$ (i.e., x is socially strictly preferred to y, because both i and k strictly prefer x to y and jointly beat j's preference). When we compare y and z, yPz, because $yP_i z$ and $yP_j z$. When we compare x and z, zPx, because $zP_j x$ and $zP_k x$. Thus, we have $xPyPzPx$, which is intransitive (more precisely, cyclical). If three alternatives are ranked transitively, one of the voters is a 'dictator' in the sense that the social ranking of all three alternatives coincides with the ranking of that voter (for example, if it happens to be the case that $yPzPx$, then j is the dictator). The simple majority rule which is extensively used as a democratic decision-making rule allows the existence of a person whose preference is decisive over other people's preferences.

Now to turn to Arrow's theorem: let X and $N := \{1, 2, \ldots, n\}$ be the set of all states of affairs and the set of all individuals in the society, where $2 \leq n < +\infty$ (the number of individuals is finite and at least two) and $3 \leq \# X$ (there are at least three states of affairs). For each $i \in N$, R_i denotes the individual i's weak preference relation on X, which is assumed to be reflexive, transitive, and complete. Let R be a *social welfare ordering* defined on X. A social welfare ordering ranks the states of affairs from the social point of view. A *social welfare rule* (Arrow calls it 'constitution') is a function f that specifies one social welfare ordering R for any n-tuple of individuals' preference orderings $\{R_i\}$. In plain words, a social welfare rule aggregates individuals' preference orderings to a social welfare ordering. There is an important assumption here about individuals' preference orderings; individuals' preference orderings are assumed to be *ordinal* and *interpersonally incomparable*. In other words, these preference orderings merely represent the ranking of states of affairs, and the level (or the unit) of preference satisfaction among different individuals cannot be compared.

in Kenneth J. Arrow and Michael Intriligator (edited), *Handbook of Mathematical Economics*, volume 3 (Amsterdam: North-Holland, 1986); and Kotaro Suzumura, *Rational Choice, Collective Decisions and Social Welfare* (Cambridge: Cambridge University Press, 1983).

Arrow's impossibility theorem holds that there exists no social welfare rule that satisfies four seemingly uncontroversial conditions simultaneously. The four conditions are:

Condition U (unrestricted domain): The domain of the social welfare rule includes all logically possible n-tuples of individual orderings of X (the social welfare rule can take all logically possible preference orderings as its domain).

Condition P (weak Pareto principle): For any $[x, y]$ in X, if everyone strictly prefers x to y, then xPy (if all individuals strictly prefer x to y, then society would strictly prefer x to y).

Condition D (non-dictatorship): There is no individual i such that for all preference n-tuples in the domain of the social welfare rule, for each ordered pair $x, y \in X$, if $xP_i y$, then xPy (the ranking of the social welfare ordering does not coincide with the ranking of an identified individual whatever others may rank).

Condition I (independence of irrelevant alternatives): If any pair $x, y \in X$, for all i: ($xR_i y$ if and only if $xR'_i y$) and ($yR_i x$ if and only if $yR'_i x$), then $f([Ri])$ and $f([R'_i])$ rank x and y in exactly the same way (the social ranking of two alternatives depends only on individuals' preferences over these two alternatives).

Arrow's theorem is stated as follows:

Arrow's impossibility theorem: *If a social welfare rule f satisfies conditions U, P, and I, then f is dictatorial.*

In other words, there exists no social welfare rule satisfying conditions U, P, D, and I simultaneously. There are many proofs of the theorem in the literature. In what follows, I shall present Amartya Sen's proof.[5] In doing so, we need to introduce the notion of decisiveness.

Decisiveness: *For any pair of states of affairs x and y, a group $G \subset N$ (a proper subset of N) is decisive for x over y if xPy when everyone in G strictly prefers x to y and everyone in $N - G$ strictly prefers y to x.*

We prove the theorem through two lemmas (proven statements used as stepping stones towards the proof of another statement). The first lemma is:

Field-Expansion Lemma: *If a group of individuals is decisive over any pair of states of affairs, then that group is decisive over every pair of states of affairs.*

---

[5] Amartya K. Sen, *Collective Choice and Social Welfare* (San Francisco: Holden-Day, 1970), chapter 3; and Amartya K. Sen, 'Rationality and Social Choice', *American Economic Review*, 85/1 (1995), pp. 1–24. For different types of the proof see, e.g., John E. Roemer, *Theories of Distributive Justice* (Cambridge, MA: Harvard University Press, 1996); and Suzumura, *Rational Choice, Collective Decisions and Social Welfare*, chapter 3.

Proof: Take two pairs of states (x, y) and (a, b). Suppose that group G is decisive over (x, y). We need to show that the same group G is decisive over (a, b), too. By unrestricted domain, let each individual in G prefer a to x to y to b. Let all others prefer a to x, and y to b, leaving the ordering of a and b completely unspecified. By the weak Pareto principle, aPx and yPb. By the decisiveness of G over (x, y), clearly xPy. Thus, by (quasi-)transitivity, aPb. By the independence of irrelevant alternatives, this must depend only on the individual orderings of a and b. Therefore, G is decisive over (a, b) as well, completing the proof of the lemma.

The second lemma is:

Group-Contraction Lemma: *If a group is decisive, then some smaller group in that group is also decisive.*

Proof: Take a decisive group G and partition it into G_1 and G_2 ($G_1 \cap G_2 = \emptyset$ and $G_1 \cup G_2 = G$). Let the preference orderings of the three groups be the following in strict descending order, over some triple $\{x, y, z\}$:

$G_1: z, x, y$

$G_2: x, y, z$

$N{-}G: y, z, x$

By the decisiveness of G, xPy. Now, a question arises: how is z ranked? By completeness, either zPy or xPz. If zPy, then G_1 is decisive over for z over x. If xPz, then G_2 is decisive for x over z. Therefore, either G_1 or G_2 is decisive. This completes the proof of the lemma.

In either case, we have a pair of states of affairs and a decisive group that is strictly smaller than the smallest decisive group. But this is a contradiction. Hence the smallest decisive group must contain a single person.

We have now proved the main theorem. By the weak Pareto principle, the group of all individuals is decisive. Since the number of the individuals is finite, by successive partitioning, we find an individual who is decisive over the others. This means that the same individual is a 'dictator' (hence, the violation of non-dictatorship). This completes the proof of the theorem.

This theorem is remarkable and upsetting. It is remarkable because it shows that there exists no social welfare rule that satisfies four seemingly uncontroversial conditions. It appears to be upsetting because the four conditions are seen to be weak in democratic society, but, logically speaking, there exists no social welfare rule satisfying these conditions simultaneously. But we need not feel too pessimistic. This theorem should be seen as a constructive challenge rather than the dead end of democratic social welfare rules. There are several possibility theorems in the extensive literature. Some possibility theorems are not very illuminating as far as normative political theory is concerned, because the axioms or assumptions are revised in such a way that the substantive implication for normative political theory is not straightforward. For example, if the number of individuals is assumed to be infinite, it is shown that there exists a class of social welfare rule that satisfies all of Arrow's conditions simultaneously.[6] Undeniably, this result helps us to understand the far-reaching scope of Arrow's impossibility theorem. But is there a substantive implication for normative political theory?

There are many illuminating possibility (and impossibility) theorems. One example is provided by Amartya Sen.[7] In the original Arrovian framework, the individual preference orderings are assumed to be ordinal and interpersonally incomparable. This is a standard assumption in what is called *new welfare economics*, after the work of Lionel Robbins and Paul Samuelson.[8] In new welfare economics, a person's utility is understood as her preference satisfaction, and it is claimed that there is no scientific basis on which to compare the mental states of different individuals. According to this view, in order for economics to be a branch of science, non-scientific elements such as interpersonal comparison of utility should be ruled out. However, given that social choice is concerned with social welfare judgements about states of affairs, the subject itself includes (or ought to include) some element of normative concerns— such as justice, equality, fairness, and so on—and these concerns inevitably demand interpersonal comparison of some sort. For example, if interpersonal comparison is ruled out, then social welfare judgements do not consider the distribution of people's utility at all. If we care about the normative issues, we would need to expand the informational basis of social welfare judgements and introduce some sort of interpersonal comparison.

One of Sen's contributions concerns this aspect of Arrow's impossibility theorem. He shows that there exists a class of social welfare rules if interpersonal comparability is admitted. For example, if it is assumed that the *level* of people's utility can be compared, we can have a position-dictatorship, such as the lexicographic extension of maximin (*leximin* for short). In ranking states of affairs, leximin first compares the level of the worst off individual across the states of affairs, and if the worst off individuals are at the same level, it then proceeds to compare the level of the second worst off, and so on. Leximin gives lexical priority to a worse-off individual, and underlies John Rawls' difference principle.[9] Needless to say, the difference principle is one of Rawls' two principles of justice, and is applied only to (*a*) the basic social

---

[6] Peter C. Fishburn, 'Arrow's Impossibility Theorem: Concise Proof and Infinite Voters', *Journal of Economic Theory*, 2/1 (1970), pp. 103–6.

[7] Sen, *Collective Choice and Social Welfare*, chapters 8–9.

[8] Lionel Robbins, *An Essay on the Nature and Significance of Economic Science* (London: Macmillan, 1932); and Paul A. Samuelson, *Foundations of Economic Analysis* (Cambridge, MA: Harvard University Press, 1947).

[9] For the axiomatic characterization of leximin, see Claude d'Asprimont and Luis Gevers, 'Equity and the Informational Basis of Collective Choice', *Review of Economic Studies*, 44/2 (1977),

structure, (b) the representative individuals of different groups, and (c) the comparison in terms of primary social goods. Our formal analysis cannot capture the rich and complex arguments in Rawls' *A Theory of Justice* fully. However, this possibility result can motivate the Rawlsian difference principle as a social welfare rule that we may adopt.

4

That was an example of axiomatic analysis. Axiomatic analysis requires some training in formal techniques. But it is possible to conduct formal analysis with much more straightforward mathematics. In this section, I consider Derek Parfit's so-called 'levelling down' objection to a version of egalitarianism,[10] and show how simple mathematics can be used to analyse ongoing discussions in contemporary political philosophy. It is not necessary to use formal methods to consider Parfit's objection, but formal methods help us to shed new light on it.

Some egalitarians contend that equality is best understood as a teleological notion; that is, inequality is a bad (or equality is a good). Other egalitarians contend that equality is a deontological notion, that is, inequality is unfair or unjust. Parfit calls egalitarianism of the first type *telic egalitarianism*, and raises an objection to this type of egalitarianism. According to Parfit, telic egalitarianism holds at least one principle, the *principle of equality*, according to which it is in itself bad if some people are worse off than others. The principle of equality alone, however, would not constitute a plausible distributive principle. This is because the distributive principle, based only on the principle of equality, would judge that a perfectly equal distribution is equally as good as another perfectly equal distribution, even though one distribution is strictly better for everyone than the other (to see this, compare $x = (10, 10)$ and $y = (5, 5)$ in the two-person case). The principle of equality would need to be combined with another principle, for example, the *principle of utility*, according to which it is in itself good if people are better off.

Parfit's 'levelling down' objection runs as follows. Suppose that the level of a better-off person is lowered to the level of a worse-off person without benefiting any person (for example, we burn some of a better-off person's resources so that she ends up at the level of a worse-off person). According to Parfit, telic egalitarianism judges that this levelling down is better at least

pp. 199–210; and Robert Deschamps and Luis Gevers, 'Leximin and Utilitarian Rules: A Joint Characterization', *Journal of Economic Theory*, 17/2 (1978), pp. 143–63.

[10] Derek Parfit, *Equality or Priority?* (Kansas: University of Kansas Lindley Lecture, 1995). Reprinted in Matthew Clayton and Andrew Williams (edited), *The Ideal of Equality* (Basingstoke: Palgrave Macmillan, 2000).

in one respect, because it makes the outcome more equal. However, Parfit believes that levelling down is not better in any respect. Thus, Parfit claims that telic egalitarianism is absurd.

The levelling down objection is widely considered a serious challenge to telic egalitarianism. It seems that there is nothing good about a levelling down. Formal methods, however, can offer another way to look at this objection. Let R be a betterness relation defined on the set of states of affairs X (let us assume R is reflexive, transitive, and complete), and g be a social welfare function such that $g(x) \geq g(y)$ if and only if xRy. Let w_i represent person i's co-cardinal welfare (ratios of differences of welfare are interpersonally determinate). We only consider people's welfare to rank the states of affairs. This means that $x = (w_1, w_2, \ldots, w_n)$ is at least as good as $y = (w'_1, w'_2, \ldots, w'_n)$ if and only if $g(w_1, w_2, \ldots, w_n) \geq g(w'_1, w'_2, \ldots, w'_n)$. According to telic egalitarianism, the social welfare function is such that it is in itself bad if some people are worse off than others. For the sake of simplicity, consider the following simple two-person case of telic egalitarianism:

$$g(w_1, w_2) = \frac{1}{2}(w_1 + w_2) - \frac{1}{4}|w_1 - w_2|. \tag{1}$$

According to this social welfare function, the relative goodness of states of affairs is judged by the average welfare of the two people and the absolute difference between these two people. This function is surely a version of telic egalitarianism. The disvalue of inequality, $1/4|w_1 - w_2|$, represents what Parfit calls the principle of equality. People's average welfare represents the principle of utility. Therefore, Equation (1) is clearly a combination of these two principles.

Does this version of telic egalitarianism encounter the objection? Suppose that person 1 is strictly better off than person 2, namely that $w_1 > w_2$. If w_1 is reduced to the level of w_2, the value of $1/4(w_1 - w_2)$ is reduced to nil, and hence the disvalue of inequality is reduced. It therefore seems as though the levelling down of w_1 is better in terms of reduction of inequality. On the face of it, telic egalitarianism as Equation (1) *seems* to be susceptible to the objection. But it is not.

There is another way to look at telic egalitarianism as expressed in Equation (1).[11] By a simple rearrangement, Equation (1) can be written as follows:

$$g(w_1, w_2) = \begin{cases} \frac{1}{4}w_1 + \frac{3}{4}w_2 & \text{if } w_1 \geq w_2 \\ \frac{3}{4}w_1 + \frac{1}{4}w2 & \text{if } w_1 \leq w_2 \end{cases} \tag{2}$$

---

[11] I owe the following point to John Broome. See also Charles Blackorby and David Donaldson, 'A Theoretical Treatment of Indices of Absolute Equality', *International Economic Review*, 21/1 (1980), pp. 107–36. Equations (1) and (2) are known as the *Gini social welfare function* in economic theory.

Equation (1) is mathematically equivalent to Equation (2). That is, for any pair of states of affairs, the two equations always reach the same distributive judgement, and rank the states of affairs in exactly the same way.

However, according to Equation (2), the levelling down is *not* better in *any* respect. Suppose again that $w_1 > w_2$. According to telic egalitarianism as formulated in Equation (2), the levelling down of w_1 is not better for person 2. It is just worse for person 1. There is no respect with regard to which the levelling down of w_1 is better. No wonder. Telic egalitarianism as formulated in Equation (2) is represented as the weighted sum of people's welfare. Thus, telic egalitarianism as formulated in Equation (2) is not susceptible to the objection. Although Equations (1) and (2) are equivalent, the levelling down *seems* to be better at least in one respect according to Equation (1), and it is not better in any respect according to Equation (2).

In Equation (1), the relative goodness of states of affairs is considered in terms of two respects: the value of aggregated welfare and the disvalue of inequality. It can be claimed that levelling down is better in the latter respect. On the other hand, in Equation (2), the relative goodness of states of affairs is not considered in terms of the individual components; it is given by the weighted sum of two people's welfare. The difference between the two equations lies in the ways of *decomposing* a state of affairs. What goes on in the rearrangement from (1) to (2) is this: the disvalue of inequality is reduced to the weight of each person's welfare. In Equation (2), the fact that person 1 is better off than person 2 decreases the weight of person 1's welfare in the overall goodness of the state of affairs, and the fact that person 2 is worse off than person 1 increases the weight of person 2's welfare in the overall goodness of the state of affairs. That is, the disvalue of inequality is reduced to the weight, or the moral importance, of each person's welfare. This reduction removes 'one respect' in which the levelling down is better.

There are many ways to decompose a state of affairs into mutually exclusive and jointly exhaustive elements. We may divide the population into men and women; we first aggregate the values of men's welfare and women's welfare separately, and then aggregate them into the overall goodness of the state of affairs. Or we may divide the population by geographical region; we aggregate the value of a state of affairs in each region separately and then aggregate the value of individual regions into the overall goodness. Thus, there are many ways to aggregate the overall goodness of states of affairs, and there are many ways to decompose the goodness of states of affairs. But telic egalitarianism is not committed to a particular way of decomposition. From our formal perspective, telic egalitarianism is one type of social welfare function. A telic egalitarian social welfare function aggregates individuals' welfare in such a way that the more equal the distribution is, the better the state of affairs. It does not aggregate individuals' welfare *and* equality. Equality is not an object of aggregation but a feature of the aggregation process. According to our formal framework, it does not make sense to say that the levelling down is better in one respect. The use of formal methods thus suggests that Parfit's levelling down objection is misguided from the beginning.

If this response to the levelling down objection is correct, a new question arises. What is telic egalitarianism all about? More precisely, how do we make sense of the claim that equality is valuable in itself? Remember that the levelling down objection sets out with a widely agreed-upon idea of telic egalitarianism, that equality is valuable in itself. If equality is valuable in itself, the objection continues, levelling down is better in one respect. Our formal analysis has rejected the consequent. This suggests that either (*a*) the antecedent is not true or (*b*) the logical inference in the levelling down objection is not valid (or both). If (*a*), telic egalitarianism cannot hold that equality is valuable in itself. Either, telic egalitarianism must hold that equality is valuable in another sense; or, telic egalitarianism should be understood in a different way. This possibility makes us reconsider the nature of equality in telic egalitarianism. On the other hand, if (*b*), it is only claimed that the consequent does not follow from the antecedent. This would be because the antecedent is not sufficiently precise. For example, suppose that the relative goodness of states of affairs is given by the following function:

$$g(w_1, w_2) = 1/2(w_1 + w_2) - \sqrt{|w_1 - w_2|}. \tag{3}$$

In this case, we cannot use the mathematical manoeuvre that we used in Equation (2); we cannot remove the respect with regard to which the levelling down is better. It might be argued that the levelling down objection picks out this type of telic egalitarianism. But, in so far as the telic egalitarianism of Equation (2) is seen as a version of telic egalitarianism, the original consequent does not follow. The antecedent must be revised in such a way that it rules out telic egalitarianism as Equations (1) or (2). In this case, the reach of the original levelling down objection is not as far as we initially thought.

5

I now wish to address two fundamental problems concerning consistency requirements. The first problem is that there would be no normative reason to satisfy consistency requirements. As I discussed earlier, one of the cases for imposing consistency requirements is that these requirements are normative: there is a normative reason to have a consistent preference ordering. Surely, it would be nice to be seen as rational rather than impulsive. It would also be the case that having a consistent preference is beneficial for a pragmatic reason. However, it is not immediately clear why there is a *normative* reason to have consistent preferences, or why we ought to have a consistent preference ordering.

A person's preference is one aspect of her mental states or attitudes. Other aspects of mental states include belief, desire, intention, and so on. We happen to have a particular mental state. But ought our mental states to be governed by consistency requirements? Suppose that you strictly prefer x to y and y to z, but z to x. Is there a normative reason for you to prefer x to z? Or, is there a normative reason to put yourself in a position to revise your preference? Your cyclical preference does not entail any wrongdoing. You are not blameworthy simply for having a cyclical preference.

Take the example of a *money-pump*. Suppose that you have the following cyclical preference over three objects; you strictly prefer apples to bananas, bananas to cherries, and cherries to apples. Suppose further that you have some cherries in hand. A trader comes along and makes an offer of some bananas in exchange for cherries at the cost of £1. As you strictly prefer bananas to cherries, you would be happy to trade cherries with bananas and pay £1. The same trader makes another offer of some apples in exchange for some bananas at the cost of £1. As you strictly prefer apples to bananas, you would be happy to accept this offer. The trader goes on to make another offer of some cherries in exchange for some apples at the cost of £1. As you strictly prefer cherries to apples, you would be happy to accept this offer, too. You now notice that you end up with exactly what you started with, but with fewer coins in your pocket. Thus, the cyclical preference is susceptible to exploitation by the trader. Prudence—if you have it—would tell you either you should not accept the trader's offer or you should revise the preference. Had you had a transitive preference, you would not have been subjected to the exploitation. So you have a good reason to have a preference that meets transitivity.

You may therefore have a pragmatic reason to have a transitive preference ordering. Why? Because you want to avoid exploitation by the trader. So, if you want to avoid exploitation, you ought to have a transitive preference ordering. But it is not clear that we detach 'you ought to have a transitive preference ordering' from the antecedent. This point concerns a difficult philosophical question about the source of normativity, and it would be too simple to claim that consistency requirements are normative, *simpliciter*.[12]

It might be argued that consistency has a distinctive role in the political domain. Many people believe, for example, that prime ministers ought to be consistent. If prime ministers act or decide inconsistently, they might be criticized for lacking political integrity and accountability. In public discussions in the political domain, such as the town meeting, parliament, electoral

---

[12] Nico Kolodny, 'Why Be Rational?', *Mind*, 114/455 (2005), pp. 509–63; and John Broome, 'Does Rationality Give Us Reasons?', *Philosophical Issues*, 15/1 (2005), pp. 321–37.

campaign, and so on, consistency would play an important role in demonstrating accountability. In the political domain, each person tries to justify her political thought or opinion to other people. But when there is inconsistency in what she says, it is hard to justify her political position because it does not appear to be accountable to other people. Therefore, it might be claimed that, from the very nature of politics, we ought to be consistent in the political domain. On this account, it is not directly claimed that consistency requirements are normative. Rather it is claimed that the explanatory role of consistency requirements has a normative force in the political domain, and hence that consistency requirements are normative in this particular sense. This view is perfectly consistent with the criticism against the normativity of consistency requirements I discussed above. This criticism rejects the direct claim such that consistency requirements themselves are normative. The view advanced here does not necessarily appeal to such a claim. It derives the normativity of consistency requirements from their explanatory role in the political domain.

The second problem is that consistency requirements can be self-defeating. In the literature of rational choice theory and game theory, there are many well-known paradoxes. Some paradoxes demonstrate that we violate some consistency requirements. For example, the Allais paradox, the Ellsberg paradox, and the framing effect suggest that, for a good reason, we violate one of the central requirements, called the independence of irrelevant alternatives, in the expected utility theory (which is distinct from the condition of the same name in Arrow's impossibility theorem).[13] Other paradoxes further illuminate that the rational choice can lead us to an undesirable consequence.

A spectacularly self-defeating case is found in the paradox of backward induction in game theory. One example of the paradox is the *centipede game*. Suppose that there are two rational individuals, players 1 and 2, who seek to maximize their pay-off. The two players make a move alternately. Each player can either stop the game or continue on each move. For each player, it is better to stop the game if the other player stops immediately afterward. But it is better to continue the game if the other player continues. It is assumed that the game comes to an end after a finite number of periods. The 6-period game is depicted below. The last player to make a choice is player 2, who would be better off stopping the game; she can walk away with 6 units. If player 1 is rational enough to predict this move of player 2, player 1 will stop the game at her third move, and get 5 units. Continuing the same induction process backward, we can see that player 1 would choose to stop on the first move, thus ending up with (1, 0). This is a unique equilibrium (which is called a *subgame*

---

[13] David M. Kreps, *A Course in Microeconomic Theory* (Princeton: Princeton University Press, 1990), chapters 2–3.

perfect equilibrium) for these two players. But this is highly counterintuitive, as both players could end up with a better pay-off.

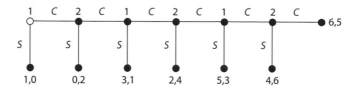

Thus, consistency requirements can be self-defeating. In order to save formal analysis, we need to revise and refine the model of individual consistency. But this is not an easy task.[14]

6

I hope that the examples included here have demonstrated that formal analysis is not shallow. It is very useful when focusing on the structure of political behaviour and phenomena. Some political philosophers dislike formal analysis, but that may be because they see formal and informal analysis as rivals to each other rather than as complements. In fact, those who conduct formal analysis can aid informal theorists, as demonstrated above, and those who conduct informal analysis can help formal analysis by discussing the meaning and plausibility of each axiom, condition, or theorem. There is no point in arguing that one approach is superior to the other. Formal analysis does, however, possess a few difficulties. I have touched here upon two fundamental problems in consistency requirements, which are simply assumed in formal analysis. I have no good answer to these problems, but they should be kept in mind whenever we use formal methods in analysing normative political theories.

---

[14] For the achievement and scope of game theory in general, see David M. Kreps, *Game Theory and Economic Modelling* (Oxford: Clarendon Press, 1990). For the philosophical discussions on the self-defeating features of rationality, see Derek Parfit, *Reasons and Persons* (Oxford: Oxford University Press, 1984). A more radical criticism of consistency is put forward by *particularism*, according to which the consistency requirements are unnecessary, impracticable, and even undesirable. See Jonathan Dancy, *Ethics Without Principles* (Oxford: Oxford University Press, 2004). Brad Hooker and Margaret Little (edited), *Moral Particularism* (Oxford: Oxford University Press, 2000) is a useful collection of papers on particularism.

5 Recognition as fact and norm: the method of critique

Lois McNay

1

This chapter considers the nature of the relation between political and social theory. It is one of the central claims of contemporary Anglo-American philosophy that these two areas of thought are distinct and necessarily separate. Normative thought does not concern itself with an assessment of existing social arrangements, rather it is free-standing and its consideration of politico-moral issues is guided by ideas of analytical clarity and argumentative rigour. There is, however, a long tradition of thought that regards normative political reflection as being intrinsically connected to a critical social theory. There is, of course, disagreement about the precise nature of this connection and this reflects the diversity of the tradition which, although it ultimately derives much of its inspiration from Hegel's dialectical thought, ranges across disciplines such as hermeneutics, orthodox Marxism, critical theory, communitarianism, and so-called postmodernism. In the last decade or so, the intertwinement of normative political thought in sociological pre-understanding has been one of the animating insights of the burgeoning field of work on the politics of recognition. Thinkers of recognition proceed from the insight that it is only possible to think meaningfully about desirable political arrangements if individuals are conceived not as abstract ends in themselves but as constitutively situated with a specific social context.

Jürgen Habermas is one of the foremost contemporary thinkers of recognition which he conceives of as a linguistically mediated process of communication. His thought arises from the tradition of twentieth-century cultural Marxism or critical theory that posits an intrinsic, dialectical connection between normative political thought and critical social analysis. Critical theorists are sceptical of the disinterested, transcendental status claimed by certain types of philosophical reflection. On their view, reason is always historically embodied and, therefore, even its most idealized forms carry within themselves unexamined givens that relate to their social conditions of emergence. The role of a critical social theory, then, is to unmask these tacit presumptions, showing how they have a determining impact on the most abstract modes of theorizing and, perhaps most importantly, how, in failing adequately to scrutinize its socio-historical elements, philosophy risks becoming ideology. This deconstructive critique of pure reason aligns the project of critical theory with other post-metaphysical strands of thought including post-structuralism, late twentieth-century pragmatism, and hermeneutics. However, unlike the latter, critical theorists argue that it is not enough for critique simply to de-transcendentalize abstract modes of reflection by situating them within their unthought social preconditions. To do only this would be to remain within a one-sided, negative metaphysics that denies that idealizing modes of thought have any context transcending import and hence any utopian or subversive potential. The reduction of reflection to social ontology—the conflation of the ideal with the real—is also self-cancelling for, if one of the aims of the historical deconstruction of pure reason is to reveal that there can be no neutral 'God's eye' view from which to consider issues of truth, justice, and morality, then the meta-perspective upon which the validity of the deconstructive critique itself is tacitly based is also thrown into question. Thus, for critical theorists, while the ideal can never be entirely freed from the real, it cannot be reduced to it either. Instead, the discrepancy between the ideal and the real, between the 'ought' and the 'is', is not a relation that normative political thinkers should attempt to overcome, disregard, or conceal, rather it designates precisely the domain in which they should situate themselves in order constructively to explore its tensions and paradoxes. This task takes the form of what critical theorists call 'immanent critique': in the absence of any objective perspective, normative political thought and critical social theory enter into a dialectical exchange where each perspective is used to probe the limitations of the other. Social theory is used to anchor the abstraction of pure speculation in concrete ways of life while the normative force of counterfactual claims is a 'thorn [that] sticks in the flesh of any social reality'.[1] The ultimate aim of this critical exchange is the exploration of the entanglement of the ought within the is, namely, the 'emancipatory' potential that pertains not to acceptability under ideal epistemic conditions but, instead, resides within existing social practices albeit obscured by current injustices and oppression. It follows too that the task of critique is ceaseless because if ideals are to retain their emancipating force and avoid instituting unforeseen types of exclusion, they must be continually tested through ongoing recontextualization.

It is within this general understanding of normative thought as critique that Habermas operates, indeed he is its most prominent contemporary proponent. The productive tension between the ideal and the real is a theme

---

[1] Jürgen Habermas, *Postmetaphysical Thinking: Philosophical Essays* (Cambridge: Polity Press, 1992), p. 47.

that pervades his work although it is developed principally in his idea of communicative recognition as both a social fact and a regulative norm. In his later work, Habermas has argued that the derivation of an ideal of communicative deliberation from concrete social practices yields a procedural concept of justice that is normatively more robust and has stronger binding effects upon its subjects than liberal concepts. Against John Rawls' idea of justice as fairness, Habermas' idea of communicative recognition asserts that democratic consensus can be achieved, not by bracketing off many of the substantive differences and conflicts of the lifeworld, but by explicitly incorporating conflicting world views into deliberative debate. I do not disagree with much of what Habermas has to say about Rawls nor do I disagree with the more general proposition that normative thought should take the form of immanent critique rather than of a free-standing idealization. My purpose in considering some of Habermas' arguments here is simply to illustrate certain difficulties in sustaining the central dynamic to critique, namely the necessary but rather indeterminate exchange between counterfactual thought and sociological analysis. I argue that Habermas fails systematically to realize the implications of this dialectical exchange for his theory of communicative recognition and this is apparent in the theory's persistent inability to deal with issues of so-called 'deep difference'. This failure is not contingent or partial but is necessary in order to maintain the universal normative scope he claims for communicative deliberation. In particular, he expediently forecloses a consideration of how embodied relations of power might undermine the exaggerated levels of fungibility and mutual empathy he envisages between participants in communicative ethics. He ultimately relies on a problematic linguistic ontology where deliberation, qua speech acts, is emptied of much determinate content. An irony of this is that it renders his work vulnerable to the selfsame criticism that he levels at Rawls, namely that it is based on an untenable abstraction from the determinate content of social life. Ultimately, then, the productive tension between the real and the ideal that is supposed not only to animate Habermas' thought but also to drive the development of emancipating knowledge becomes a frozen contradiction. Far from realizing the idea of immanent critique as a ceaseless interpretation of the 'is' through the 'ought' and a vivification of the 'ought' through the 'is', the idea of communicative recognition becomes an untenable utopia.

2

In the last decade or so, the idea of recognition has become a dominant way of representing the increasingly central role played by identity claims in social and political conflict. Although the idea has been developed in a variety of intellectual disciplines, it has been particularly influential in what could be loosely termed communitarian and communicative styles of political thought such as that of Charles Taylor and Jürgen Habermas. The attraction of the idea of recognition for such thinkers is that it provides an alternative basis for normative theory beyond what Habermas has called the 'philosophy of the subject' that dominates conventional social and political thought. The recognition perspective replaces the self-contained 'monological' conception of the subject in liberal political philosophy with a 'dialogical' conception where individuals are understood, not as isolated or antecedently individuated beings, but as beings who only know themselves through interaction with others. The claim that subjectivity is dialogical in nature allows social and political theory to be recast around the insight of the central importance of intersubjective relations rather than instrumental or strategic ones to social life. Certainly many liberal thinkers acknowledge dialogical aspects to subjectivity and social life but, on the whole, the relation between self and other is attenuated by the ontological primacy accorded to the rational or prudentially self-interested individual. In liberal theory, cultural, social, and ethical differences are treated as the more or less unalterable given of value pluralism. Individuals are understood to have fairly fixed, pre-given beliefs and are regarded, therefore, as relatively impervious to democratic deliberation.[2] On the whole, any response to collective social and normative problems must be based on an appeal to their rational self-interest, rather than on any particularly empathetic orientation to the other or on an appeal to the intrinsic importance of certain normative ideals. This leads to an emphasis on normatively thin political arrangements that focus on procedures for protecting the liberty of all and that leave the seemingly irreconcilable differences of value pluralism intact. Against this, the inclusive inflexion that thinkers of recognition give to the dialogical constitution of the subject means that individuals have the capacity, indeed in some cases are predisposed, to empathize and identify with the other rather than being mutually indifferent. The introduction of empathy into the process of deliberation means that difference is no longer reified as an insurmountable obstacle to social and political arrangements based on normatively thick consensus. The proposition that subjectivity is dialogical in nature is closely related to a second characteristic of the subject of recognition, namely, that it is ineluctably situated in a particular social context. The situated nature of subjectivity can be elaborated in many ways but, in general, it denotes the way in which our sense of self and our understanding of what is good and what is just are not trans-historical, universal phenomena but are inseparable from specific cultural and social contexts. Recognition thinkers focus on social context not to highlight difference, however, but to draw out

---

[2] This is an abstract typology and, of course, there are many liberals who are critical of such monological approaches. See, e.g., Cass R. Sunstein's critique of liberal preference theory, *Free Markets and Social Justice* (Oxford: Oxford University Press, 1997).

the commonalities of situated existence that might form the potential grounds for shared understanding and action. The inclusive proclivities of the dialogical subject are reinforced therefore by drawing attention to the underlying shared regularities, assumptions, and norms that structure embodied social existence. On this view, difference is not denied but nor is its significance exaggerated. As Kruks puts it: 'the commonalities of embodiment point beyond the solipsistic tendencies of . . . subjects each of whom objectifies the other'.[3]

The emphasis placed by recognition thinkers on the situated nature of the subject of political thought also extends to a more general understanding of the nature of political theory. Contra the claims of Anglo-American political thinkers, political thought is conceived not as a free-standing abstract mode of reflection on the nature of justice, liberty, and so forth, but rather as a form of normative reflection that is historically and socially contextualized. It is not possible, as Habermas puts it, to 'jump out of the particular life history or form of life in which [we] actually find [ourselves] and with which our identities are "irrevocably bound up" '.[4] The idea that all thought is ineluctably embedded within what, the hermeneutic thinker, Hans-Georg Gadamer has called historical 'prejudice' has various entailments for political critique, one of the most fundamental of which is that the very attempt to set up a universal, normative theory that explicitly brackets off issues connected to the organization of existing social relations is epistemologically misguided. All ideal thought inevitably carries within it certain sociological presuppositions and the failure to acknowledge or scrutinize them is to fall into the danger of attributing a universal status to what, in fact, might be more limited, socially specific concepts and norms. In *Between Facts and Norms*, for example, Habermas discusses the way in which supposedly neutral paradigms of law are tacitly upheld by latent background assumptions about society. The implication of his argument, as Thomas McCarthy points out, holds *ceteris paribus* for political theorists too: 'such understandings, images, or models of society, which are always at work, though usually only tacitly, in normative theorizing, have to become an explicit theme if political theorists hope to avoid exalting intuitive pre-understandings of their social contexts into universal ideals'.[5] The idea that thought cannot be entirely detached from sociological context need not undermine its universal scope; it seeks, however, to locate the source of transcendental critique in a reconstructive social theory rather than logically correct arguments. Indeed, without social theoretical content,

---

[3] Sonia Kruks, *Retrieving Experience: Subjectivity and Recognition in Feminist Politics* (Ithaca, NY: Cornell University Press, 2001), p. 33.

[4] Habermas, quoted in Thomas McCarthy, *Ideals and Illusions. On Reconstruction and Deconstruction in Contemporary Critical Theory* (Cambridge MA: MIT Press, 1991), p. 186.

[5] Thomas McCarthy, 'Political Philosophy and Racial Injustice: From Normative to Critical Theory', in Selya Benhabib and Nancy Fraser (edited), *Pragmatism, Critique, Judgement: Essays for Richard J. Bernstein* (London: MIT Press, 2004), p. 166.

normative reflection becomes an empty, abstract universal that is unable to 'guide criticism with a practical interest in emancipation'.[6] The force of normative thought resides in part, therefore, in the extent to which it realizes an emancipatory kernel latent in social practices and thereby connects practical to ideal reason.

Where Habermas diverges, however, from hermeneutic thinkers like Gadamer and communitarians such as Taylor and MacIntyre is that he is also wary of the potential dangers of an empiricist reduction of the 'ought' to the 'is'. The situating of ideals within their social context can too easily become a 'negative metaphysics' which underplays the context transcending and therefore critical potential of counterfactual norms.[7] The reduction of utopian thought to what Hannah Arendt calls the 'social question' undermines, *inter alia*, the important function of ideology critique. The problem with communitarian thinkers, for example, is that they are too uncritical in locating the source of an ethical way of life within the established practices of certain communities or pre-modern traditions. The potential moral authority of traditional practices cannot be derived simply from the weight of settled convictions, rather, latent or explicit claims to validity must be reconstructed and justified according to the idealizing suppositions of emancipatory thought. By failing to build into their theories a sufficiently independent process of reflexive scrutiny, communitarian thinkers underplay the anti-democratic and oppressive aspects of received traditions and fall into a problematic ethical relativism. The conflation of the ideal with the real risks losing the critical and utopian perspective that comes from holding these two moments apart in the recognition that, although the kernel of emancipation might reside in actuality, it can never be exhausted by it. Mindful of this, Habermas frequently argues that although the idea of communicative ethics is derived from practical action, it is an ultimate standard which, in reality, can never be attained: 'No prospect of such forms of life can be given to us, not even in the abstract, this side of prophetic teachings'.[8]

Normative thought is thus understood as a type of immanent critique or 'determinate negation', where a given social reality is scrutinized from an explicitly evaluative perspective in order to reconstruct its suppressed emancipatory potential. Accordingly, Habermas' key idea of communicative recognition has a dual status as both fact and norm; it both describes a fundamental mode of pragmatic social interaction and expresses a political ideal against which empirical forms of democratic deliberation can be evaluated. The ideal is derived from what Habermas regards as the universal core to practical interaction which he defines as the 'unavoidable supposition[s] reciprocally

---

[6] Iris Marion Young, *Justice and the Politics of Difference* (Princeton: Princeton University Press, 1990), p. 5.
[7] Habermas, *Postmetaphysical Thinking*, p. 145.   [8] Ibid. 146.

made in discourse'.[9] The most fundamental of these presuppositions is that intersubjective communication is driven by an orientation towards achieving mutual understanding. Habermas claims that significant normative advantages flow from his extrapolation of a democratic ideal from practical linguistic exchanges. He spells out some of these advantages in his engagement with John Rawls, whom he criticizes for constraining the nature and scope of rational deliberation by imposing a veil of ignorance upon participants which enshrines an ego-logical perspective at the heart of the original position. On the ego-logical view, individuals have an essentially negative relation to each other predicated on the Kantian idea that nobody can be free at the expense of anybody else's freedom. Individuals thus relate to each other on the basis of enlightened self-interest; the substantive differences that arise from diverging world views are set aside in order that they may relate to each other on the normatively thin grounds of the most stable procedures required to protect the liberties of all. Rawls claims that this placing of 'morally substantive situational constraints' behind the veil of ignorance is necessary in order to reach consensus in the face of entrenched ethical pluralism. Habermas argues, however, that it results in a cluster of conceptual difficulties which throw into doubt the plausibility and robustness of his procedural framework. Echoing many other commentators, he claims that one of the central difficulties is that the separation of the just from the good, upon which Rawls' political liberalism is predicated, is untenable because notions of what is universally valid for all individuals are inextricably bound up with particularist ethical beliefs. Formal neutral procedure can never be separated from substantive content; it is not possible to achieve what is just without achieving some measure of agreement on what is good. Any consensus that is reached about principles of justice on the basis of such a separation lacks sufficient binding force upon its subjects because its legitimacy is primarily functional rather than based on sound normative justification. Justice is equated with stability rather than with universally agreed upon moral norms.[10] The assumption that citizens will willingly accept the supremacy of political procedures of overlapping consensus over their deeply held moral convictions is based upon a further unsustainable separation of the political identities of citizens from their non-public identities. This splitting of public from private autonomy not only reifies the historically shifting boundary between the public and private spheres but it also runs against the republican intuition that the practices of individuals in civil society are intrinsically related to, not withdrawn from,

---

[9] Habermas, quoted in Jonathan Culler, 'Communicative Competence and Normative Force', *New German Critique*, 35 (1985), pp. 133–44, 141.

[10] Rawls robustly rejects this accusation. See his 'The Idea of Public Reason Revisited', *The University of Chicago Law Review*, 64/3 (1997), pp. 765–807. For a critical assessment of the Habermas–Rawls debate, see Kenneth Baynes, *The Normative Grounds of Social Criticism: Kant, Rawls and Habermas* (Albany: State University of New York Press, 1991).

their activities as political citizens.[11] Rawls' separation of the determinate content of individual beliefs from the public use of reason creates a further potential difficulty, namely whether, by according his principles of justice an inviolate, transcendental status, he does not in fact empty the political realm of any determinate content once the veil of ignorance has been lifted. Citizens cannot 'reignite the radical democratic embers of the original position' in their actual civic life and, therefore, democratic deliberation can no longer be about fundamental guiding values and norms but must be oriented to the preservation of already sedimented principles of political stability.

Habermas claims that rational deliberation on the nature of justice must proceed from an explicit consideration of conflicting world views and not on the basis of a Rawlsian deprivation of information. It is only from a monological conception of subjectivity that it becomes necessary to set aside normatively thick, ethical beliefs in order to achieve consensus because the self-interested perspective of actors renders them impenetrable to each other in some basic sense. On a dialogical view, this problem disappears because individuals are ontologically predisposed to empathize with others and this endows them, *inter alia*, with the capacity for 'ideal role taking' in rational deliberation. In the Habermasian ideal of communicative debate, individuals are able to accord equal weight to the desires of others as well as their own: 'everyone is required to take the perspective of everyone else and thus to project herself into the understandings of self and world of all others'.[12] Unlike the original position, then, communicative debate proceeds from a consideration of the particular preferences and values of citizens; however, these are not treated as unalterable givens because they have to be rationally reconstructed in order to render their underlying claims to validity amenable to deliberation. In this emphasis on idealizing reconstruction, Habermas also diverges from communitarian thought because the formation of a democratic will draws its legitimating force not from a previous convergence of settled ethical convictions but from communicative presuppositions that allow the power of the 'better' argument to come into play. Communicative debate forces individuals to reconfigure their often intuitive, commonsensical beliefs in rational terms so as to expose underlying claims to legitimacy to democratic scrutiny. It is through this twofold process of rational reconstruction and ideal role taking that it becomes possible to create some measure of agreement over 'good' practices but, more importantly, to filter a consensus over universally binding moral norms from a multiplicity of divergent ethical perspectives. The interlocking of perspectives that is intrinsic to communicative deliberation engenders a third, transcendental 'we' perspective 'from which all can test in

---

[11] Jürgen Habermas, *The Inclusion of the Other: Studies in Political Theory* (Cambridge: Polity Press, 1998), p. 71.
[12] Ibid. 58.

common whether they wish to make a controversial norm the basis of their shared practice'.[13] Consensus that is achieved under the conditions of communicative recognition does not simply have a functional validity, therefore, but a normatively thick one in so far as it is the outcome of free and rational deliberation on moral claims. The binding force of these communicative outcomes over democratic citizens is accordingly stronger than in Rawls because individuals regard themselves as not simply subject to the law but as authors of it. Private autonomy is no longer untheorized as the spontaneous pluralism that forms the natural backdrop to legal and political intervention. Rather public and private autonomy are conceived of as co-original. They are simultaneously constructed and protected through the communicatively regulated interaction of discrete processes of legal, political, and social recognition. The political realm is therefore not free-standing from moral life rather it is a 'reflexive form of substantial ethical life' and the means through which reciprocal recognition is constantly developed.

There is certainly much force to Habermas' criticisms of Rawls and, ultimately, to the more general intuition underlying his idea of communicatively achieved recognition that normative thought must proceed from the productive tension between the ought and the is, between the general and the particular. Despite the frequency with which he asserts the co-implication of social and political thought, I consider now how Habermas fails to sustain this basic claim throughout his work and therefore defaults on the animating method of critique. This ultimately relates to the normative exigencies of the framework of communicative recognition that require Habermas to posit unfeasible levels of fungibility and mutual understanding between participants in deliberation. In order to achieve this dialogical transparency, Habermas resorts to a questionable linguistic abstraction that empties deliberation of much determinate content. In certain crucial respects, then, Habermas' normative theory can be said to be no more grounded in a sociological appreciation of the actual constraints of the lifeworld than Rawls' thought. In short, the 'productive tension' between the ideal and the real turns into an antagonism where the latter is discounted by the former.

3

Many of the normative strengths of the idea of communicative recognition follow from the claim that it is not an abstract ideal but is derived from the presuppositions that are 'inevitably' made in the practical reasoning of everyday life. Habermas regards the most fundamental of these

---

[13] Ibid. 58.

communicative presuppositions as that of an orientation towards reaching understanding. This claim that mutual understanding is the *telos* of speech is related to the further claim that the universal core of speech acts consists in the raising of validity claims. According to this idea of universal pragmatics, anyone performing a communicative speech act necessarily raises validity claims and presupposes that they can be vindicated or justified when challenged. In everyday interaction, these validity claims are often implicit and unexplored, but in the ideal speech situation they have to be made explicit and expressed in a rational manner. The ideal speech situation is characterized then as pure intersubjectivity, that is by the lack of any barrier which would hinder communication. Although actual speech situations rarely if ever correspond to this ideal, nevertheless, such an ideal is always presupposed in all communication. The ideal speech situation is therefore a 'metanorm' that delineates aspects of an argumentation process—around the validity claims raised by speech—which would lead to a rationally motivated agreement, as opposed to a false or apparent consensus. It is on this notion of an ideal speech situation that Habermas rests his definition of truth as rational consensus: 'The condition for the truth of statements is the potential consent for all others...Truth means the promise to attain a rational consensus'.[14] Emancipatory critique is governed by the idea that a rational consensus could be achieved not only with regard to problematic truth claims but also with regard to problematic norms.

In order to allow this rationally motivating core to speech acts to be fully realized, Habermas sets up a series of conditions governing discourse ethics about the nature of speech and equality between participants. Central to these conditions of deliberation is the separation of the illocutionary from the perlocutionary dimensions of speech acts. The illocutionary dimensions of speech acts enact what they are saying in the moment of saying whereas, from the perlocutionary dimensions, certain effects follow, rather than being synchronous with the act of speech. For example, the speech act 'shoot her' has both an immediate effect (illocutionary) in that it is an order and deferred consequences (perlocutionary) in that it may or may not have persuaded me to shoot her. The intersubjective binding effects of speech acts, that is, the commitments that speakers and hearers make and reciprocally recognize when they enter into communication (such as ideal role taking) are necessarily illocutionary. The communicative situation is based upon 'the unreserved and sincere pursuit of illocutionary aims'.[15] Perlocutionary effects must not be present in discourse ethics because they belong to the 'latently strategic' use of language and involve some form of concealment in the sense that their

---

[14] Habermas, quoted in John B. Thompson and David Held (edited), *Habermas: Critical Debates* (London: Macmillan, 1982), p. 124.
[15] Habermas, *Postmetaphysical Thinking*, p. 80.

consequences are deferred rather than instantaneous. Illocutionarily strong speech acts are the means by which the sincerity of participants is assured and the only way in which the original *telos* of language as reaching understanding can be fully realized. Not only should the perlocutionary effects of speech acts be minimized in the communicative situation but also, more generally, they are to be understood as secondary or parasitic to illocutionary effects: 'The latently strategic use of language is parasitic because it only functions when at least one side assumes that language is being used with an orientation toward reaching understanding. Whoever acts strategically in this way must violate the sincerity condition of communicative action inconspicuously'.[16] In democratic deliberation, it is justifiable to consider, therefore, only 'those linguistically mediated interactions in which all participants pursue illocutionary aims, and only illocutionary aims, with their speech acts'.[17]

The idea that speech can be purified of its rhetorical and figurative aspects in order to minimize distorting perlocutionary effects and to render it a transparent medium for sincere communication has been widely criticized from a linguistic perspective. The establishment of a hierarchy between the illocutionary and perlocutionary functions of speech rests on an excessively stringent separation of what are, in fact, inextricably intertwined elements in linguistic interaction. The telling of a joke, for example, may have both an illocutionary aim (perhaps to make myself understood) and a perlocutionary one (entertaining an audience). Furthermore, if it is the aim of entertainment which is being pursued it is questionable that it should be relegated to a secondary form of communication as Habermas suggests.[18] In such a vein, Jonathan Culler argues that even if the illocutionary and perlocutionary aspects of speech could be held apart so rigorously, they do not correspond to the distinction between communicative and strategic action. So that establishing the priority of the illocutionary over the perlocutionary does not advance Habermas' argument about the primacy of communicative action. Culler concludes that Habermas' claim that reaching understanding is the inherent *telos* of speech is one of the least justified aspects of his theory of communicative action. Indeed, in most cases of speech, it is arguably more plausible to assume that its *telos* is not reaching understanding but rather that something significant is being said: 'the presumption of all interpretive activity, that there is some point to what seems to need interpretation, even if the point is an absence of point'.[19] The requirement that sincerity is the overriding characteristic of the orientation towards understanding can only plausibly be understood as a 'special feature of particular situations

---

[16] Ibid. 82.

[17] Habermas, quoted in John B. Thompson, *Studies in the Theory of Ideology* (Cambridge: Polity Press, 1984), p. 295.

[18] Thompson, *Studies*, p. 296.   [19] Culler, 'Communicative Competence', p. 139.

rather than a universal norm'.[20] In short, Habermas is only able to main-tain the insistence on sincerity by outlawing as derivative all other types of communicative activity that do not privilege the illocutionary elements of speech.

The purification of communication to a putative illocutionary essence is not only linguistically problematic but also questionable in so far as it rests on an abstraction of speech from embodied context and, more generally, of language from power. For Pierre Bourdieu, for example, Habermas' claim that illocutionary force is a property of speech acts is the result of an internalist approach to language which ignores its status as a social institution. Bourdieu argues that illocutionary force is, in fact, a delegated force or power originating in the social context of the speech act: 'By trying to understand the power of linguistic manifestations linguistically, by looking in language for the principle underlying the logic and effectiveness of the language of institution, one for-gets that authority comes to language from outside...Language at most *rep-resents* this authority, manifests and symbolizes it'.[21] The illocutionary efficacy of a speech act is, then, the effect of a set of interdependent conditions which constitute social rituals. The 'social magic' of a given illocutionary speech act depends on it being uttered in a legitimate situation, uttered according to legitimate forms and, above all, being uttered by a person legitimately entitled to do so. The extent to which the illocutionary force of speech acts is dependent on its social conditions of utterance can be illustrated by disputes over whether women priests have sufficient authority to utter the liturgy or by the moral philosopher J. L. Austin's example of a passer-by who christens a ship 'Mr Stalin'. For Bourdieu, language and power are coextensive; indeed, language is a form of symbolic power or violence. It is a medium through which individuals are accommodated to social hierarchies in a process that is neither forced nor freely assumed:

all symbolic domination presupposes, on the part of those who submit to it, a form of complicity which is neither passive submission to external constraint nor a free adherence to values...it is inscribed, in a practical state, in dispositions which are impalpably inculcated, through a long and slow process of acquisition, by the sanctions of the linguistic market.[22]

Habitus is the concept that expresses how symbolic violence shapes embodied being in the most profound and insidious ways. It follows from this that linguistic *habitus* is defined as a certain propensity to speak and to say certain determinate things rather than others. This involves 'both the linguistic capac-ity to generate an infinite number of grammatically correct discourses, and the social capacity to use this competence adequately in a determinate situation'.[23]

---

[20] Ibid. 140.
[21] Pierre Bourdieu, *Language and Symbolic Power* (Cambridge: Polity Press, 1991), p. 109.
[22] Ibid. 50–1.   [23] Ibid. 37.

These capacities and propensities are not abstract potentials but are physical and psychological dispositions that are inseparable from the position that an individual occupies within a social formation. In other words, linguistic capacities are shaped by class, gender, and race relations.

For Habermas, in contrast, power is extrinsic to language, indeed it must necessarily be so for him to assert that its original *telos* is orientation towards understanding. The disassociation of language from power allows Habermas to set up an account of communication as a linguistic process divorced from embodied situation. This in turn sets up a problematic ontology of recognition where subjectivity emerges from a primal linguistic dyad centred around untrammelled and symmetrical communication.[24] The operations of power that distort communicative interactions follow *ex posteriori*, they are secondary and contingent to a linguistically mediated 'intact intersubjectivity...marked by free, reciprocal recognition'.[25] This purification of language 'has the practical effect of removing from relations of communication the power relations which are implemented within them in a transfigured form'.[26] There is no recognition in Habermas' model that language and power are coeval in that the subject's entry into language is a simultaneous entry into society. It is certainly the case that Habermas recognizes the distorting effects of power upon communicative structures which is why he sets out procedures to ensure equality between participants in discussion. These procedures seem ineffectual, however, if power is not understood as a *post hoc* distortion of pure understanding but, *pace* Bourdieu, as ineluctably inscribed upon bodies and embedded in the structure of speech. The formation of the *habitus* takes place 'without passing through language or consciousness' and therefore there are significant forms of power and inequality that operate below the scope of Habermas' rules governing discourse: 'ways of looking, sitting, standing, keeping silent, or even of speaking...are full of injunctions that are powerful and hard to resist precisely because they are silent, insidious, insistent and insinuating'.[27] The theory of universal pragmatics divorces the formal ability to produce speech acts from the social conditions in which they are always produced and thus treats interlocutors in the ideal speech situation as disembodied linguistic beings. By separating the ideal from the real in this way, it thus fails to appreciate fully the subtle forms of symbolic domination whereby the formal capacity to produce a comprehensible speech act by no means ensures that a particular subject's speech acts will be listened to or understood.[28] The divorcing of linguistic from social competence cannot regulate, for example, the operation of prejudices which, in subtle and insidious ways, incline individuals to hear some speakers and some arguments rather

---

[24] I have developed this idea of an ontology of recognition in my *Against Recognition* (Cambridge: Polity Press, 2007).
[25] Habermas, *Postmetaphysical Thinking*, p. 145.
[26] Bourdieu, *Language and Symbolic Power*, p. 257.   [27] Ibid. 51.   [28] Ibid. 55.

than others. Although the rules of deliberation ensure formal equality between participants in Habermas' communicative ethics, prejudice escapes regulation in this manner because it operates at a prior, embodied level. As Lynn Sanders puts it: 'Prejudice and privilege do not emerge in deliberative settings as bad reasons, and they are not countered by good arguments ... one cannot counter a pernicious group dynamic with a good reason'.[29]

On such a view of speech acts as expressions of embodied power relations, the neutral language of rational discourse may be, in fact, the imposed discourse of the cultural elite which has been naturalized through processes of social inculcation. The apparently neutral status of a certain discourse conceals the gap that always exists between the universal recognition of a language as legitimate and the much more limited competence or authority to operate within this language. Habermas cannot address this structural disparity because he takes competence within rational discourse as a universal given rather than as a skill whose acquisition is often closely connected to position within social order. Agreement may not be the result of the most rational argument prevailing but of the tacit operation of symbolic forms of distinction which are themselves expressions of social privilege. In 'linguistic markets', language rarely functions as a pure instrument of neutral communication, rather it more often functions as a tool through which symbolic profits are consciously or unconsciously pursued. Any given linguistic market is governed by its own immanent rules which establish the value of linguistic expressions. All speakers within the market operate with a sense of the probable value of their own linguistic productions and with an orientation towards maximizing their profits. This sense is not a form of rational calculation but is a tacit social sense which expresses itself in forms of linguistic adjustment to render one's speech socially acceptable. The inseparability of language and power denoted in the idea of linguistic *habitus* draws attention to the tacit, embodied cues that render communication successful. Indeed, as Culler puts it: 'we would not be very competent if we invariably approached language with the presumption that it is always true, truthful, right and serious'.[30] In locating the essence of communication in the rational justification of validity claims, Habermas not only disregards a crucial dimension in the reproduction of social inequalities but he also fails adequately to address the potentially anti-democratic implications of his own idea of deliberation. The insistence on a certain type of disembodied, rational deliberation potentially compounds rather than challenges the under-representation of disadvantaged groups, in Sanders' words: 'learning to deliberate ... might be inseparable from indoctrination in familiar routes of hierarchy and deference'.[31]

---

[29]   Lynn Sanders, 'Against Deliberation', *Political Theory*, 25/3 (1997), pp. 347–76, 353–4.
[30]   Culler, 'Communicative Competence', p. 143.   [31]   Sanders, 'Against Deliberation', p. 362.

4

Habermas' idea of communicatively mediated recognition seems to foreclose, then, a cluster of issues connected to the way in which inequalities are sustained through embodied power relations. In other words, the intertwinement of the real and the ideal, which is so central to Habermas' understanding of critique, and where each is used to interrogate the other, appears to be abandoned. The irony of this foreclosure is that while Habermas criticizes Rawls for his abstract conception of the individual in the original position, his idea of communicative ethics is underpinned by a similarly insubstantial concept of personhood. This emptying out of determinate social content is not achieved, however, through the imposition of explicit informational constraints but through a process of linguistic abstraction. The suspicion that subjects in communicative debate are perhaps no more situated than those behind the veil of ignorance is reinforced rather than allayed by further statements that Habermas makes about how the substantive social differences connected to conflicting world views can be incorporated into a deliberative framework. Even if it were possible to derive consensus over universal moral norms from clashing ethical standpoints, there remain outstanding questions such as how it is possible, in the first place, to persuade individuals with radically divergent world views to debate with each other, to submit their metaphysical convictions to the supposedly neutral demands of rational reconstruction, and, indeed, to accept that their views may embody particular values which cannot be generalized as universal norms. Such issues of 'deep difference' are familiar from debates over the politics of recognition and Habermas responds to them, not by expanding the scope of communicative debate, as some of his followers have done, but by setting them aside. He does this by resorting to a sharp delineation between the universal status of the just and the particular nature of the good. In other words, having criticized Rawls for his arbitrary and dichotomous separation of the just from the good, he proceeds to institute a similar problematic distinction. Given his commitment to the inclusion of the substantive content of world views into communicative debate, Habermas cannot separate the just and the good by relegating the latter to the private realm of value pluralism as Rawls does. Instead, he sets up a troubling deliberative hierarchy which relies on the superordination of a questionable ideal of communication over actual practice. In a familiar argumentative manoeuvre, he claims that, like the orientation towards understanding and the raising of validity claims, recognition of difference is yet another of the 'unavoidable presuppositions' of communication. Communicative disputation over moral norms could not take place unless others in the debate had already recognized the speaker as a unique and autonomous being: 'Among the universal and unavoidable presuppositions of action oriented to reaching understanding is the presupposition that the speaker qua actor lays claim to recognition both as an autonomous will and as an individuated being'.[32] Recognition claims must be fully realized, therefore, within all the communicative structures of social life before any debate about overarching normative constraints can proceed: 'In communicative action everyone thus recognizes in the other his own autonomy'.[33] Thus far from effacing difference, the linguistic structure of communicative ethics necessarily enshrines an acknowledgement of the uniqueness of the individual as its ethical starting point. Yet, although inter-subjectively generated claims for recognition precede communicative debate, they themselves cannot be the subject of such debate because they represent particular ethical claims that do not have universal moral relevance. This relegation of recognition claims to a stage prior to normative deliberation is problematic for many reasons, some of which are exemplified in Habermas' debate with Carole Gilligan about whether issues pertaining to gender are universalizable or not.[34] His deliberative hierarchy leaves unanswered the question of how plausible or desirable it is to expect individuals to lay aside their deeply held ethical convictions about the good when they debate the just. Rather than answering the question, Habermas sidesteps it by an expedient separation between the good and the just, which is maintained, ultimately, through a linguistic abstraction from embodied existence that renders identity little more than a formalizable set of propositions. This linguistic abstraction enables him to empty identity claims of any emotional content and consider them not as expressions of the suffering that emerges from misrecognition but in a formalistic way as 'epistemic inputs' into the deliberative process. Through this linguistic rendering of identity, he can ignore fundamental issues such as how it is possible to persuade individuals with deeply held grievances and convictions to abandon them at the threshold of deliberative debate. As Newey puts it: 'The requirement that the conceptions of the good be treated as epistemic inputs prejudices both the deliberative framework's ability to model political negotiations and the willingness of rational individuals to make themselves a party to it'.[35]

Habermas' linguistic abstraction ultimately renders his theory of communicative recognition vulnerable to the same criticism that he levels at Rawls, namely that the separation of the just from the good is an unjustifiably arbitrary device used to guarantee an otherwise implausible democratic consensus. Furthermore, Habermas faces the additional problem, that Rawls does not, that this distinction between the just and the good undermines his claim that communicative ethics does not neglect the substantive conflicts of the

---

[32] Habermas, *Postmetaphysical Thinking*, p. 191.   [33] Ibid. 190.
[34] See Selya Benhabib, *Situating the Self. Gender, Community and Postmodernism* (Cambridge: Polity Press, 1992), chapters 5–6.
[35] Glen Newey, *After Politics: The Rejection of Politics in Contemporary Liberal Philosophy* (Basingstoke: Palgrave, 2001), p. 168.

political lifeworld, which, in turn, reflects the more general claim that critique is situated in the productive tension between the real and the ideal. It is this arbitrary separation of the 'ought' from the 'is' that Charles Taylor invokes in his criticism of Habermas' reliance upon a formalist concept of morality. An individual's self-understanding and conceptions of the good are continuous with their understanding of broader questions of morality and justice rather than standing on one side or the other of an artificial division between the particular and the universal. Taylor claims that, in the face of radical doubt about why one should prefer a proceduralist mode of deliberation over other forms of disputation, Habermas cannot really provide a satisfactory answer. His answer, that communicatively reached understanding is based on the basic structure of speech, is too formalist to persuade someone who would prefer to reach their desired goal 'at the cost of being slightly inconsistent'.[36] The only compelling answer to the communicative sceptic, according to Taylor, is one that necessarily makes reference to a 'substantialist' conception of human nature in order to justify the primacy of rational understanding over all other purposes: 'I must be able to show why it is that I attach a value to rational understanding so great that it should be preferred to all other purposes'.[37]

Habermas does, in fact, underpin his idea of rational deliberation with a substantive conception of human nature which can be defined as an ontology of recognition. This ontology is based on a linguistic abstraction from embodied context which ultimately allows Habermas to set up a moral psychology where individuals are a priori predisposed to communicative debate. Thinkers of radical difference and 'agonistic' democracy frequently criticize ideas of deliberative democracy on the grounds that the reasonable and open-minded attitudes adopted by participants in debate are not borne out by the actuality of political discussion. Given the volatile and biased nature of actual political debate, it is reasonable to enquire of deliberative democrats where these required attitudes should come from. In the case of Habermas, it is clear that these attitudes are generated by his ontology of communicative recognition that tacitly predisposes individuals towards cooperative and open-minded debate. It is not that individuals are never empirically capable of deliberating in such a manner but that the delimited linguistic construal of identity enables Habermas to downplay the dimensions of embodied existence that are often the source of deep division and hostility in political debate. In short, communicatively mediated recognition is conceived in such a way that there is little friction between its sociological and normative senses; it becomes what

---

[36] Charles Taylor, 'Language and Society', in Axel Honneth and Hans Joas (edited), *Communicative Action: Essays on Jürgen Habermas' The Theory of Communicative Action* (Cambridge: Polity Press, 1991), p. 31.
[37] Ibid.

Düttmann has called 'presupposition and result'.[38] This linguistic abstraction ultimately undermines one of the animating insights of Habermas' thought, namely that normative critique should proceed from an explicit consideration of the determinate content of social life. It would seem then, that at least with respect to his speech act theory, Habermas' dialogical concept of the subject is no more situated than the disembodied philosophy of the subject to which he is ostensibly so opposed.

5

To criticize Habermas' idea of communicative recognition for its lack of determinate social content is to move close to the above mentioned danger of constraining normative reflection upon freedom and justice by reducing it to social ontology. To emphasize the inseparability of language and power in embodied speech acts in the way that Bourdieu, Sanders, and many others do can be seen as tantamount to denying the possibility of any kind of critical perspective on actuality. Domination may exert itself in an insidious fashion but, nonetheless, individuals seem to have the capacity to reflect critically upon their actions and to act in a subversive and resistant fashion.[39] Bourdieu's conflation of linguistic with social competence appears to reduce speech to its narrowly strategic functions and consequently forecloses an account of agency based on the communicatively generated capacity of individuals to reflect on the conditions under which they act and speak. In James Bohman's view, by failing to attribute this capacity for practical reflection to actors: 'the possibility of innovation and transformation becomes improbable and dependent on external social conditions'.[40] The force of the Habermasian idea of communication is that it is a second order form of discourse that transcends the first order, strategic use of speech. The reflective functions of language can be used both in the disputation of norms and also in scrutinizing the form and style of discursive deliberation with the aim of transforming it if it proves to be exclusionary. Communicative reason is thus capable of challenging the basis on which any antecedent consensus has been established. In Bohman's view, Bourdieu 'one-sidedly emphasizes the suppression of modes of expression

---

[38] Alexander Garcia Düttmann, *Between Cultures: Tensions in the Struggle for Recognition* (London: Verso, 2000), p. 140–1.

[39] For example, James Scott, *Domination and the Arts of Resistance: Hidden Transcripts* (New Haven: Yale University Press, 1990); and Michel de Certeau, *The Practice of Everyday Life* (Berkeley: University of California Press, 1984).

[40] James Bohman, 'Practical Reason and Cultural Constraint', in Richard Schusterman (edited), *Bourdieu: A Critical Reader* (Oxford: Blackwell, 1999), p. 141.

through relations of power, rather than the way public institutions could promote voice through open and fair procedures of public justification'.[41]

It is a misrepresentation, however, to claim that an emphasis on the embodied workings of power necessarily pre-empts an account of reflexivity. As a sociologist, Bourdieu accepts that it is possible for individuals to have a critical understanding of their conditions of existence but maintains that this reflexive knowledge is always limited and open to contestation. He frequently discusses different types of reflexivity: the 'lucidity of the excluded' that arises from social exclusion, the insight generated from the competitive and dialogic structure of expert knowledge production, the critical awareness of the self that arises from societal detraditionalization.[42] Indeed, in many respects, Bourdieu's idea of reflexivity resembles the critical theorists' notion of historically embedded critique, namely that, in the absence of a God's eye perspective, limited critical understanding is generated from the dialogue between competing perspectives and different disciplinary standpoints: 'sociocultural critique is best thought of as a polymorphic, multi-layered and multidimensional enterprise'.[43] A difficulty with the way in which Habermas develops the idea of communicative deliberation is that it tacitly moves away from the original, delimited understanding of reflexive critique towards a more absolute version where if actors' critical awareness does not reach certain conclusions based on pre-given epistemological or normative criteria then they cannot be said to be autonomous at all. The Habermasian idea of rational reconstruction implicitly invokes something akin to what Richard Flathman calls a 'biblical' view of autonomous agency where 'knowing the truth is a necessary or at least a sufficient condition of freedom'. It is undeniable that 'knowing the truth can contribute towards one's freedom' but it does not mean to say that agents are not autonomous if this knowledge does not reach 'established or envisioned criteria of correctness'.[44] It is such notions of untrammelled reflexivity which form the underpinnings of Habermas' theory of communicative competence that are justifiably problematized in Bourdieu's insistence on the inescapably embodied nature of speech acts. Habermas' requirement of sincerity through the privileging of the illocutionary elements of speech over the perlocutionary ones underpins his untenable account of self-reflexivity. It locks the account of reflexivity into a zero sum logic where understanding can be acquired only on the basis of complete self-transparency or not at all. Anything less than absolute sincerity on the part of participants exposes the deliberative process to the distortions of strategic interests. The possibility that this false antinomy

[41] Ibid. 148.

[42] Bourdieu discusses these different types of reflexivity in *Pascalian Meditations* (Cambridge: Polity Press, 2000).

[43] Hoy and McCarthy, *Critical Theory*, p. 18.

[44] Richard Flathman, *Freedom and Its Conditions: Discipline, Autonomy and Resistance* (London: Routledge, 2003), p. 9.

does not allow is that efficacious political deliberation and agency can emerge from linguistic processes that are much more 'impure' and indeterminate. Judith Butler, for example, argues against the censorship of 'hate-speech' on the illocutionary grounds of unacceptable intention because one of the unforeseen perlocutionary effects of these speech acts has been to animate acts of resistance and subversion. The appropriation of derogatory terms such as 'nigger' and 'queer' by the very groups against whom they are directed has been an effective strategy in subverting their hateful effects.[45] Communicative exchange will always potentially have a spontaneous and uncertain dimension that can be generative of new knowledges and critical self-understanding. This critical understanding cannot be guaranteed, however, in the form of a purified, communicatively mediated reflexivity; it is always necessarily partial, incomplete, and subject to permanent revision. The idea of linguistic *habitus* highlights how speech is an indeterminate ensemble of motivations and effects and cannot be reduced to a putative essence of the communicative disputation of validity claims. Indeed, as Paul Ricoeur argues in his mediation of Habermas' debate with Gadamer, the choice that the former presents between the possibility of critical distantiation and uncritical belonging is a false one. The possibility of critical reflexivity is necessarily immanent in the interpretative process that embeds individuals within a particular cultural or social order.[46]

6

In principle, Habermas claims that political thought as critique can never be free-standing, that it derives its normative relevance from its dialectical connection with a sociological account of the injustices and conflicts of social life. In practice, however, he deploys the normative status of the idea of recognition to circumvent some of the destabilizing implications that a perspective on embodied social hierarchies potentially has for his theory. This is, ultimately, because it would undermine the claims he makes about the universal status and binding force of the outcomes of communicative deliberation. His formulation of communicative recognition rests on a series of questionable linguistic reductions starting with the assertion that that orientation towards understanding is a universal constant within the most significant types of human interaction. This allows him further to delimit understanding to the narrowly cognitive idea of the disputation of validity claims that is allegedly presupposed in all significant speech acts. Speech acts are further purified

---

[45]   Judith Butler, *Excitable Speech: A Politics of the Performative* (London: Routledge, 1997).

[46]   Paul Ricoeur, *Hermeneutics and the Human Sciences: Essays on Language, Action and Interpretation* (Cambridge: Cambridge University Press, 1981).

by being conceptualized as the utterances of disembodied beings. In other words, the political ideal of communicative recognition is only maintained by emptying it of much determinate social content.

It is too easy to argue in response to such criticisms, as Habermas and his followers often do, that the interrogation of ideal thought from a non-ideal sociological perspective on power is tantamount to falling back into a resigned pragmatism that undermines the hopeful possibilities held out by utopias.[47] Indeed, in making these arguments, Habermasians seem to want to have it both ways. On the one hand, they wish to criticize abstract normative theories, such as Rawls' justice as fairness, for the failure to reflexively scrutinize the latent sociological presuppositions embedded in their philosophical paradigms. On the other hand, when the shortcomings of their own sociological pre-understandings are pointed out, they retreat to the assertion that it is illegitimate to criticize transcendental norms from a sociological concern with actual power relations. The potentially fruitful dialectic between social and political thought, between the real and the ideal, that is avowedly the animating impulse behind Habermas' idea of critique is turned thereby into an aporia. If the idea of recognition is posited on a fundamental misunderstanding of the conditions of social existence then it is necessary, according to the idea of critique, to scrutinize its validity as a regulative ideal. Furthermore, if the idea of communicative recognition presupposes narrow or untenable notions of subjectivity and identity, then it is also legitimate to question its desirability, in so far as, if it were to be realized, it might result in conformist social orders.[48] To criticize normative political theory in terms of its sociological pre-understandings is not necessarily to forestall it. It is rather to continue the dialectical engagement between the two areas of thought and, in using each to expose the limits of the other, to provide renewed grounds for critical debate. Normative theory can only develop in tandem with a continuous sociological self-critique that, as McCarthy puts it, is oriented to uncovering the exclusions that it makes: 'the search for a genuinely inclusive theory of justice is a never ending, constantly renewed effort to rethink supposedly universal basic norms and reshape their practical and institutional embodiments to include, what, in their limited historical forms, they unjustly exclude'.[49]

---

[47] See also Selya Benhabib, *The Claims of Culture. Equality and Diversity in the Global Era* (Princeton: Princeton University Press, 2002), chapter 5.

[48] Düttmann, *Between Cultures*, pp. 156–7.   [49] McCarthy, 'Political Philosophy', p. 163.

6 Dialectical approaches

David Leopold

1

Students are sometimes frustrated by what they see as the dominance of the analytical approach in contemporary political theory. Those frustrations can take a variety of forms, and be more or less justified. They can also make students receptive to the siren call of alternatives, both real and imagined, to that methodological mainstream. In this chapter, I cast a sceptical, but not dismissive, eye over one of the more seductively esoteric candidates for that role—the idea of a dialectical approach.

The concept of dialectic is not a new one. Few discussions—including this one—can resist some passing mention of its ancient origins, although there is little consensus about where to begin. The linguistic derivation from the Greek *dialectikē* (meaning conversation or, more literally, reasoning by splitting in two) suggests the ancient world, but also generates a confusing breadth of associations. Dialectic is variously linked with the paradoxes propounded by Zeno of Elea, with the Socratic mode of argument known as *elenchus*, with the 'deformation' of that discursive method by the Sophists, with the architectonic science (built on mathematical knowledge) which is utilized by the guardians in Plato's *Republic*, and so on.

In short, from the very beginning, the term 'dialectic' and its various cognates have been used in a variety of very different ways. There is certainly no consensus about what dialectic is, no single model that we can examine and interrogate here. Given that variety, and the desire to avoid an extensive but shallow historical survey, my discussion proceeds in a highly selective manner. First, I consider only the treatment of dialectic within one (albeit broad) intellectual tradition. Second, from among the range of views on dialectic which can be found within that tradition, I examine only two (albeit contrasting) accounts in any detail.

Students of political theory are most likely to come across the notion of dialectic in accounts of G. W. F. Hegel, of Karl Marx, and (perhaps especially) of the contested intellectual relationship between these two nineteenth-century German thinkers. It is the Marxist tradition, broadly construed, which will form my subject here. That tradition contains a wide variety of views, both *extravagant* and *modest*, about dialectic. In this chapter I consider one exemplar from each of these categories, linked by a discussion of (some aspects of) Hegel's own system. I begin with an extravagant account.

2

My example of an *extravagant* account of dialectic is provided by the Hungarian Marxist Georg Lukács (whose life spanned the remarkable period 1885–1971). More precisely, it is taken from Lukács' essay 'What Is Orthodox Marxism?', a piece first written in 1919 but best known in the revised version which appeared in *History and Class Consciousness* (an important collection of Lukács' essays first published, in German, in 1923).

This volume of essays is widely thought to have played a significant role in both Lukács' own intellectual evolution and the wider history of Marxism. The simplified version of that contextual story identifies *History and Class Consciousness* as both the point at which the (largely apolitical) cultural pessimism of Lukács' earlier 'anti-bourgeois' radicalism was replaced by a commitment to Marxism, and as a founding document of the intellectual movement sometimes called 'Western Marxism'. That simplified contextual story does some considerable violence both to the continuities in Lukács' intellectual evolution and to the complexities of his relation to the Western Marxist tradition. However, since my concern here is with some aspects of the argument of one particular essay, and not with the wider historical significance of the collection as a whole, it can suffice.

'What Is Orthodox Marxism?' is a striking essay in many ways. One of its most noticeable features is its juxtaposition of plausible and familiar advice alongside some rather more contestable and surprising remarks. Lukács' opening observations are entirely representative in this regard.

Lukács begins with the claim that 'orthodoxy' in Marxism does not mean a belief in the truth of any particular thesis that Marx might have endorsed; a thesis, for instance, such as the labour theory of value (which maintains that the value of a commodity is determined by the socially necessary labour time required to produce it). Indeed, Lukács recommends rather that Marxists adopt a critical—we might say 'non-religious'—attitude towards the results of Marx's own intellectual investigations. This seems eminently sensible advice. After all, Marx's writings contain a wide variety of claims about a wide variety of subject matters, and there seems no good reason to presuppose that all of those claims are coherent and true.

However, alongside these unexceptional comments about how to approach Marx's work, Lukács ventures some more remarkable thoughts concerning the relation between the intellectual standing of Marxism and the nature of empirical evidence. In particular, he maintains that even if recent research had disproved—decisively and once and for all—everyone of Marx's substantive claims, then the intellectual standing of Marxism would remain intact. The original targets of Lukács' remarks here include the German revisionist Eduard Bernstein, who had long argued that the standing of orthodox Marxism was in doubt because empirical evidence had invalidated Marx's account of the falling rate of profit, the immiseration of the proletariat, the timing of the transition to socialism, and so on. Lukács' response is to insist that all these, and other, substantive claims made by Marx might turn out to be unfounded and yet the character and value of Marxism would remain entirely unscathed. (In an earlier version of his article, Lukács had responded to Bernstein's account of the tension between Marxist theory and certain facts about the contemporary world with a notorious quotation from the German idealist philosopher Johann Gottlieb Fichte—'so much the worse for the facts'.[1])

Lukács' claim—that the standing of Marxism would be unaffected by proof that all of its substantive claims were unfounded (that nothing in the social and political world could disprove it)—needs to be unpacked with care. Whatever else they may include, Marx's writings contain a theory of history, a critical account of the workings of capitalism, a philosophical anthropology (i.e., a model of human nature), and a vision of socialism. The role that is played by empirical evidence in Marx's views on these topics is, no doubt, complex and contested. Nonetheless, justifying at least some of his views on these topics would seem to require their being supported by the appropriate empirical evidence. Moreover, Marx seems to have understood that this was the case. For example, it seems certain that he intended his account of the workings of capitalism (as developed in *Capital* and elsewhere) as, at least in part, a work of social science supported by appropriate empirical evidence. *Capital* is not only full of claims whose justification would seem to require some appeal to empirical evidence but also it is precisely by such an appeal that Marx does attempt to generate support for them. (To give a small but entirely representative example: in his discussion of the 'Reserve Army' of the unemployed, Marx seeks to substantiate his claim that the introduction of capitalist production in agriculture results both in a reduced demand for agricultural labour and in the migration of the rural population to urban centres, by marshalling detailed statistics from the official census in Great Britain.[2]) However, the bearing of such remarks on Lukács' account is less certain. Note that the latter

---

[1] Georg Lukács, *Political Writings 19191–1929. The Question of Parliamentarism and Other Essays*, translated by Michael McColgan, edited by Rodney Livingstone (London: NLB, 1972), p. 27.

[2] See, e.g., Karl Marx, *Capital, Karl Marx Frederick Engels Collected Works* (London: Lawrence & Wishart, 1996), volume 35, p. 625 note 1.

does not deny the relevance of empirical evidence to these various substantive claims (about history, capitalism, human nature, and socialism). Rather, Lukács insists that those various claims do not constitute the fundamental core of Marx's work. The fundamental core of Marxism is said to consist rather in a *dialectical* method, and it is this method which is seemingly impervious to the weight or character of empirical evidence.

I am sceptical about such claims but also interested in trying to understand the reasoning behind them. In tracing Lukács' explanation and defence of these claims, I am especially interested in what he means by a dialectical method.

Lukács begins straightforwardly enough. He discusses a series of views of the world—the views of revisionists like Bernstein or economists like Léonard Simonde de Sismondi—which are said to be 'one-sided' and 'static'. Lukács goes on to portray these ('one-sided' and 'static') views of the world as both *mistaken* and *revealing*. Those latter two characteristics can usefully be considered in turn.

In the first place, 'one-sided' and 'static' views are mistaken. It seems they are mistaken because they fail to capture the structure of society. Social reality has the structure of what Lukács calls a 'totality'. We might doubt whether—at least in this particular essay—Lukács gives anything like a complete account of what being a 'totality' means, but he does give some content to the notion. The idea of a 'totality' seems to suggest a structure which is many-sided and which develops. Since reality, on Lukács' account, has this structure, it seems that it cannot properly be understood from a one-sided and static vantage point.

Lukács' positive suggestion is that society can be comprehended best in what might be called organic terms, in that its component parts are to be understood in relation to a whole which is itself developing. Although controversial, such claims that the world is best understood as an evolving organism are not wholly unfamiliar. Nor are organic views—at least when considered at this level of generality—the sole property of any one intellectual tradition. Hegelianism and Marxism are certainly not the only intellectual traditions that contain enthusiasts for such views. In addition, not all of these various organic accounts are hopelessly extravagant. (Less controversially, it might be said that not all versions of this organic view are equally extravagant.) At the risk of anticipating subsequent discussion, what makes Hegel's version of the organic view, for example, an extravagant one, is less his claim that the world should be conceived as an organic structure, than that he conceives it as a structure analogous to a human subject, a structure that is in some way (potentially) self-aware, a structure of the kind that is sometimes called a *macroanthropos*.

In the second place, 'one-sided' and 'static' views are revealing. It is important not to lose sight of this additional element in Lukács' account. He insists not only that these 'one-sided' and 'static' views are mistaken but also that they are *illuminating*. They are, of course, mistaken because they are 'one-sided' and static' (and thus fail to capture a reality which is many-sided and develops). It emerges that they are *illuminating* because they constitute precisely the kind of (mistaken) ways of thinking about the world that the contemporary world engenders and promotes. The social structure of capitalism, Lukács writes, 'in great measure encourages such views'.[3]

This is an important and striking claim. On Lukács' account, capitalism is an opaque form of society, in that it appears to be other than it is. In addition, that opacity encourages, and is reflected in, the kind of mistaken views about the world we've been considering. The opacity in question—which characterizes both the social world and certain popular ways of thinking about the social world—is usually called 'reification' in English translations of Lukács. Reification is the Latinized equivalent of a German word (namely, *Verdinglichung*) which literally means 'thingification'. In capitalist societies, dynamic social relations are said to appear, and be (mis)understood, as the static characteristics of things.

Lukács' claims about reification are usually seen as building on Marx's discussion of the 'fetishism of commodities' in *Capital*. Such analogies can be helpful, but it is important to see that Lukács transforms as well as adopts elements of that discussion. Marx suggests that certain false beliefs about economic life are engendered and encouraged by the manner in which capitalist society presents itself. Lukács—drawing also on the writings of the sociologists Max Weber and Georg Simmel—expands these remarks into a complete account of what capitalism does to humankind. Lukács maintains that reification infects all areas of social life, including, of course, attempts to make sense of social life. Isolated facts, isolated complexes of facts, certain conceptual distinctions, and separate specialist disciplines (such as law and economics) are all treated by Lukács as evidence of the deceptive self-understanding at the heart of capitalism.

At this point, it might seem that the broad outlines, at least, of Lukács' methodological advice should be relatively straightforward. In order to embrace a dialectical approach we need (negatively) to dump standpoints which are contaminated by reification, and (positively) to embrace standpoints which are not in that way tainted. Moreover, in places, Lukács does indeed appear to recommend that we abandon 'one-sided' and 'static' views in favour of a dialectical vantage point which is 'totalizing' and 'historical'. No doubt, a 'totalizing' and 'historical' standpoint, unlike its 'one-sided' and 'static' counterpart, would understand the world along organic lines (understanding the various parts of society, for example, in relation to an evolving whole).

However, some care is needed here. Although dialectic is often associated with notions of systematic interconnectedness and development, Lukács is

---

[3] Georg Lukács, *History and Class Consciousness. Studies in Marxist Dialectics*, translated by Rodney Livingstone (London: Merlin Press, 1971), p. 5.

keen to avoid the suggestion that he is simply recommending that we replace one way of looking at the world with another. Such a suggestion, he maintains, would seriously misrepresent his views. Adopting a dialectical approach is not simply a matter of learning to look at the world in the right way, namely in a more interconnected and historical manner. Indeed, in so far as we read his comments in this way, Lukács suggests that we remain trapped within a reified (and thus misleading) framework. In particular, such comments show that we are still thinking of 'method' as distinct from 'reality', and of 'theorizing' and 'changing' the world as distinct activities. However, these distinctions— between 'method' and 'reality', and between 'theorizing' and 'changing' the world—are said to be paradigmatically reified ways of thinking. Reading his comments in this way would, Lukács insists, massively understate their radical character. On such an interpretation, it might appear that 'the dialectical relation between parts and whole were no more than a construct of thought', just another way of looking at the world.[4] Lukács is scathing about such an interpretation. On such an account, the dialectical vantage point would turn out to be just as remote from social reality as the partial and static views that he has already dismissed.

Lukács maintains that the real differences between dialectical and reified approaches are much deeper and more fundamental than this issue of focus. It is not simply that the dialectical view examines the whole rather than the part, or that it considers reality in a dynamic, rather than in a static, fashion. What distinguishes the dialectical view, properly understood, is that it is not separate from social reality, it is already somehow present in the world (which is itself dialectically structured). On Lukács account, it seems that dialectic, properly understood, primarily concerns what is sometimes called social ontology rather than method in any conventional sense. Yet more strikingly, Lukács tells us that Marxism—like Hegelianism—conceives of 'theory' proper, that is, the truth about the world, 'as the self-knowledge of reality'.[5] He maintains that we should think of the truth about the social world, not as a possible result of applying the right kind of technique to some external object, but rather as embodied in the 'self-knowledge' of that world.

Trying to work out what Lukács means by this is not easy. He seems to be saying not only that there is a vantage point from which we can gain a correct (and uncontaminated) understanding of the social whole, but that this vantage point is equivalent to the self-knowledge of reality. Thinking of the world as having self-knowledge would appear to commit us to the (Hegelian) view that the world should be understood not simply as an organic structure but as an organic structure which has the shape of a self and which is somehow (at least, potentially) self-aware.

---

[4] Ibid. 15.   [5] Ibid. 16.

Scarcely less surprising is Lukács' account of where that self-knowledge is to be found. Having suggested that there is an agent whose self-knowledge constitutes the self-knowledge of the world, he subsequently identifies that agent as the *proletariat*.

I should note an important clarification of this claim. Lukács is not suggesting that the truth about the world is necessarily revealed by the views that might at any particular moment be held by actual proletarians. There could, he allows, be a gap between those empirically revealed views and the truth about the world. Rather the proletarian views which are identical to the truth about the world are not the actual empirical views that workers may happen to have at any particular time, but rather their 'ascribed' or 'imputed' class consciousness—the views which individuals in a particular life-situation *would* have, *if they were able fully to comprehend* this situation.[6] It is *this* proletarian understanding which is equivalent to the self-knowledge of reality.

However, even with this clarification, many will remain suspicious of Lukács' claim. Not least, it is sometimes thought that the association of particular social theories with particular social groups creates a presupposition against the truth of those theories. This kind of worry needs careful formulation if it is to avoid the 'genetic fallacy' of assuming that revealing the origins of a set of beliefs demonstrates anything about their truth or falsity. Nonetheless, that a set of beliefs have a particular social origin might well make us wary of those beliefs, and make us worry, in particular, about their partiality. For example, in the present case, the claim that Marxism is equivalent to the proletarian world view might seem to cast doubt on its aspirations to genuine knowledge, to jeopardize its claims to have grasped the truth about the world.

However, Lukács maintains that this worry gets matters entirely the wrong way round. On his account, Marxism provides us with a correct understanding of the world precisely *because* it is the self-knowledge of the proletariat. Knowledge of reality, he insists, can arise only from the point of view of a class of a certain kind. Marxism is thus identified as a peculiarly privileged theory. Although it is the self-knowledge of a class, that class occupies a special position such that in understanding itself it thereby comes to understand the truth about the world. That truth is equivalent to the self-knowledge of the world.

At the heart of this account is a set of happy coincidences. The truth about the world consists in the 'self-knowledge' of the world, and the 'self-knowledge' of the world is identical with the 'self-knowledge' of the proletariat. In order to understand the peculiarly privileged position occupied by the proletariat, we need to work out what guarantees or explains these

---

[6] See, e.g., ibid. 51 and 73. (The relevant German term is *zugerechnete*.)

various coincidences. The answer seems to lie in one of Lukács' most audacious ideas, namely that the proletariat is 'the identical subject-object of history'.

3

Anyone whose head is already spinning will be pleased to discover that, in order to unpack the idea of an identical subject-object of history, a short detour through some of the denser parts of Hegel's metaphysics is required. This is not the easiest—nor the least controversial—bit of Hegel, and the outline that I offer here involves some considerable simplification. Hegel scholars will need to grit their teeth, and remember that my aim is not to give a thorough outline of his science of logic, but rather to sketch Hegel's explanation of the happy coincidence between the self-knowledge of some agent and knowledge of the world. (The happy coincidence that, in a revised form, plays a central role in Lukács' essay.)

Metaphysics, on Hegel's account, is concerned with knowledge of what he calls the absolute. The absolute, on this account, is that which is independent of, and unrestricted or unconditioned by, anything else. One clue to what Hegel has in mind here is provided by his insistence that the absolute can be seen as the philosophical expression of the Christian notion of God. Like God, the absolute is said to create and govern the finite world.

As part of his contribution to the intellectual discipline that he calls the science of logic, Hegel offers an account of the structure of the absolute considered apart from that creation. Glossing over a number of complications, we can describe the result as a categorical system with a distinctive triadic dynamic. The constituent concepts in this categorical system are purportedly embodiments of pure thinking (devoid of empirical content and independent of history and culture). They form a series with a repeated triadic pattern, within which progression is said to be generated by 'contradiction'. Dialectic is sometimes associated with this triadic pattern as a whole, and sometimes associated with the driving force involved in the second stage of the triadic pattern (namely, 'contradiction').

A paradigmatic triad might take the following general form. Hegel starts with a particular category which appears fixed and distinct. Conceptual analysis, however, reveals that this first category contains a contrary category and that this contrary category contains it. Further analysis of the relation between these self-contradictory categories reveals a third category which unites the previous two. More precisely, the third category unites the previous two in a highly distinctive manner. The third category is said to cancel, preserve, and elevate, the previous concepts in a way which renders them no longer contrary. (This notorious combination of cancellation, preservation, and elevation is captured by the concept of *Aufhebung*, a term which lacks a single uncontroversial English equivalent.) Perhaps the best-known triad appears at the beginning of Hegel's discussion of the categorical system. He starts from the category 'being', and attempts to show that it contains its contrary, namely the category of 'nothing' (and that the latter contains the former). He then seeks to demonstrate that there is a third category, namely 'becoming', which unites these two in a way which renders them no longer contrary. Hegel associates each of these three developmental stages with forms of thought. The first stage is linked with 'understanding' which fixes and separates concepts (and is associated with deductive argument); the second stage is linked with 'dialectic' which reveals the apparent 'contradictions' that result from such an approach (and is associated with scepticism and sophistry); and the third stage is linked with 'speculation' which incorporates those contraries into a positive and stable result. Hegel describes his own metaphysics as speculative in that it unifies apparently opposed entities, and he characterizes German as a paradigmatically speculative language, in part, because it contains a word— namely, *Aufhebung*—which captures the distinctive dynamic that this unification involves.

It will be apparent that even this brief outline raises a number of thorny questions, including concerns about the character of Hegel's attitude towards formal logic, and whether he endorses the idea of 'contradictions' existing in the world (not merely in claims about the world). There is scarcely room to treat these topics properly here, but I will risk two asides. First, despite the keenness of some modern interpreters to declare Hegel wholly innocent of any conventional intellectual sins, it seems hard to deny that he embraced the idea of 'contradictions' in reality. Second, while Hegel is clearly critical of some of the uses to which conventional logical principles were put, he does not simply reject the laws of identity, contradiction, and excluded middle. (One might think this is just as well, since the notion of rational argument and the distinction between truth and falsity do not obviously survive the abandonment of these principles.) If this combination of claims is to be made consistent, we would seem to require an account of 'contradictions in reality' which is compatible with an endorsement of the law of non-contradiction (the principle, roughly speaking, that a self-contradictory proposition cannot be true, or that contradictory propositions cannot both be true).

It is important to realize that, on Hegel's account, there is nothing arbitrary in the developmental pattern that is revealed by his conceptual analysis. Once an appropriate starting point has been found—and ignoring the considerable difficulties which attach to that issue—each particular category has a unique successor as its necessary result. The kind of necessity involved here is far from certain, but it is crucial to see that progression is supposed to be internal to the categories (not imposed on them from outside). Thought is somehow self-moving, and Hegel claims simply to be following and recording the movement of a self-determining conceptual system. At some point—and in a way which is also controversial—the beginning and end of the series of categories meet up, confirming that the series (and thus the description of the absolute) is complete. We might think of the resulting categorical structure—which Hegel sometimes refers to as *the* concept—as an account of the structure of reason.

Note that it is this categorical system which provides the necessary structure of reality. Modern readers are liable to think of a study of the necessary relations between concepts (Hegel's 'logic') as independent of any study of reality, of what actually exists. However, Hegel maintains that his account of the necessary relations between the categorical concepts is also an account of the necessary structure of reality. Indeed, he maintains that it is the conceptual structure revealed by the 'science of logic' which provides the essential structure of the world. The Hegelian 'concept' is not a set of categories invented by humankind in order to make sense of what actually exists, but is rather to be understood as the non-finite entity on which the finite world depends.

When Hegel refers to the speculative method (of which dialectic is a part), he does not think of himself as having come up with a set of artificial rules or guidelines which might be applied to any subject. Speculative method refers rather to his broad understanding of the essential structure of the world (and only secondarily, and as a consequence, does it suggest anything about the intellectual models or approaches which might best unearth or represent that structure).

The sense in which the finite world depends on the concept is contentious, but Hegel is perhaps best understood as advancing two related claims. The categorical structure unearthed by the science of logic is responsible for both the existence and the development of the finite world. In this way, Hegel sees his account as the philosophical expression of the Christian claim that the world is both created and governed by God. Here, as elsewhere, Hegel's use of religious analogy manages to be both helpful and (potentially) misleading.

The first element in the dependence claim is that the relation between reason and the sensible world is a relation between reason and its own creation. Here, the Christian analogy would seem to be helpful. The precise manner in which the concept creates the natural and social worlds is far from certain—perhaps no two Hegel scholars agree about what precisely is going on here as thought 'spills over' into the finite—but the divine creation *ex nihilo* is clearly the relevant parallel. Reason is not only necessarily embodied—that is, it requires the existence of the sensible world in order to be what it is—but also somehow produces its own embodiment. The temptation to portray this relation, between the concept and the sensible world, in terms of the categorical structure of the logic making an impact on some pre-existing or independent material, should be resisted. Hegel explicitly rejects such an account—he has the demiurge of the ancients in mind—because it would demote God from being the creator of the world to being the mere architect of it. The natural and social worlds are rather the product of the self-realizing activity of the concept (whose actualized form Hegel calls the idea).

The second element in the dependence claim is that thought governs (as well as creates) the sensible world. Here the Christian analogy would seem rather less helpful. Commentators sometimes characterize the Hegelian absolute as a cosmic subject, but it is important not to be misled by such labels. The absolute is not a transcendental entity and it is only potentially a subject. Thus the concept does not exist prior to, or apart from, its embodiment in the social and natural worlds. It is not a puppeteer controlling the social and natural worlds like marionettes, but rather a developmental plan (wholly) immanent in the sensible world. Moreover, although Hegel does maintain that the absolute has the structure of a subject, and not merely the structure of substance, it is (to begin with) only potentially a subject. The conditions for actually becoming a subject are no doubt many, but they crucially include 'self-knowledge', and the 'self-knowledge' of the absolute is reached only at the end of the unfolding of the developmental plan embedded in the world.

The concept is self-actualizing; it strives to be effective, to be embodied in the world. However, although both the social and natural worlds embody the categorical structure, they do so in very different ways. On Hegel's account, the natural world embodies no cumulative development, no history proper. In a striking phrase—borrowed from Friedrich Schelling—Hegel describes the natural world as 'ossified reason'. In sharp contrast, the social world is a sphere of genuine progress. Here the idea (the concept as actualized in the world) functions as a purposeful activity developing through a series of historical stages towards its goal. The concept is embedded in social arrangements, but those social arrangements initially take a form which does not adequately reflect their rational underpinnings. That lack of fit between the concept and the various forms in which it is embodied is what generates historical progress. The result is a series of historical epochs, each of which can be said to provide a more adequate *realization* of reason than its predecessor. It is in the last of these historical epochs—the epoch that, to the evident discomfort of some modern commentators, Hegel calls 'the Germanic world'—that we arrive at a society which is not only fully rational (because its social arrangements adequately reflect the structure of reason) but which is also understood to be fully rational by its members. Hegel characterizes this historical goal in a variety of ways. Not the least striking of these is the claim that it embodies the 'self-knowledge' of the absolute.

Hegel's account of self-knowledge is suggestive but fiddly. He holds that self-knowledge requires a particular developmental relation between a (potential) subject and something (apparently) other than itself (an object). More precisely, it requires the projection of a subject into something (apparently) other than itself, and the subsequent recognition by that subject of itself in that other. The paradigmatic location of this requirement is in the relation between the concept and the finite world. Indeed, for Hegel, the creation and development of the finite world constitutes the necessary detour by which the self-knowledge of the absolute is achieved. There are many complexities here. Not least, Hegel insists that it is humankind which functions as the vehicle of the self-knowledge of the absolute. The process by which humankind comes to understand the world is, as a result, also the process whereby the absolute achieves self-knowledge. Importantly, that process of self-knowledge has practical as well as cognitive aspects. It is the historical progression of ever more rational cultures which constitutes the development of the self-knowledge of the absolute. It is only at the end of this historical process that the absolute can be accurately described as a subject as well as substance. Realizing that end requires not only that the social world be rational but also that it is understood to be so by its members.

On Hegel's account, the identical subject-object of history is the absolute, whose self-knowledge is embodied in humankind. Perhaps the key point to notice here is that the happy coincidence with which we began—between the self-knowledge of this particular subject and knowledge of the world—is guaranteed by the structural identity between that subject and the world. The self-knowledge of the absolute (whose vehicle is humankind) is only equivalent to the self-knowledge of the world, because that subject (the absolute) created the world *ex nihilo* and governs it immanently. In short, it is because the absolute provides the essential structure of the world, that the self-knowledge of this subject (the absolute) and knowledge of the world are the same thing.

However, once we realize this, we are unlikely to be persuaded by Lukács' substitution of the proletariat for the Hegelian absolute. Hegel's account may be hard to swallow but it has a coherence precisely because the agent in question also provides the essential structure of the world. It is that identity which guarantees the happy coincidence between the self-knowledge of that agent and knowledge of the world (and which makes it possible to conceptualize the latter as the self-knowledge of the world).

However, no sane account of the proletariat can appeal to the same rationale. As some contemporary critics of Lukács—such as József Révai—noticed, the proletariat is peculiarly ill-equipped to be the subject-object of history. This particular collective subject does not constitute the essential structure of the social world; indeed, it is not even present during most of the historical process. The worry here is not a trivial one. If the subject in question (here the proletariat) does not constitute the essential structure of the social world, then its self-knowledge cannot plausibly be seen as identical with knowledge of that world (still less equated with the self-knowledge of that world).

Lukács himself seems subsequently to have acknowledged that the idea of an identical subject-object which realizes itself in the historical process was not easily separated from its roots in an idealist metaphysics, and that his ambitious attempt to cast the proletariat in this role was ultimately unsuccessful. In a critical introduction (written in 1967) to a new edition of *History and Class Consciousness*, Lukács characterized his earlier position as an attempt 'to out-Hegel Hegel' which had failed.[7]

More recently, Marshall Berman has characterized Lukács' account as embodying a kind of 'cosmic *chutzpah*'.[8] This seems to me exactly right. *Chutzpah* is, of course, a Yiddish word which connotes hard-to-believe effrontery. (It is the quality famously demonstrated by the man who murders both of his parents, and then asks the court to take pity on a poor orphan.) Once it is unpacked, Lukács' argument might lack plausibility, but it is hard to resist a sneaking admiration for its audacity.

4

I turn now to consider more *modest* accounts of dialectic. From within the wide range of viewpoints that might fit that description, I will sketch (some aspects of) the account of dialectic advanced within the intellectual current often called Analytical Marxism.

Analytical Marxism as a self-conscious tradition of thought—embodied in some of the writings of G. A. Cohen, Jon Elster, Adam Przeworski, John Roemer, Philippe Van Parijs, Erik Olin Wright, and others—emerged in the anglophone world in the late 1970s. The term itself seems to have been coined by Elster, and was perhaps first used publicly as the title of a collection of essays, including pieces by some of the best-known members of the school, published in 1986.[9] Analytical Marxists have been intellectually active in an impressively wide range of subjects, ranging from philosophical anthropology to empirical class analysis, from medieval history to questions of socialist design.

The proper characterization of Analytical Marxism is a difficult and disputed issue. A satisfactory account would seem to require a detailed explanation of both what is 'analytical' and what is 'Marxist' about the work in this tradition. It would also take us some way from the central concerns of this chapter. Instead, it is perhaps helpful to begin, slightly obliquely, with

---

[7]   Ibid. xxiii.   [8]   Marshall Berman, *Adventures in Marxism* (London: Verso, 1999), pp. 183–4.
[9]   John Roemer (edited), *Analytical Marxism* (Cambridge: Cambridge University Press, 1986). Analytical Marxism extends well beyond, but remains closely associated with, the so-called 'September Group' (founded in 1979 by G. A. Cohen and Jon Elster). On the latter, see G. A. Cohen, *Karl Marx's Theory of History: A Defence*, expanded edition (Oxford: Oxford University Press, 2000), pp. xviii–xix.

the self-understanding of this school, that is, with Analytical Marxism's own account of its component parts. In an often repeated description, Analytical Marxism depicts itself as the self-conscious product of both Marxist and non-Marxist traditions. (Note that non-Marxist here is intended as a neutral descriptive term. It is not, for example, equivalent to the pejorative use of 'un-Marxist' by what might—equally pejoratively—be called 'true believers'.)

This self-description of Analytical Marxism appeals to a clear division of labour. On the one hand, it is the Marxist tradition which supplies not only many of the Analytical Marxists' *substantive concerns* (such as their interest in historical explanation, class, and exploitation) but also some of their *normative commitments* (such as the belief that some kind of socialism is superior to existing capitalism). On the other hand, it is the non-Marxist approaches which are largely responsible for the *methods*—the plural here is important—of Analytical Marxism. These methods include conceptual analysis, formal logic and mathematics, game theory, and other conventional tools of statistical, econometric, and historical research. Notice that there are, on this account, no methods which are *both* defensible *and* uniquely Marxist. What properly divides Marxist and non-Marxist accounts are their substantive concerns and normative commitments, not the methods that they adopt.

This division of labour is apparent, for example, in Cohen's opening remarks in *Karl Marx's Theory of History. A Defence*, the book (first published in 1978) which is often portrayed as the founding document of this school, its declaration of independence as it were. Cohen describes his project as a creative mixture of Marxist substance and non-Marxist methods. Seeking to construct a theory of history which met two constraints, the book was intended to be in broad accord with what Marx said on the subject, and to respect 'those standards of clarity and rigour which distinguish twentieth-century analytical philosophy'.[10] Analytical method is construed in broad terms here. It refers to techniques which involve, and enable, clear and precise statement together with rigorous argument.

Analytical Marxism, in short, seeks to combine Marxist subjects with non-Marxist methods. It is important to use the plural here (in speaking of non-Marxist methods), not only because different methods may be appropriate in different contexts but also because there exists some disagreement within Analytical Marxism about the merits of particular methods in the same context. Indeed, methodological concerns have been a central and recurring element in disagreements between individual members of the school.

For example, Cohen and Elster have famously disagreed about the utility of formulating certain of the central theses of historical materialism in functional

---

[10] Cohen, *Karl Marx's Theory of History*, p. ix.

terms, and about the extent to which rational choice accounts might substitute for functional explanation in this context. Cohen maintains that the only way of making the main explanatory claims of historical materialism consistent is by interpreting them as involving functional explanations, and he defends functional explanation as an explanatory device. Functional explanations, speaking very roughly, are those in which something which has a certain effect is explained by the fact that it has that effect. (An example would be the Darwinian claim that birds have hollow bones because hollow bones facilitate flight.) While Elster does not deny the legitimacy of functional explanation in certain circumstances (for example, he accepts that it is a methodologically respectable procedure in evolutionary biology), he is sceptical about its application in this particular context. Functional explanations of macro-phenomena are methodologically acceptable, he maintains, only where it is possible to indicate, at least schematically, the mechanisms at the level of individual behaviour through which the aggregate behaviour emerges. Macro-explanations of the social consequently require what he calls 'microfounda-tions' at the level of the processes of individual choice and action. It is in this context that Elster recommends that Marxism should abandon (insufficiently supported) functional explanation and utilize rational choice explanation in its place. Cohen accepts that such microanalysis is always desirable, and in principle possible, but notes that we are not always in a position to provide it. Moreover, while the provision of microfoundations—what he prefers to call 'elaborations' of a functional mechanism—would improve the functional explanation, their absence does not necessarily invalidate it. A functional explanation can explain even when the mechanism that it involves cannot, as yet, be specified. (The Darwinian claim that birds have hollow bones because hollow bones facilitate flight, for example, provided an 'excellent' explanation which was subsequently rendered 'even better' through developments in the science of genetics.) In addition, Cohen expresses some doubts about the alter-native offered here. While game theory potentially offers imaginative accounts of some aspects of class struggle (of class alliances and revolutionary motiva-tion, for example), class struggle is not the most basic of the phenomena that historical materialism is trying to explain. In short, Cohen argues, both that the absence of microfoundations does not necessarily invalidate functional explanation, and that Elster's proposal to replace functional explanation with game theoretic accounts is, in this particular context, an unpromising one.

What matters here is not the rights or wrongs of this particular dispute—I might have preferred to use the disagreements between Elster and Wright (and others) regarding methodological individualism as an illustration—but the character of these competing methods. Neither Cohen's version of functional explanation nor Elster's preferred alternative of rational choice is the unique property of the Marxist tradition. Analytical Marxists might claim that these methods are (at times, to some extent, and more or less explicitly) adopted by Marx, but there is no straightforward sense in which they are what distinguishes Marxist from non-Marxist theory.

What does distinguish Marx's work, on this account, is not its investigative tools, but its substantive concerns (and normative commitments). Those substantive concerns, as noted earlier, include a theory of history, an account of the workings of capitalism, a philosophical anthropology, and a vision of socialism. Marx's primary achievement is said to lie in his insights into those substantive subject areas, and not in his methodological approach.

From these remarks, one might suppose that the attitude of Analytical Marxism towards the notion of dialectic would be an unremittingly negative one. That supposition is encouraged and reinforced by much of the surrounding literature. It has become a misleading and unfortunate commonplace that Analytical Marxists shun the notion of dialectic.[11] The claim that there is no distinctive Marxist method, no tools and approaches which are available to Marxists that are not available to anyone else, is probably most likely to be resisted by those who identify 'the Marxist method' with some variety of dialectical talk. However, it does not follow that those who accept that claim have to reject all talk of dialectic.

As evidence of a surprisingly open and positive attitude towards dialectic among Analytical Marxists, consider the treatment of this topic by Elster. He has identified three strands of 'Hegelian' reasoning in Marx's work which might be said to embody a dialectical method. Moreover, far from dismissing these out of hand, he finds something of value in two of them.[12]

The first (and least promising) of these three strands is the 'quasi-deductive procedure' which appears in parts of the *Grundrisse* and *Capital*, and which Marx seemingly adopts in order to present the results of some of his economic analysis, in a manner analogous to, and inspired by, the developing categorical system of Hegel's science of logic. Elster is wholly unsympathetic to this notion of dialectic as a method of presentation. Indeed, he purports to find both the relevant passages and their underlying motivation scarcely intelligible. Less fiercely, we might concede that the advantages of presenting the results of a

[11] One commentator even suggests that 'a good test to follow if in doubt whether a particular writer supports the analytic school is to see whether he mentions dialectics with favour. If he does, he must immediately be crossed off the list. Even to cite the word at all counts against membership'. David Gordon, *Resurrecting Marx. The Analytical Marxists on Freedom, Exploitation, and Justice* (New Brunswick: Transaction, 1990), pp. 22–3.

[12] The account that follows is based closely on the discussion of dialectic in three works by Jon Elster: *Logic and Society. Contradiction and Possible Worlds* (London: John Wiley & Sons, 1978), chapters 3–5; *Making Sense of Marx* (Cambridge: Cambridge University Press, 1985), pp. 37–48; and *An Introduction to Karl Marx* (Cambridge: Cambridge University Press, 1986), pp. 34–9. See also Philippe Van Parijs, 'Perverse Effects and Social Contradictions', *British Journal of Sociology*, 33 (1982), 589–603.

complex empirical investigation in the form of an a priori deductive process are far from obvious.[13]

The second (and more promising) of these three strands is the so-called 'dialectical laws' whose general, and overly mechanical, formulation is associated with the later writings of Friedrich Engels, but which also find some partial echo in Marx's own work. In the well-known formulation of the later Engels (in *Anti-Dühring* and elsewhere), these laws include the 'negation of the negation', the 'transformation of quantity into quality' (and vice versa), and the 'interpenetration of opposites'. There is much in Engels' account that Analytical Marxism would reject. For instance, Elster demotes the relevant ideas from their status (in Engels' work) as universal 'laws of nature', to something more akin to descriptive characterizations of patterns of change. These patterns of change might be found in a variety of contexts, including the spheres of nature, society, and consciousness. However, the extent to which these patterns might be evidenced in the world is an open question. There is certainly no echo here of Engels' conviction that all developments in nature, consciousness, and society follow these patterns. But with these and other health warnings, Elster allows that these ideas may be of qualified interest. They are, he concludes, vague but suggestive.

Take, for example, the transformation of quantity into quality (i.e. processes which involve the passage of quantitative change into qualitative transformation). Elster interprets Engels as drawing attention to the possibility, in both the natural and social worlds, of processes with the properties of discontinuity and non-linearity. Engels' discussion of the transformation of water to ice at $0°C$ (and of water into a gaseous state at $100°C$) is treated as an example which draws attention to a discontinuous relation (between an independent variable and a dependent one) from the natural world. While his discussion of the complex relation between numbers and success in cavalry tactics is treated as an example emphasizing a non-linear relation from the social world. Engels—who had a long-standing interest in military tactics (earning him the nickname of 'the General' within the Marx household)—utilizes an example drawn from the memoirs of Napoleon, noting that whereas two Marmelukes would invariably defeat three Frenchmen in military combat, a 1,000 Frenchmen would invariably defeat 1,500 Marmelukes. (Engels' informal explanation of the process here includes claims about the relative superiority of French discipline, the relative superiority of Marmeluke horsemanship, and the minimum size of cavalry detachment in which the advantages of discipline outweigh those of dexterity.[14]) On Elster's account, the (social and natural) world contains, but is not wholly composed of,

---

[13] For a more enthusiastic account of what is sometimes called 'systematic' dialectics, see, e.g., Christopher J. Arthur, *The New Dialectic and Marx's 'Capital'* (Leiden: Brill, 2002), chapters 4–5.

[14] See Friedrich Engels, *Anti-Dühring, Karl Marx Frederick Engels Collected Works* (London: Lawrence & Wishart, 1987), volume 25, p. 119.

discontinuous or non-linear processes of this kind. Given that theorists are often tempted to study the world using continuous, or even linear, models, it is helpful to be reminded that such phenomena do exist.

The negation of the negation can provide another example of a suggestive dialectical pattern. Suitably reinterpreted, this idea describes a triadic development from a stage of 'undifferentiated unity' (where some subject is undivided from some object), through a stage of 'differentiated disunity' (where some subject is divided from some object in a manner which involves discord), to a stage of 'differentiated unity' (where the distinction between subject and object remains but unity is restored). Analytical Marxism is happy to allow that there might be social and individual developments which are usefully described in terms of this dialectical pattern. Cohen, for example, often utilizes an example drawn from Marx's work concerning the historical development from pre-capitalist society, where a collective structure and consciousness inhibit individualism (a stage of undifferentiated unity), through the divisions of capitalism, which stimulate an unbridled individualism (a stage of differentiated disunity), to a communist future, which will preserve (aspects of) individuality in a context of regained community (a stage of differentiated unity). There is no suggestion here of the development being a necessary one (of each stage having to generate the next); society is said to undergo a dialectical transformation simply by virtue of experiencing the relevant stages in turn.[15]

As may be apparent, there is no Marxist monopoly on the identification of such patterns. These dialectical motifs can be found in a wide variety of places. Their use is certainly not restricted either to Marxism or to the wider German philosophical tradition on which Marxism might be thought to draw at this point. Elster has noted the occasional appearance of dialectical patterns in Alexis de Tocqueville's *Democracy in America* (a two-volume work first published, in French, in 1835 and 1840). For example, at one point, Tocqueville characterizes individual belief formation in terms which might fit without much struggle into the pattern of 'the negation of the negation'. Tocqueville identifies what he calls three 'distinct and often successive' stages of human understanding, which we can elaborate in terms of the relation between the individual and their religious beliefs.[16] The first stage, perhaps characteristic of childhood, involves individuals identifying in a wholly unreflective way with their religious beliefs (this is a stage of undifferentiated unity). The second stage, perhaps characteristic of adolescence and early adulthood, involves individuals rejecting their religious beliefs out of doubt and distrust (a stage of differentiated disunity). And the third stage, perhaps characteristic

---

[15] See G. A. Cohen, *History Labour Freedom. Themes from Marx* (Oxford: Oxford University Press, 1988), p. 185.

[16] Alexis de Tocqueville, *Democracy in America*, translated by George Lawrence, edited by J. P. Mayer (London: Fontana, 1994), p. 187.

of maturity, involves individuals reaching a reflective reconciliation with their religious beliefs (a stage of differentiated unity). There could be other features of such a developmental story—for example, it might be claimed that it is not possible either to step directly from the first to the third stage or to revert from the third to the first—but what most matters here is simply the overarching dialectical structure.

The third (and most fruitful) of these three strands is what might be called a theory of social contradictions. Dialectic here is associated with attempts to explain (certain kinds of) social change in terms of underlying real contradictions. Elster is critical of much Hegelian discussion of the idea of 'contradictions in reality'. In particular, he resists any account of 'contradictions in reality' which would imply a denial of the law of non-contradiction. There is no suggestion here that both a statement and its negation can be true at the same time and in the same respect. Nonetheless, Elster maintains not only that there obtains a meaningful sense in which one can talk of 'real contradictions' but also that Marx was a pioneer of their study (although not always using the term 'contradiction [*Widerspruch*]' when rehearsing the relevant line of argument). Real contradictions, on this account, are understood as situations in reality which can only be described with reference to the concept of (logical) contradiction. These real contradictions can take either a psychological form or a social form, although only the latter will be discussed here.

One kind of social contradiction consists of what Elster—adopting a term initially used by Jean-Paul Sartre—calls 'counterfinality'.[17] Counterfinality is a complex notion intended to capture unexpected and undesirable consequences which result from the fallacy of composition. First, counterfinality involves a particular kind of unintended consequence (i.e., a situation in which an unexpected—or unanticipated—outcome arises in the place of the intended one). In addition, it involves unintended consequences where the relevant outcome is undesirable (i.e., where the outcome is detrimental, rather than beneficial, to the interests of the agents bringing them about). Finally, it involves cases where unexpected and undesirable consequences result from the fallacy of composition. The fallacy of composition—on this somewhat nonstandard account—is the inference that what is possible for any single individual must be possible for all individuals simultaneously. (It is a fallacy because there are cases where the antecedent is true and the consequent false.) Speaking generally, we can say that these undesirable unexpected consequences are the result of a discrepancy between the local and the global, between what is possible for a particular agent and what is possible for all agents in that position. (Elster wants the non-universalizability here to rest on logical—rather

---

[17] Other social contradictions, not discussed here, include what Elster calls 'suboptimality' and games without a non-cooperative solution.

than, for instance, on conceptual or causal—grounds, in order to maintain the close link between logical and social contradictions. Whether this limitation is required, and, moreover, whether Elster's own examples respect it, has been questioned. However, these issues will not be pursued here.)

A concrete example should help make the basic idea of counterfinality clearer. Take the, no-doubt familiar, paradox that each capitalist wants his own workers to have low wages (to generate high profits), and wants the workers of other capitalists to have high wages (to generate high demand). Each individual capitalist wants to be in a position—namely of 'having his cake and eating it'—which not all capitalists can occupy. The desires of each individual capitalist are internally consistent, but taken together their desires are contradictory. They are contradictory in the sense that there is no possible world in which all capitalists can have their desires satisfied.

Given certain conditions, the 'real contradictions' here are said to be at the heart of certain kinds of social change. Not least, contradictions tend to generate collective action aimed at overcoming those contradictions. Developing the above example, we might consider the response of individual capitalists to some exogenously induced fall in demand. Imagine that each individual capitalist responds rationally and reduces the wages of his own workers (in order to maintain profits). The collective result, contrary to those intentions, would be a further reduction of workers' buying power (and thus of profits), and the possibility of starting a vicious spiral. The eventual result of such a spiral might be mass unemployment, or pressure for certain kinds of state intervention, or some other form of collective action, in an attempt to overcome the contradiction.

Elster concludes that this notion of 'real contradiction' is both clear and fertile. It is clear, in that it is impervious to some standard 'analytical' objections to dialectical talk (it does not, for instance, conflict with the law of non-contradiction). And it is fertile, in that it generates a method which can be operationalized and which yields substantive results. This method is seen as especially fruitful in identifying potential causes of social instability and change.

Marx was, no doubt, an important pioneer in the study of social contradictions, but—as with the negation of the negation—Elster notes that these ideas are both prefigured and developed in the work of authors who are not (all) to be located within the Marxist tradition. (In a historical survey of the idea of 'counterfinality', Elster identifies Bossuet, Mandeville, Vico, Adam Smith, and Hegel, as figures whose work also includes significant adumbrations of the relevant core idea. And he singles out the writings of Oskar Morgenstern, Sartre, Robert Nozick, and Trygve Haavelmo, as contributing to more recent refinements of that core.[18])

---

[18] Elster, *Logic and Society*, p. 106.

5

The approach I have adopted towards dialectic in this chapter is not dismissive—both because I have sought to take the notion seriously and because I would happily admit some modest version of it into my preferred collection of approaches—but it is sceptical. Two sources of that scepticism might be mentioned here. It is, in part, a reaction against the grandiloquent and obscure claims that are sometimes made on behalf of dialectic. And it reflects, in part, a more general suspicion about the recommendation of a single methodological approach over all others. Some methods and approaches are, no doubt, superior to others in some particular contexts, or for some particular tasks. However, one can reasonably doubt that the complexity of the world can be captured by a single theoretical model, making all others redundant. The metaphor of a toolkit may be overused but it effectively suggests the methodological pluralism I have in mind here. (A good toolkit will include a variety of different implements, no subset of which can replace all the rest. Indeed, it is its very diversity which appears to constitute the strength of a collection of tools.)

In these brief closing remarks, I want both to acknowledge the limited remit of this chapter and to venture some general conclusions. From among a huge range of views about dialectic, I have focused on only two examples in the present chapter. Moreover, these are both taken from within the Marxist tradition. Even with the significant nod to Hegel which bridged the discussion of Lukács and Analytical Marxism, I have clearly not exhausted very many of the possibilities here. As a result, it seems inappropriate to offer too much by way of a general conclusion. Nonetheless, I would like to rehearse, and thereby reinforce, three observations from the above discussion: that a huge variety of very different things have been called dialectic; that some accounts of dialectic are more extravagant (and implausible) than others; and that, in some more modest (and plausible) guise, dialectic should not be seen as antithetical to an analytical approach.

In the first place, even within the confines of the present discussion, it is apparent that the term 'dialectic' gets used to suggest a large number of different ideas. They include interconnectedness and development, a reciprocal relationship between theory and practice, a social ontology (of an evolving organic kind), a grand idealist metaphysics underpinned by a triadic conceptual structure, the driving force of (the second stage of) that conceptual structure (namely, 'contradiction'), a form of thought (associated with scepticism and sophistry), a method of presentation, a pattern of change (found, at times, in nature, society, and consciousness), and an explanation of social change (in terms of underlying 'real contradictions'). In addition, it is certain that not all of these notions will be judged equally clear and persuasive. I suspect that there will be few takers for a full-blown Hegelian idealism which understands the world as an organic structure analogous to a human subject, a structure which is created and governed by a categorical system formed on a triadic pattern. However, perhaps equally few would deny the contrastingly modest possibility of ever usefully ascribing a dialectical pattern—such as the negation of the negation—to some process in nature, society, or consciousness. Finally, in many of the cases discussed above, dialectic is not to be construed as a methodological alternative to analytical approaches (at least, on any appropriately broad account of the latter). A commitment to clear and precise statement together with rigorous argument is not incompatible with dialectical talk. And defending the idea of dialectic need not offer any support for those who would insist on the existence of a radical gulf between 'dialectical' and 'analytical' reasoning.

7 Political theory and history[1]

Mark Philp

1

Every graduate student of political theory faces a series of choices about
what to study and how best to study it. In the natural sciences topics are
generally located in a well-defined research programme rooted in a shared
view of what the most interesting and current problems are and what the
appropriate methods are for approaching them. In political theory, issues of
method are themselves so much part of the contested terrain of the subject
matter that identifying the problem may itself be a function of commitments
that derive from the position one takes in methodological debates. For that
reason the student of political theory cannot remain methodologically naive
or uncommitted; part of choosing a topic involves decisions about how one
should approach it methodologically. This is particularly true in relation to
history and the history of political thought—an area that has seen dramatic
challenges in relation to the appropriate methods for the study of political
thought and political theory over the last thirty or forty years in the work of
Quentin Skinner, John Dunn, J. G. A. Pocock, Reinhart Koselleck, and Michel
Foucault.

This chapter does not pretend to offer a complete overview of those
challenges—attempting to do so would at best replicate work that others
have done in recent years, to which I refer in the bibliography. My concerns,
moreover, are slightly different from those who have approached the debate
mainly as historians with an interest in political thought, in that the question I
address is how far *political theorists* have reasons for being interested in history
and the history of political thought, and how far the discipline of politics has
demands that distinguish its activity and interests, and its methods, from those
of history. There is no doubt that the history of political thought has things of
importance to say to those who work in political theory, and that the very
wide range of methodological issues tackled by, for example, Skinner's work,

[1] My thanks to the members of the Centre for the Study for Social Justice in Oxford for their
contribution to a spirited debate on these issues, and to Dan Butt, Jerry Cohen, David Miller, Joe
Philp, Adam Swift, and the editors of this collection.

speaks to concerns about the nature of social understanding, rationality in thought and action, and problems in interpretation that are central to any social scientist who crosses a minimum threshold of intellectual awareness and competence. But, against at least some of those who propose a more historical approach to political theory, I argue that such an understanding does not (and, more normatively, must not) wholly displace the distinctive character or concerns of political theory itself. To that extent, this chapter addresses what it is that political theorists should concern themselves with, methodologically, when they turn to history and the history of political thought.

2

There is a good deal of disagreement about how to characterize political theory but, as a starting point, let us say that it is a practice involving systematic reflection on the character of politics, the causal forces underlying political stability and change, the institutional frameworks within which certain types of political activity are sustained, and, more normatively, the values or objectives that political activity and organization might realize, and conditions under which they can be realized. Political theorists differ over how far these components can be separated and split off into relatively discrete enterprises with some suggesting, for example, that the analysis of concepts focusing on the values that politics should pursue can be separated off from the descriptive analysis of conceptual change or reflection about the causal conditions necessary for the development and stabilization of certain institutional structures. And in those discussions lines are often drawn (often very much in the sand) between political philosophy and political theory and political and social theory.[2]

In one sense it seems obvious that history—our past—has made us what we are. In so far as all the forces, causal or intentional, that can be distinguished from what we are at this point in time are credited to the side of 'history', then it seems that they must contain within them the necessary and sufficient conditions for explaining any of the features we care to pick out on the side of 'what we are'. But the statement, if true, is in need of substantial further specification simply because the historian's craft involves sifting through that mass of information and identifying certain specific elements in that mass of historical data as the salient elements in understanding some event, action, or feature of our contemporary world (or, more commonly among historians, to look at features of history prior to time T_n, to understand or explain features of X—where X is itself some historical event or occurrence at T_n). To that extent,

---

[2] But for a 'sand-free' version, see G. A. Cohen, 'Facts and Principles', *Philosophy & Public Affairs*, 31/3 (2003), pp. 211–45.

it is not 'history' that explains but the subset of causal and intentional elements that are identified; and the selection of that subset involves making a number of assumptions and theoretical claims that are not always clearly articulated but that are nonetheless central to the construction of an explanation or interpretation. Moreover, in at least one important sense, the idea that history has made us what we are is false. To think it true we need to place ourselves pretty firmly on the side of accounts that give structure ascendancy over agency; whereas, the more weight we accord to agency and to the understanding of action (rather than its causal explanation) the more difficult it is analytically to distinguish 'what we are' from the world of intersubjective understanding in which we interpret and react to the world and make it our own. We may not choose the conditions under which we are born and come to consciousness, but we do nonetheless, in some important sense (albeit to different degrees under different conditions), make our own futures.

There are two central ways in which political theory and history intersect. The analysis of what is politically possible (which may or may not include in its scope any part of what we think normatively desirable) is developed through understanding the interaction between individual motivations, political culture, institutions, and structural preconditions, each of which is inflected by the past; and one laboratory for developing and testing such generalizations is the past. However, while a comparative political science with no sense of history—something resolutely modernist and presentist—is undoubtedly poorer as a result, it is not clear that it is fatally flawed (consider some of the insights of rational choice theorists in political science or economics). Moreover, it is also unclear that we want something specific to history itself, rather than looking for case studies that are illuminating about some aspect of politics, where it is a contingent truth about those case studies that they occur at different points in time. The past is one field on which people can draw for insights and evidence, and the methods of the professional historian (which are often deeply contested)[3] provide a set of tools to work that field, but it is certainly not the only field or discipline in which political theorists should be interested—philosophy, sociology, psychology, anthropology, law, and economics are also often equally relevant. Moreover, as I have suggested, in drawing on history we always select—in the very presentation of information as 'evidence' it has already been worked over to form part of an argument or theory about the meaning of events and their causes and impact—so there is no question about simply going to history for either evidence or answers.[4] Politics may look to history, but it does so because it is concerned

---

[3] On contests over the nature of history as a discipline see, e.g., Joyce Appleby, Lynn Hunt, and Margaret Jacobs, *Telling the Truth About History* (New York: W. W. Norton, 1993); and Jacques Le Goff and Pierre Nora, *Faire de L'histoire: Nouvelles Approaches* (Paris: Gallimard, 1974).

[4] See, e.g., Quentin Skinner, 'The Practice of History and the Cult of the Fact', *Visions of Politics*, volume 1:*Regarding Method* (Cambridge: Cambridge University Press, 2002), chapter 2.

to understand events, to construct explanations and models of political order, and to develop a sense of what is politically possible and desirable. It comes to history with specific purposes that derive from the nature of its own discipline and its object—the understanding of politics—and it addresses historical material with greater or lesser degrees of attention according to its purposes (and it is as possible to over-invest as it is to underinvest). But its object is not identical with history, and its aim is not merely historical.

The second way in which political theory and history intersect is more complex. The activity of reflecting on politics is of long-standing, and the history of that reflection both has an impact on current thinking and practices (within the discipline and more widely in the political system as a whole) and offers us a range of competing narratives of our past, and thereby of our present. The study of that process of reflection raises a number of intractable philosophical and methodological disputes that have been amply illustrated in the rich literature on the history of political thought over the last forty years or so.

3

In Britain the major methodological dispute over political theory and the history of political thought was initiated by Quentin Skinner in a series of articles in which he attacked a number of aspects of the interpretation of the history of ideas drawing on the work of philosophers of language, especially the later Wittgenstein, Grice, Austin, Davidson, and Quine, together with the philosopher of history, R. G. Collingwood.[5] Skinner argues against the study of ideas across time on the grounds that the meaning of terms depends on the function they have in particular contexts. To insist on the continuity of ideas (such as the state of nature, or social contract theory, or Lovejoy's 'great chain of being') across time both fails to grasp that meaning is context-dependent, and that it needs to be articulated in relation to the issues and questions that

---

[5] These articles are now amended and collected in volume 1 of *Visions of Politics*. Earlier versions can be found in James Tully (edited), *Meaning and Context* (Cambridge: Polity Press, 1988), which also has a good bibliography of Skinner's early writings, together with a collection of critical essays, of which Charles Taylor's piece, 'The Hermeneutics of Conflict' is both deep and accessible. The salient works are Ludwig Wittgenstein, *Philosophical Investigations* (Oxford: Basil Blackwell, 1958); H. P. Grice, 'Meaning', *The Philosophical Review*, 66/3 (1957), pp. 377–88; H. P. Grice, 'Utterer's Meaning and Intention', *The Philosophical Review*, 78/2 (1969), pp. 147–77; J. L. Austin, *How to Do Things with Words* (Oxford: Oxford University Press, 1980); Donald Davidson, 'On the Very Idea of a Conceptual Scheme', *Inquiries into Truth and Interpretation* (Oxford: Clarendon Press, 1984), pp. 183–98; W. V. O. Quine, *Word and Object* (Cambridge, MA: MIT Press, 1960); W. V. O. Quine, 'On the Reasons for the Indeterminacy of Translation', *The Journal of Philosophy*, 67/6 (1970), pp. 178–83; and R. G. Collingwood, *The Idea of History* (Oxford: Oxford University Press, 1946).

a particular author was trying to address.[6] Treating 'unit ideas' across time rips them from their context and assumes an essentialist understanding of concepts that cannot be defended.[7] A second, related target against which Skinner inveighs is the purely textual study of political theorists, which treats them as if they are contributing to discussion of timeless issues and concepts— what Skinner calls 'the mythology of doctrines'.[8] And that target is related to the attack on the idea that certain texts anticipate or influence certain later theorists. A further, more independent line of criticism is aimed at reduction-ist analysis of ideas to the social and material conditions of their production. In each case, one central line of argument that has remained consistent in Skinner's methodological oeuvre is the view that the identification of the meaning of a statement or text depends on seeing what act the author is undertaking by making that statement.[9] And to answer that question is to make a stab at understanding the intersubjective world of meaning that the actor occupies, the textual context, and the particular set of reference points in that world to which he or she orientates his or her action.

Skinner's work is also often coupled with that of J. G. A. Pocock, and the 'Cambridge School' is often taken to encompass both (as well as the early work of the political theorist John Dunn).[10] In fact, while there are broad similarities, the terminology used by Pocock has consistently pointed towards the idea of larger unities of thought within which, and against which, one reads particular texts, starting with 'paradigms', but moving increasingly to speak of vocabularies, rhetorics, languages, or discourses of political thought. These units are not simply the sum of terms and their usages but are made up by linguistic conventions that shape what can be said and done (not unlike Wittgenstein's 'language games'). They also cover often extended periods of time, so his *Machiavellian Moment* traces a discourse of civic humanism or classical republicanism that passes from Machiavelli's Renaissance to the

[6] See A. O. Lovejoy, *The Great Chain of Being* (Cambridge, MA: Harvard University Press, 1936); and Skinner, *Visions of Politics*, volume 1, pp. 83–5.

[7] Skinner, *Visions of Politics*, volume 1, pp. 82–6.

[8] Ibid. 59–60. See also Melvin Richter, 'A German Version of the "Linguistic Turn": Reinhart Koselleck and the History of Political and Social Concepts (*Begriffsgeschichte*)', in Dario Castiglione and Iain Hampsher-Monk (edited), *The History of Political Thought in National Context* (Cambridge: Cambridge University Press, 2001), chapter 4; and Iain Hampsher-Monk, 'The History of Political Thought and the Political History of Thought', in Castiglione and Hampsher-Monk (edited), *The History of Political Thought in National Context*, chapter 8.

[9] Or by not making a particular statement—e.g., Locke's silence on the 'Ancient Constitution'. See John Dunn, 'The Identity of the History of Ideas', *Philosophy*, 43/164 (1968), pp. 85–104.

[10] J. G. A. Pocock's best-known work is his *Machiavellian Moment* (Princeton: Princeton University Press, 1975), but see also the methodological essays that open each of his collections *Politics, Language and Time: Essays on Political Thought and History* (New York: Athaneum, 1973), and *Virtue, Commerce and History* (Cambridge: Cambridge University Press, 1985), and 'The concept of a language and the *metier d'historien*: some considerations on practice', Anthony Pagden, *The Languages of Political Theory in Early Modern Europe* (Cambridge: Cambridge University Press, 1987), pp. 19–40. For John Dunn, see previous note.

American Revolution, via Harrington and the English Country Party traditions of argument. Moreover, different discourses or languages coexist at the
same time, so that every moment will find a range of competing languages
available for discussing political institutions and ideas.

There are a number of potential sources for this historicizing of political
thought. In part their position was a reaction against Marxism[11] and what
was seen as the reductionism in its analysis of political agency and ideas; in
part it was a response to the 'linguistic turn' in philosophy (the view that there
is no place outside of language from which to have access to facts, truth or
value, and that these meaningful utterances on such matters are a function
of the language games or linguistic units within which they operate).[12] But
another influential, if rather different, source for many writing in the late
1960s and early 1970s was work in the philosophy of science, and the history
of the philosophy of science, on scientific research and theoretical change,
notably in the work of Thomas Kuhn. Kuhn's work on paradigms has two
dimensions.[13] One is the view that to understand scientific research one has
to understand the intellectual framework or paradigm within which it is
conducted. Rather than reducing scientific claims to statements and hypotheses that are straightforwardly open to verification or refutation by evidence,
we need to understand that the way in which questions and hypotheses are
framed and tested is a function of the broader intellectual framework of the
particular discipline. For the most part scientific research is 'normal science',
conducted within the paradigm of the discipline, where results that do not
fit the model are treated, not as refutations, but as anomalies that the framework serves to marginalize. In periods of revolutionary scientific activity we
witness paradigm shifts that replace the old orthodoxies with new models that
better explain the anomalies of the previous paradigm, but which generate,
over time, further results that cannot be satisfactorily explained within its
framework. Theoretical paradigms, then, frame scientific work and shape the
way that questions are asked and answers pursued. This more holist understanding of scientific activity, as a process of revolutionary paradigm shifts,
interspersed with long periods of 'normal' science, invited the interpretation
that the 'stickiness' of paradigms is partly a function of the power wielded by
those who are centrally attached to the dominant paradigm in an area, and

---

[11] Although rarely attacked directly, Marxism was a clear target for Skinner as an example of a failed
account of the relationship between action (including the speech acts of texts) and circumstance. See,
e.g., 'Meaning and Understanding in the History of Ideas', *History and Theory*, 8/1 (1969), p. 42. In the
history of ideas one major target of the Cambridge school was C. B. Macpherson's *The Political Theory
of Possessive Individualism: Hobbes to Locke* (Oxford: Oxford University Press, 1962).

[12] See, e.g., Richard Rorty, *The Linguistic Turn: Recent Essays in Philosophical Method* (Chicago:
University of Chicago Press, 1967); and Richard Rorty, *Philosophy and the Mirror of Nature* (Princeton:
Princeton University Press, 1980).

[13] Thomas Kuhn, *The Structure of Scientific Revolutions* (Chicago: University of Chicago Press,
1963).

who have a disproportionate impact on controlling the flow of resources, the publication of results, and admission into the profession, so that a paradigm shift threatens not simply an intellectual edifice but also a social world and its accompanying power structures. Kuhn doubted that the social sciences were fully paradigmatic, although that did not stop the application of his ideas to them, but in many respects the interest that his ideas generated among social scientists was with the development of a more social, less rationalist, account of scientific change. By playing down the role of rationality and scientific truth in accounting for a shift between paradigms Kuhn offered those hostile to or sceptical of the ideals of modern science an understanding in which truth is relativized to the dominant paradigm.[14]

The work of Kuhn and others in this field remains of importance precisely because of the question it raises about the relativizing of truth to domains of practice—a relativization in relation to political thought that is also an explicit component of the work of the Cambridge school. Statements and theories are true within the paradigm, discourse, language, or context: given how we do things today and given the methods we consider appropriate, then we can validate certain hypotheses or statements—but we cannot talk of their truth more generally. And if this is true for physics, it must certainly be true for the less evidently scientific activities of political and social scientists, which suggests that truth in these domains is relativized and essentially a social artefact. Those attracted to that view have often been drawn also to the work of Michel Foucault who, while coming from a very different angle (albeit one shaped by the work of the French philosopher of physics Gaston Bachelard and the philosopher of the life sciences, Georges Canguilhem), developed a way of thinking about the discourses of the human sciences that both relativized truth and came increasingly to identify what counts as 'true' as the effect of power.[15]

These approaches share a concern with the identification of discontinuities or breaks in the meaning and use of concepts. To relativize a concept to a framework, paradigm, or discourse is also to create the possibility of recognizing that at one point of time a concept has a certain meaning, within a particular discourse, while at another it is different, and to have no way of saying that one or other has greater validity, warrantability, or value. For some, like Kuhn and Foucault, the interest of this recognition lay precisely in the way that these differences add up to a shift in fundamental paradigms or

---

[14] Interestingly, Lakatos' work, on scientific research programmes, which is often bracketed with Kuhn, but which retains a subtle form of scientific rationalism, was less popular with social scientists. See Imre Lakatos, *The Methodology of Scientific Research Programmes, Philosophical Papers*, volume 1 (Cambridge: Cambridge University Press, 1978), and the profoundly influential collection edited by Lakatos and Alan Musgrave, *Criticism and the Growth of Knowledge* (Cambridge: Cambridge University Press, 1970).

[15] See Foucault's *The Archaeology of Knowledge* (London: Tavistock Publications, 1972); Colin Gordon (edited), *Power/Knowledge* (Brighton: Harvester Press, 1980); and 'Orders of Discourse', *Social Science Information*, 10/2 (1971), pp. 7–30.

discursive frameworks. But for many the idea of conceptual change became itself an attractive option for the contextual study of the history of concepts. This has taken various forms, notably in Germany, under the influence of the hermeneutics of Gadamer and Heidegger and in the theory of *Begriffs-geschichte* developed by Reinhart Koselleck, while in the English-speaking world the most influential work, thus far, has been the collection on *Political Innovation and Conceptual Change* edited by Ball, Farr, and Hanson and Melvin Richter's essays on Koselleck.[16] There is no single orthodoxy in this field, not least with respect to how far this is a history of language that is to be partly or wholly distinct from social and cultural history (with some seeing the latter as necessarily encapsulated in the linguistic), but there is a shared sense that the historicizing of concepts and the tracking of the way in which meanings change over time gives us a more sophisticated way of understanding the history of a society or a set of practices. For some this implies that meaning is relativized to context and that our own conceptual tools and frameworks should be understood wholly historically, but there is nothing intrinsic to the study of conceptual change that requires that we make that move.

4

In a number of essays Leo Strauss inveighs against what he refers to as 'historicism' in political thinking. As he defines it, historicism abandons the fact/value distinction, denies the authority of modern science, rejects the view that history is progressive or reasonable, and rejects an evolutionary perspective as the basis for value.[17] This is a rather freighted view of historicism, but the central claim that it involves the relativizing of fact and value (and thereby truth) to

---

[16] Reinhart Koselleck, 'Linguistic Change and the History of Events', *The Journal of Modern History*, 61/4 (1989), pp. 649–66; Reinhart Koselleck, *The Practice of Conceptual History* (Palo Alto: Stanford University Press, 2002), especially essays 1, 2, 13, and 14; Melvin Richter, *The History of Social and Political Concepts: A Critical Introduction* (New York: Oxford University Press, 1995); Melvin Richter, 'A German Version of the "Linguistic Turn" ', in Castiglione and Hampsher-Monk (edited), *The History of Political Thought in National Context*, chapter 4; and Melvin Richter, 'Reconstructing the History of Political Languages: Pocock, Skinner, and the *Geschichtliche Grundbegriffe*', *History and Theory*, 29/1 (1990), pp. 38–70. This note, and the paragraph to which it refers, is an inadequate discussion of what has been, for historians, an attractive enterprise, and an extremely productive one in Germany. There are clearly tensions between the emphasis in Skinner on what people are doing with words and concepts, and the view that sees a gradual process of conceptual change over time and which focuses not simply on single authors but on the language as such. But work is ongoing in exploring the extent to which there may be common interests and concerns between the different traditions. See also Terence Ball, James Farr, and Russell L. Hanson, *Political Innovation and Conceptual Change* (Cambridge: Cambridge University Press, 1987).

[17] Leo Strauss, *An Introduction to Political Philosophy: Ten Essays* (Detroit: Wayne State University Press, 1989), p. 23.

particular historical periods certainly captures the force of the proposal. The cruder versions of historicism (initially influenced by Marxist commitments to seeing thought as functional to the development of the productive forces in the economy) read texts as expressive of the social and material conditions under which they were written. More sophisticated versions, many of which were influenced by developments in later Marxism, sought more plausible ways of thinking about the nature of the relationship between the social and the ideational and have given greater weight to language, discourse, and ideology, both in the sense of according them more independence from material and non-discursive elements and by treating language and ideology as constitutive of the political and social world. Nonetheless, these positions are for the most part versions of historicism. They are so because each context is historicized, each language, discourse, or conceptual scheme is local, so that, if we want to understand what a classical text is arguing, we have to root it in its (variously identified) context, from which it cannot be extracted without violence to the subtleties and particular meanings that it conveys.

In some of the more ambitious versions of historicism, 'the local' develops a higher significance for us by becoming a part of the history of the present. The tracking of conceptual change and development, and the evolution of discursive formations and political languages through history, allows us, on this view, to write a history of our own present, and thereby to gain some reflexive purchase on our own political discourse. That purchase may be positive, in that an excavation of the historical roots of our conceptual vocabulary can empower us through allowing us a better understanding of the possibilities (and distortions) inherent in the political language that we have inherited;[18] or it may be negative, revealing to us through a genealogy of our present a past that we cannot endorse, and which consequently disconcerts our current discursive practices.[19] On the latter view, political theory becomes wholly historicized; but on either version of the story, there is an issue of whether there is any place outside the language or discourse that escapes this historical specificity. The conclusion that there is not is something that is enthusiastically embraced by many advocates of this approach to political thought—but it comes at a price.

Political theory involves normative, analytical, and explanatory theorizing about politics. If we historicize politics so that it is always a local phenomenon—if it is only ever what counts as politics round here—then we have no grounds for believing that people are thinking about the same thing at all and there becomes a basic untranslatability of each local discussion. Those who resist this relativizing do so on the grounds that while the terms

[18] See, e.g., John Dunn's *Setting the People Free* (London: Atlantic Books, 2005), and Skinner's reconstruction of the neo-Roman concept of liberty in *Liberty before Liberalism* (Cambridge: Cambridge University Press, 1998).

[19] Perhaps most strikingly in Foucault's *Discipline and Punish* (London: Allen Lane, 1977).

of debates on politics certainly change over time, there remains a core set of concerns that mark political activities off from other activities and provide the basis for a sense that there are continuities in the discussion that revolve around political rule and the attempt to exercise political authority. As we have seen, this suggestion was roundly attacked by many in the 1960s who saw it as imposing a straightjacket on the interpretation of classic texts—one that might ride roughshod over the intentions of particular authors and the meaning of their text. There was, and is, considerable good sense in the objections raised to the idea that there are perennial debates in politics, not because there are no such debates, but because those debates need careful reconstruction in which we give close attention to what people said, and what they meant by saying that, and (as Skinner has importantly insisted) what they were trying to do by saying what they said—and responding to those injunctions does rely on an understanding of context. But, for the fruits of that investigation to contribute to political theory (even to see them as contributing to a history of political thought), they must themselves be shown to link to concerns and problems that are intelligible to someone who is not steeped in that context, but who has a sufficiently deep understanding of politics to recognize the nature of the contribution. The very attempt to understand a text presumes the possibility of its intelligibility and of communicating that to our contemporaries, and that possibility rests on our ability to recognize within the foreignness of a particular past and its texts at least some common referents that provide a bridge for understanding.

It is also important to insist that political theory is not the same as writing history. The two practices certainly meet in the territory of the history of political thought but that does not make them identical. Clearly, if one wants to say something about what Hobbes said, or thought, or was trying to do in *Leviathan*, then an attention to the context in which he developed and advanced his views is required—and, although there are many ways in which that context can be defined, the crucial issue is to ensure a match between what one seeks to understand in relation to Hobbes and the identification of the particular context. We may talk about the language of sovereignty on which he draws to understand what the Hobbesian theory of sovereignty is, from where it was derived, or against what orthodoxy it was articulated; or we may use Hobbes' familiarity with certain pamphlet debates to show what Hobbes was trying to do in certain sections of *Leviathan*. There are a wide number of interpretations of Hobbes (indeed, of most political thinkers) that fall clearly short of such standards. Nonetheless, there remains a question about what we might learn from Hobbes and his perspective on the nature of sovereignty, authority, and government; and that is certainly not restricted to what he intended to do. This would, however, give us two Hobbes, the historically reconstructed Hobbes and 'Hobbes' the person whose texts we find stimulate certain ideas whose contemporary significance we are keen to explore. That tension might be eased by calling the latter 'Hobbesian', but that solution must not obscure the fact that neither 'Hobbes' nor 'Hobbesian' ought to be allowed to escape completely from Hobbes.[20] By referencing Hobbes at all, some constraint is placed on what we can say in his name. But is that constraint so absolute that the only thing we can do in his name is to provide the most faithful possible historical contextualizing of a text like *Leviathan*? As political theorists we may also want to argue about competing understandings of sovereignty, and about how we should understand and relate to sovereignty and its associated issues in the modern world. If we think the context of *Leviathan* sufficiently unique to preclude translation between it and other contexts, then Hobbes has nothing to say to us—much as John Dunn once felt forced to conclude about Locke.[21] But many modern political theorists, including many who are interested in historical context and in attaining a deeper understanding of what Hobbes and others were doing, are also interested in thinking about contemporary politics in terms that an engagement with thinkers from a range of different contexts can facilitate. To have that engagement often requires a certain amount of loose translation, and while those who rely on this certainly have an obligation to be clear about what it is that they are trying to do and about how far their faithfulness, or lack of it, to a particular author's intentions is necessary to their project, to argue that this thereby wholly vitiates their project is to take a resolutely historicist line with respect to the activity of contemporary political theory. Naturally, just as there is good and bad history, so too there is good and bad political philosophy, but it is simply illegitimate to think that good political philosophy is something for which meeting the criteria for good history is a necessary and sufficient condition. That is to historicize every discipline, and is to overreach.

5

Political theorists and philosophers who resist these forms of relativism may do so on a number of grounds and may do so without ignoring the importance of an understanding of historical context in grasping a particular text's meaning. In the first place, there is something colossally self-defeating about claims for method that are not reflexive. To say that truth is relative to intellectual

---

[20] See, e.g., Gregory S. Kavka, *Hobbesian Moral and Political Theory* (Princeton: Princeton University Press, 1986), who gives two interpretations of Hobbes' work, one as providing a descriptive theory and the other as providing a moral theory. It is inconceivable that Hobbes meant his ideas in these two different ways, but the analysis is often extremely illuminating, sometimes of the ideas, and sometimes about what Hobbes might have meant.

[21] See John Dunn, *The Political Thought of John Locke* (Cambridge: Cambridge University Press, 1969); and John Dunn, 'What Is Living and What Is Dead in the Political Thought of John Locke?', *Interpreting Political Responsibility* (Cambridge: Cambridge University Press, 1990), pp. 9–25.

frameworks is to make a claim that if true would render itself false. Similarly, historicist approaches must somehow account for their own emergence, and cope with their own historical relativity, to be plausible. And to argue that we cannot understand a text except historically leaves open the question of what earlier political theorists, including many in the canon, were doing when they engaged across historical divides with their predecessors—as, for example, in Locke's use of Filmer and Hooker. The proclamation of relativism is cant simply because it is not itself a relativist claim. This does not mean that there are not considerable insights to be drawn from the linguistic turn and related arguments but we do need to take care to avoid the methodological fallacy of assuming a type of validity for method that one then denies to the objects studied by that method.[22] Nor does it mean that we can grandly proclaim certainty about interpretative or historical matters; instead it involves the recognition that when we engage in enquiry we may pursue truth, using the canons of enquiry that have been tried and tested and that allow us some degree of confidence, without ever guaranteeing certainty or a place to stand from which objectively to assess our degree of success. This means that there is room for a good deal of context in understanding what people were trying to do, but without thinking that everything that they do, and everything we do with them, must be wholly relativized to their context.

A second ground for political theorists to be less than discomfited by these claims is that political theory is itself a complex practice, with conventions and rules of procedure, and criteria for distinguishing better and worse arguments and interpretations. On a historicist understanding of that practice its findings may lack enduring truth value, but there is nowhere firm to stand to make that claim, and while the suggestion of relativism might make people hope for a little humility in the claims that people make for their work it undercuts any ground we might have for asking for this. What that practice should be understood as asking of us is that we do not study, think, or analyse sloppily— that we are aware of methodological issues, that we reflect on the criteria by which we give greater weight to some arguments or interpretations than others, that we are clear about what it is we are trying to do in any given instance, and so on. But that is simply to take seriously what it is to participate in a discipline.

A third ground for comfort for those engaged with the more analytic and normative concerns of political theory concerns the character of their arguments. In a comment at the end of his introduction to his methodological essays that have had such a powerful influence over the history of political thought in the UK and more widely, Quentin Skinner notes that 'the principles governing our moral and political life have generally been disputed

---

[22] See, e.g., the historically sophisticated non-relativism of Charles Taylor, in his 'The Hermeneutics of Conflict', in Tully (edited), *Meaning and Context*.

in a manner more reminiscent of the battlefield than the seminar room' and that it may therefore 'be right to view with a certain irony those moral and political philosophers of our own day who present us with overarching visions of justice, freedom, and other cherished values in the manner of dispassionate analysts standing above the battle. What the historical record suggests is that no one is above the battle, because the battle is all there is.'[23] The claim that moral and political dispute is a battlefield offers an apt metaphor, but one that is undeveloped in one crucial respect. We might take it to mean that the rhetorical strategies of those involved in political theory, and the history of political thought, are such that we have to take what they say as wholly instrumental to some set of purposes vis-à-vis their opponents. What they say, they say in order to win, not because they have any commitment to the content of what they say. But, if that is the case, it is difficult to think that anything of moral or political substance underlies this war—it is effectively one group or side seeking domination over and against another. However, while it is clear that this sometimes happens, it seems a remarkably reductive (and, paradoxically given Skinner's own critique, a rather Namierite) view of political argument, historical or contemporary. Battles can be fought solely for ascendancy, but they are more often fought for other things as well, including moral and political values; and where those values enter in (where they are not simply terms instrumental to some other purpose) they generally involve two sorts of claim. On the one hand, to claim something as a value, not simply as a preference, is to claim that it has a cognitive status that others could recognize. It is to suggest that one's commitment to the value arises *from* its value, rather than the commitment creating that value, and that others who view things to some degree reasonably or impartially will also recognize and, all things being equal, come to accept that value. Moreover, that commitment makes certain forms of argument, justification, and counter-argument possible and gestures towards a set of standards for truth-claims that certainly evolve over time, but that also involve a different character of argument and assessment, revolving around implicit criteria of rational acceptability, than we find in rhetoric. Of course, given how inchoately we grasp most values, there is a complex mix of passion, rhetoric, and truth-claims in the values for which we fight, but these are not battles over nothing, nor is what people say solely camouflage for more sinister purposes. So, while a full analysis must certainly pay attention to rhetorical strategies, it must also seek to identify the values and commitments in relation to which such strategies are deployed.

The second claim implicit in many values is that these are goods for others, and while that perspective can legitimate a fair amount of paternalism, some values constrain paternalism by their very nature. When constrained, the realization of the value depends in part on its endorsement by those in

---

[23]   Skinner, *Visions of Politics*, volume 1, p. 7.

whose lives it will play a regulatory role, and that endorsement cannot be undertaken in error. Not to see the point of liberty but to endorse it because of the powerful rhetorical strategies of those in politics is not (on most accounts) to experience the value of liberty. And those who care about liberty (under whichever of its several possible descriptions) do so because they care about its realization.

On both these views, the values endorsed have an impact on the strategies by which we 'fight' for them. In both cases, it matters to their proponents that others recognize their cognitive status and, to that end, part of the argumentative strategy involves the development of (or the attempt to develop) a form of discussion and deliberation that appeals to people's reasonableness and capacity for impartiality. To discount that possibility is to discount the possibility of there being values rather than simply preferences or assertions of authority. Impartiality may be an aim or regulative ideal rather than a clear reality but, as such, it constrains what we can say and do and, while we understand all this rather imperfectly, it matters greatly for what we try to do in political theory and for the methods we use, both in contemporary political philosophy and in approaching the history of political thought.

6

There is justifiable scepticism towards political theorists who approach the classical canon of texts and identify in them a set of perennial values or issues for political thought. At least some of that scepticism derives from the thought that if you approach classical texts in that frame of mind you will find in them only what you read into them. But, while we clearly do need historical work to get some sense of what a given author was arguing for and what values and commitments were central to his or her understanding of politics (and how he or she understood politics and its proper scope and domain), to reduce that reading to an analysis of rhetorical strategies in a way that washes out a sense of the values to which an author was committed, is to fail that text both philosophically and historically.

For example, in the first part of his *Rights of Man* (1791), Tom Paine gives us an account of events in France and of the French Constitution that treats the actions of the French crowd as instances of regrettable but understandable retaliatory violence. He also defends the property-based franchise of the Constitution. We might read this as Paine exhibiting his distance from the more radical elements of the Revolution and their sense of revolutionary justice, and as evidence of his own conservatism towards the populace at large. On this view, Paine is essentially in the camp of Lafayette and the liberal aristocratic wing at the onset of the Revolution. However, we might also read the pamphlet quite differently—as a carefully constructed reply to Burke that is designed to demonstrate the unreasonableness of Burke's reading of French events and to defend the institutions of the Revolution, such as the constitution, in ways that would appeal to a wide section of the British public. On that reading, the text is a carefully constructed piece of political rhetoric aimed at a particular (English) audience that presents French affairs in a light that will strike his target readership of the literate middling orders as reasonable and justifiable. On the first reading, the subsequent second part of *Rights of Man* (1792) was radicalized by Paine's association with Condorcet and others in the Girondin camp, and breathes the spirit of Girondin revolutionary enthusiasm. On the second reading, it responds both to the increasingly complex and messy reality of the French revolutionary struggle and to Paine's success in communicating to a very wide English audience, including many artisans and tradesmen, by switching its primary focus to America and providing a theorized narrative of the American Revolution as an example for English imitation and pop-ular aspiration. Indeed, there are points at which these interpretations can interact—even if we do recognize the signal change of focus to America it is also the case that many of the practical proposals that fill the last chapter of the second part are indebted to Paine's acquaintance with members of the Comité de Mendicité in France.[24] Moreover, while these two interpretations have led various writers to insist that the proper way of reading Paine is to refer to his French context, or his American context, or both (largely because of the difficulty of knowing what sort of intellectual tradition we might fit him to in relation to British political thought), neither is wholly satisfactory since it remains the case that Paine's target audience remains, for the most part, Britain—and Ireland.[25] In so far as he is trying to do things with this text, he is doing so in relation to a British audience, and while he certainly draws on experience, example, and traditions of thought that come from both America and France, his target is 'the ear of John Bull'.[26] So that, to understand what he was arguing, requires that we have a sense of what he was trying to do with *that* audience in particular.

These potentially diverse contexts for understanding Paine leave us with a problem of identifying what his commitments were. It is not difficult to see that we need a grasp of context, and an understanding of popular political rhetoric, and a subtle sense of the intertextual play between Paine's work and that of Burke and others in the period. We also need a broader sense of context to avoid getting things wrong. For example, in support of the view

---

[24] See Gareth Stedman-Jones, *An End to Poverty* (London: Profile Books, 2004), pp. 16–26.

[25] Pocock expresses the concern about the difficulty of fitting Paine to any category in his *Virtue, Commerce and History*, p. 276.

[26] See Paine's letter to John Hall, London 25 November 1791: 'I have so far got the ear of John Bull that he will read what I write—which is more than ever was done before to the same extent.' Philip Foner (edited), *The Complete Writings of Thomas Paine* (Secaucus: Citadel, 1948), volume 2, p. 1322.

that Paine is responding to French influences, it has been argued that Paine comes to redefine the meaning of 'republic' through his contact with Brissot. Kates, for example, argues that the section in the second part of *Rights of Man* in which Paine defines a republic as, not a form of government, but as 'the purport, matter, or object for which government ought to be insti-tuted...RES-PUBLICA, the public affairs, or the public good; or, literally translated, the *public thing*'—is 'lifted practically verbatim from his friend Bonneville's daily newspaper, *Bouche de fer*' in July 1791.[27] In fact, Paine used this phraseology in his 'To the Authors of "Le Républicain"' written in June 1791 to Condorcet and others planning to establish a republican paper, and in doing so he was effectively repeating commitments he stated in his *Dissertations on Government* written in 1786, two years before his major trip to France and several years before his association with Girondin circles.[28] This argues against the view that Paine's commitments were profoundly influenced by events in France. There is, however, a significant change in his position at some point between 1790 and 1792, but this is not from support for a constitu-tional monarchy to republicanism, but from the view that European states are capable of only a limited republicanism to the view that they can fully emulate the American example and the republican ideal (although it might in fact have been a question not of what he believed but of what he believed it prudent and opportune to say!). That ideal, sketched in his American writings, is encapsulated in his insistence that republicanism means the expression of the sovereignty of the people in the founding of the constitution and in the view that government shall be elective, directed to the common good, and should be a government of justice and law, in contradistinction to a government by will. That makes him a partial democrat only, because he insists that the will of the people is constrained by rights and justice; but he is a democrat nonetheless (and from the beginning) because he believes in the sovereignty of the people over the political system, and believes that they must be represented through

[27] Paine's definition is to be found in *Rights of Man: Part the Second*, chapter 3. See Mark Philp (edited), *Rights of Man, Common Sense and Other Political Writings* (Oxford: Oxford University Press, 1998), p. 230. Gary Kates, 'From Liberalism to Radicalism: Tom Paine's *Rights of Man*', *Journal of the History of Ideas*, 50/4 (1989), p. 581.

[28] See 'To the Authors of "Le Républicain"' (dated June 1791), in Philip S. Foner (edited), *The Life and Major Writings of Thomas Paine* (Secaucus: Citadel, 1948), volume 2, pp. 1315–18. Foner in fact relies on a different translation than that in volume 3 of M. D. Conway (edited), *The Writings of Thomas Paine* (New York: Putnam's Sons, 1894). The salient phrase in the Conway version is, with respect to Republican: 'This word expresses perfectly the idea which we ought to have of Government in general—*Res Publica*—the public affairs of a nation' (which essentially indicates the ideas we ought to have of the ends of government). In Foner this is rendered: 'The words "Republican" imply that it is solely concerned about the *Res*-publica, namely, the interests of the state, and that includes all the ideas we should entertain of government in general' (1316). But the use of 'the interests of the state' in this way is not recognized by Paine, since the proper concern of government is the interests of the people or nation. Moreover, his 'Dissertations on Government' really cannot be explained away as in some sense offering a different doctrine: 'the word *republic* means the *public good*, or the good of the whole...' Foner, volume 2, p. 372.

election in the institutions of government. In the summer of 1791 Paine comes to see full republicanism (in his sense) as a plausible and desirable aim for European revolution. This does involve a change of view as to what is possible in France (and Britain), but it is not a change of view as to what is desirable, and so is not evidence of France radicalizing his basic principles. Indeed, the evidence opens up the question (thus far under-researched) of whether some influence may be working the other way—that Paine's distinctive (American) understanding of republics, and his associated commitment to representative forms of government, may have had an impact on the French revolutionaries, their presses, and their political agendas. But that is a distinct (and historical) question, not one about the core commitments of Paine's thought.

Given these very different contexts and the way in which they provide us with very different readings of what Paine was arguing, of what he was trying to achieve with his audience, and of to what he himself was really committed, we have to have a clear sense of what it is that we want to understand about him. For some the concern has been to fit him into a tradition, or to a political language or discourse; for others it has been to understand his importance in the re-evaluation of democracy and popular government at the end of the eighteenth century; and for yet others it is a task of understanding his impact on popular politics in the period. Each is a legitimate question, and some questions (such as that of his impact) may be answered without reference to what he intended, or what he really meant by what he said.[29] But for a political theorist, who is interested in the way in which democracy comes to be re-imagined and re-presented at the end of the eighteenth century, after enduring a long-standing reputation as the worst of all forms of government, it matters that we establish what Paine himself really thought about the core values of a democratic polity, and to what he was really (and not just rhetorically) committed. We should not underestimate either the difficulty of attaining that depth of understanding or the contribution that historical evidence and argument can make to its formation. But, in so far as we gain a sense of those core values and commitments, we may then have a distinct set of questions of a less historical character to ask about how far those commitments map onto our own political values and practices, how far they raise issues that are critical of our contemporary institutions, and how far they provide insights and distinctions that can modify or enhance the way in which we understand and defend our own practices and values. This is not an exhaustive list of the possibilities, but it indicates that a charitable reading of texts, that attributes to them, where it can be defended, a commitment to certain values for other than merely instrumental purposes, opens up the possibility of a dialogue across historical periods, and legitimates a form of contemporary political

---

[29] The word 'may' is meant to indicate a logical possibility, not a substantive claim that in Paine's case his intention had no connection with his impact.

discourse that tracks value and aims to persuade others of those values—where that persuasion is not entirely composed of rhetorical strategies that instrumentalize the values referred to.

On this sort of account, we also have to recognize the 'pretensions' to impartiality among some modern moral and political philosophers as more than a strategy—that certain forms of argument aim to provide the basis for reasonable agreement between reasonable people. And while it is easy to overreach with such claims—often by starting from premises that, while they justify the conclusions drawn, are not themselves wholly persuasive—it is difficult to dispute that in aiming for such impartiality one can achieve considerable clarity and perspicuity, and can demonstrate that certain commitments or values entail certain claims and responsibilities. Much the same can be said for methodological discussions. The strategies of argument used there cannot be reduced to a rhetorical battle—were this so it would be a pretty pointless exercise. Rather, the concern with method is a concern with identifying how to make claims about a subject matter that are genuinely insightful and faithful to their object—claims that are true or meet standards (to some degree) of impartial enquiry. If method cannot give us that it becomes utterly opaque why it should hold any interest for us. But, if it can give us that, it seems odd to insist that the objects/texts into which it enquires must not be understood as in any sense tracking value or issuing in truths about the world of politics.

If these arguments hold water then contemporary political philosophers have no grounds for embarrassment for their attempt dispassionately to develop systematic analytic distinctions and arguments—although they would be foolish to think this is in any respects a simple exercise: entailments from premises are hard enough to demonstrate, unless the true is simply trivial; providing premises that it would be unreasonable to deny is substantially more difficult. Hence the tendency among many to be clear and unapologetic about the premises and to focus on the conditional argument—if one is to be a consistent egalitarian, and one defines an egalitarian position as a commitment to the metric of resources, what follows from that in relation to, for example, health care, or education, or physical endowment?

Nonetheless, there are certain canons of enquiry that political theorists must observe with respect to the history of political thought, and history more generally. Most importantly, the arguments that they make must be clear and explicit in their use of classical texts and the arguments they derive from classical texts; and the use to which such texts are put must have a high degree of fit with the argumentative purposes pursued. It is no good to use Hobbes as an authority on some subject, and then fail to attempt to understand what he was arguing—since if he has authority we need to respect what he is actually arguing in his work. But to mine a text for a particular line of argument that we then seek to defend on its own merits means that while it may be

Hobbes, the claim for the argument is made independent of any
t what Hobbes really meant. Of course, political theorists may
ns of political thought—and where they are the methodological
have discussed in this chapter cannot but be of value for their
ng one does not entail being the other.

Political theorists and political philosophers do not need to be historians
of political thought, although they may learn much from it, but they must be
absolutely clear in their own minds (and to their readers) about what it is that
they are really doing, and in so far as it involves a task of historical reconstruction then the methods of the history of ideas are certainly of relevance. But
should political theorists feel any obligation with respect to the past? Is there
some sense in which political philosophy demands that contemporary writers
have a relationship with writers in the past?

7

There are three main reasons why a political theory that has no sense of its
history is likely to be impoverished. The first is that political theorists need
a degree of critical purchase on the language in which they express, describe,
and evaluate political values, institutions, and practices, and the past. A great
deal of the recent historical work undertaken on those languages provides
political theorists with a basis for interrogating the terminology we use, and
for reflecting on the values we espouse. For example, John Dunn's work, on
democracy and its long and distinctly intermittent historical journey, cannot
leave us viewing with any complacency contemporary democratic institutions
or attempts to impose democracy on other states. It raises fundamental questions as to how far the classical ideals and practices of democracy have any
place in the modern world, while simultaneously weakening the otherwise
axiomatic entailment between democracy and legitimacy. Quentin Skinner's
reconstruction of a neo-Roman conception of liberty similarly raises profound
questions for the political theorist about the nature of liberty in the modern
world, not least in challenging those who treat government as wholly a constraint on liberty, rather than as a condition for it.[30]

A second reason for political theory to look to its past is that the profes-
sionalization of the activity, and the dramatic growth in the number of its
practitioners in the last fifty years, has led to increasing specialization and,
often, a narrowing of focus onto very tightly defined issues. Current debates
on the metrics for equality, Rawlsian political theory, and a range of other
issues exemplify this intensity of focus. Moreover, like chess, the narrowing

---

[30] See above, n. 17.

of focus and clarity about the parameters and rules of the debate can allow intensely accomplished performances, but this is achieved by bracketing out a whole range of other questions, ones that are germane to areas in which values compete and in relation to the conditions under which such values could be realized—including concerns about the way in which the practicalities of politics themselves constrain and distort the realization of objectives and values. If we think of political philosophy as involving this focus on values, and political theory as including concerns about the conditions under which these values can be realized, or the extent to which they can be realized under current conditions—with the latter shading at times into political science— then, even if we recognize the distinctive character and independence of the different activities, we can see that having an understanding of a body of past thinking about politics and a grasp of the context and the imperatives and constraints facing earlier thinkers is likely to be a considerable asset to any political theorist even if it has no direct impact on the work of the philosopher.

Finally, there are considerations of the quality of the historical legacy. Leo Strauss famously took the view that political philosophy was born with the Ancient Greeks and reached its highest form with them, since every sub- sequent generation lives and thinks derivatively within the tradition set by these originators.[31] I leave aside his more contentious claims that each text has an esoteric meaning disguised beneath an exoteric surface intended for consumption by the uninitiated, motivated by the fear of persecution. This claim seems to me to be highly dubious and it is difficult to see method- ologically how it can be established except by something that comes closer to initiation than to reason and method. Nonetheless, the writings of the Ancient Greeks do have an enduring fascination that is partly due to the power and sophistication of Plato's dialogues in pressing the distinction between knowl- edge and opinion—a distinction Strauss makes central to the very character of political philosophy: 'political philosophy is the conscious, coherent, and relentless effort to replace opinions about political fundamentals by knowl- edge regarding them...the political philosopher is primarily interested in, and attached to, the truth'.[32] It is also partly because, in denying that he has knowledge of things, Socrates thereby simultaneously insists on the possibility of such knowledge and on its difference from opinion, giving us a sense of what the standard is even if we invariably fall short of it. It is also partly a function of the sweep of their philosophical concerns and achievements—the oeuvres of both Plato and Aristotle are daunting for the comprehensiveness of their scope. But, perhaps above all, it is their striking freshness and relevance to so many issues in moral and political life. That impression is partly a function of their influence—the West has inherited much from that brilliant

---

[31] Strauss, *An Introduction to Political Philosophy*, p. 25.   [32] Ibid. 6.

hical moment over two millennia ago—but it is also the case that ressed issues and questions about political organization and political have continuing salience. Implausible as many consider that claim to be it can be justified almost entirely on the ability of Greek political thought to distinguish forms of political rule that rest on coercion, rhetoric and imposition, from an implicit other, in which reason, truth, and value rule. Plato himself formulated the distinction in a number of ways and produced various sketches of this 'other' of the struggle for ascendancy, but it is his unwillingness to take the actual as the only possible order and his capacity to demonstrate that we can ask intelligible questions about our own political and ethical values that reveal their shortcomings that identifies a space for thinking about politics in relation to value and truth, not simply in relation to stability and dominance, that subsequent generations of political thinkers have either inherited directly or discovered for themselves, and which consequently blocks attempts to reduce political philosophy either to a descriptive and explanatory political science or to the wholly historical study of political thought.

8

Political theory, much like political science, need not be historical. There are many other disciplines to draw on for insights into the nature of politics and the challenges it faces at any one point of time. And yet the language of politics and vocabularies and lexicons we draw on in reflecting on its character and demands is profoundly shaped by the events and the writing of the past— shaped, influenced, shaded, and nuanced, but not wholly determined. We are more in control of what we say the more we understand the tools and materials with which we work, and a historical understanding of those tools and materials can be a powerful source of illumination and can contribute dramatically to the self-awareness with which we engage with difficult conceptual and theoretical problems. To that extent there is a clear case for ensuring that political theorists understand something of the history of their discipline. Developing that understanding does not entail becoming a historian. In fact, many political theorists do develop a strong historical bent and some cross over (occasionally or systematically) and work essentially as historians. I do so myself. But the difference in the activities remains important; political theory has a concern with the past that serves its disciplinary interests in understanding the character of political rule, the conditions for social and political order, the parameters of political possibility, and the values we should pursue within that set of possibilities. But those interests also demand contributions from other disciplines. Moreover, while the past certainly sets us in conditions that are not of our choosing, it does not determine how we should choose, and while the standards by which we judge the truth and falsity of claims are similarly inherited, they too are open to interrogation and question. In that possibility lies the distinctive philosophical moment for those who argue about politics, and in that moment is embedded an essential distance for political theory from history.

8 Using archival sources to theorize about politics

Sudhir Hazareesingh and Karma Nabulsi

1

It might seem incongruous to think of archives and political theorizing, the two elements which constitute the subject matter of this chapter, as sharing much by way of affinity. Archival sources, after all, are concrete, tactile, material entities, whereas political theory deals primarily with abstraction; archival records are relics of the past, whereas political theorizing (especially normative theory) occupies a sort of timeless horizon; archives are almost invariably fragmentary in their scope, whereas political theory is comprehensive; above all, archives are by their nature tied to contingencies of time and space, whereas much political theorizing—even the sort which explicitly recognizes the value of exploring the historical dimension of political thought—aspires to universalism.

The opposition between archival sources and political theorizing thus forms part of a broader question which has been discussed by other contributors to this book: the relationship between the history of ideas and political philosophy. The aim of this chapter is to argue that these two realms are interdependent. Indeed our argument is that archivally based political theory provides a rich and complex understanding of the political sphere, an understanding that is necessary in order to engage in theorizing about political questions. Answers to transcendent and universal questions of justice and freedom emerge from an appreciation of the nature of these concepts, which in turn can only emerge from an understanding of the complex forms they take, and an appreciation that they are rooted in history.

The argument will proceed as follows: first, we will briefly describe what we understand by 'archives', before providing an overarching framework for using archival sources for political theorizing, namely that of political traditions. Defined as an active site of theorizing, political traditions will be broadly illustrated with reference to republican doctrines, which will be viewed from a variety of levels and historical settings. Archival sources will be used to shed light on a passage from a Rousseau text, the intellectual relationship with the past, the elaboration of the concept of patriotism, the definition of the republican good life, and a particular manifestation of the republican ideal of liberty. Before concluding with some general observations, we will offer a concrete illustration of an archival source (and a republican doctrine in action) by analyzing a proclamation issued in October 1870 by a French republican popular organization, the Ligue du Midi.

2

A few words, first, about what we mean by 'archives'. The simplest way to define archives is by distinguishing between 'primary' and 'secondary' sources. Primary sources are written and visual documents which provide a record of the deliberations, activities, and thoughts of an individual or collectivity— the reports of state officials, legal resolutions, the strategic and organizational discussions of a political party, the collected papers of a cultural or business association, propaganda images, and even an individual political or intellectual figure's private notes. What makes a document 'primary' is its original character as a record: most remain unpublished, even though some of these types of documents (foreign policy records, parliamentary proceedings, personal correspondence) might subsequently be gathered and published in book form. They do not cease being 'records' even though they become publicly available (and increasingly, now, online): it is their original character that makes them primary. Similarly, a primary source is not defined exclusively by its whereabouts: archival records can be found in specifically designed locations, such as the Public Record Office in London and the UN archives in New York or Geneva, but also in public libraries (the British Library in London, the Bodleain in Oxford, the Bibliothèque Nationale in Paris, the American Presidential libraries), in the holdings of institutions and associations (such as the Freemasonry) or even in private homes (family archives).

Secondary sources consist of works of reflection, analysis, or imagination which either draw upon primary sources or rely upon other secondary sources; they are therefore commentaries and interpretations rather than records. There are grey areas between these two spheres. Newspapers and periodicals fall somewhere in between, because they are both records of past events and commentaries on them—but by convention they tend to be considered as primary sources. Diaries, likewise, are not considered 'secondary' because they are generally private comments, not intended for wider dissemination at the time (Anne Frank's diaries; or the jottings of a First World War soldier). But such documents cannot really be regarded as primary when they are written with the express intention of future publication, and are significantly altered and edited by their authors.

In light of this distinction, it might seem natural to consider most of today's political theorizing as falling under the heading of secondary publications. Yet there are large and vibrant traditions of political philosophizing and theorizing which draw upon archival sources. Indeed, the original drafts of many classic texts in the history of political thought are to be found in archives. For instance, the Bibliothèque Nationale in Paris possesses the manuscript of Montesquieu's *De l'Esprit des Lois*, which was written at the Château de la Brède between 1742 and 1748. The text, which abounds in annotations, corrections, and suppressions, provides remarkable evidence of how this seminal work was composed.[1] Returning to the archives to examine the manuscripts of such texts can thus provide a source of illumination, and of stimulating debate about key concepts and passages. On occasion, such forays may even provide the impetus for fundamental reinterpretations, as demonstrated by the wonderful example of Grace Roosevelt's novel account of Rousseau's writings on war, which was arrived at by folding the original manuscript of his Fragments on War [in the Geneva archives] in a different way.[2]

But archives can provide interesting material for the political theorist well beyond the concerns of textual accuracy and philology. The tradition of 'grand theory' in the human sciences is one which is deeply embedded in archival research. Karl Marx, perhaps the first of the modern grand theorists, wrote *Das Kapital* in the British Library, and drew upon its vast resources to construct and illustrate his philosophical argument about the nature of modern capitalism. And if we consider some of the most influential examples of grand theorizing in the second half of the twentieth century, for example, Jürgen Habermas' *Structural Transformation of the Public Sphere* (1962); Michel Foucault's *Surveiller et Punir* (1975); and Quentin Skinner's *Foundations of Modern Social and Political Thought* (1978) to cite but three, we find that primary and secondary sources are used throughout these works in a felicitous combination. More fundamentally, it is clear that beyond the specific questions they address (the rise and fall of a bourgeois public sphere, the emergence of modern prisons, and the transformation of early modern political thought) these works are concerned with some of the most basic questions which matter to political theorists today: the definition and scope of political freedom; the relationship between the public and the private spheres and the struggle for power among social groups; the arbitrariness of state power; and the legitimate means to resist it. It is this way of thinking about political theory, grounded in

---

[1] Bibliothèque Nationale, Paris, France (hereafter BNF); NAF 12835.
[2] Grace Roosevelt, *Reading Rousseau in the Nuclear Age* (Philadelphia: Temple University Press, 1990).

purposive action, and embedded in history and the social sciences, which this chapter will explore, in the particular context of the use of primary archival sources.

3

The first step in the exposition of the argument is to present an overarching framework within which archivally based political theorizing can be conducted. This framework is that of 'political traditions', which is drawn from our own research on the history of patterns of thought and practice about war in Europe, and on modern and contemporary forms of political culture in France.[3] We define a political tradition in terms of the transmission of a relatively coherent body of political thought and practice from one generation to the next. A political tradition can be deemed to exist when that body of knowledge and thought is concerned with defining the good life for society (both domestic and international), and serves as the principal basis for argument and theorized action by individuals, by organized political groups and movements, and by states.

Political traditions come in a wide variety of shapes and sizes, and indeed an important challenge in their analysis is to identify the ways in which they can change and adapt over time while retaining certain core elements of continuity (for example, the way in which a contemporary liberal could recognize himself in the writings of a Benjamin Constant or a John Stuart Mill; or how Catholics and Protestants in Northern Ireland self-identify with their respective 'traditions'). At the same time, all political traditions share three fundamental properties. First, they consciously seek to articulate a coherent relationship between past and present, and those who identify with them see themselves as bearers of specific forms of political continuity, often grounded in the heritage of a founding moment, episode, or political figure (for example, the American and French Revolutions, or Thatcherite conservatism). Second, political traditions operate through a distinct set of institutions which enable their continued existence and reproduction over time: these can be formal (an organization, association, or club) or informal (a shared understanding, a set of tacit conventions, or a set of common sentiments). And third (and most critically for our purposes here) these traditions embody a distinct and relatively coherent set of ideas and normative propositions about the world. Taken together, these provide an interpretive frame of reference which

---

[3] See Karma Nabulsi, *Traditions of War: Occupation, Resistance and the Law* (Oxford: Oxford University Press, 1999), and Sudhir Hazareesingh, *From Subject to Citizen* (Princeton: Princeton University Press, 1998).

describes social, economic, and moral conditions in society in order to direct and mobilize groups towards specific ends.[4]

Understood in these terms, traditions are thus active sites of political theorizing. They provide the intellectual parameters within which individuals and groups can critically engage (both internally, and with other traditions) with such fundamental questions as the defining characteristics of human nature; the meaning of key concepts such as freedom and equality; the criteria for treating other members of society (and other political communities) with fairness; the types of political institutions which can best guarantee social order, justice, and good government; and the conditions of membership of a political or national community.

From the above preliminaries it is manifest that our understanding of political theorizing within the framework of traditions is one which is profoundly embedded in historical, institutional, and social contexts, and in contingencies of space and time. 'Context' here is not to be considered as mere background, but an active, dynamic force which can define the very identity of a political actor, and decisively shape (and constrain) the deployment of political discourse and rhetoric. As it encompasses a broad range of actors at all levels of both state and society, the concept of a political tradition also rests upon an ecumenical definition of what constitutes a political 'text': for our purposes, theoretically significant material can be found in standard literary forms produced by political and cultural elites (books, articles, speeches, notes) but also in various manifestations of popular politics: pamphlets, manifestos, funereal orations, songs, poetry, and even graffiti; film and electronic media can also provide important sources for the study of political traditions.

The framework of political traditions operates on the assumption that there is no separation of any significance between a philosophical and a historical approach to political theory, and believes that an integration of the two is all at once possible (given the absence of any serious methodological or heuristic obstacles to the enterprise), desirable (because of the powerful effects of this combined approach for our understanding of political theory), and, above all, necessary (given that a theory of politics has to make sense in the real world and in a shared political culture, and not only in the abstract realm of theorists). In its emphasis on locating theoretical activity in specific spatial and temporal settings, our approach naturally shares many commonalities with the 'Cambridge school', and in particular the work of Quentin Skinner. Skinner posits that the significance of political texts can only be understood in historical terms, as expressions of distinctive 'speech acts' in which the authors' discursive interventions (both theoretical and practical) are analysed. He thus argues that the texts of classical authors should not be viewed as free-standing

---

[4] Sudhir Hazareesingh, *Political Traditions in Modern France* (Oxford: Oxford University Press, 1994).

entities, but rather as the products of intellectual and political engagements with other writings (either contemporaneous or steeped in earlier traditions of thought); these classical texts can only be properly appreciated if the body of writings with which they were directly engaging are also analysed—which is precisely how we understand the interpretation of texts within the framework of political traditions. Above all, we completely share Skinner's articulation of one of the main purposes of political theorizing, which is to recover how collective groups conceptualized the world, and what chains of reasoning they followed in order to make sense of their social, political, and cultural environments.

Our framework of political traditions therefore dovetails the contextual approach of Skinner, but it also has its own specificity. Indeed (and this is one of the main reasons why archival material is integral to the exercise) our approach encourages the analysis of a specific form of political activity: the nexus between theoretical endeavour and political practice. This intersection occupies a space which is analytically distinct, on the one hand, from traditions of thought which are purely intellectual and lack any practical political dimension (for example, a moral or philosophical tradition); and, on the other, from those forms of political practice which are not grounded in any prior theoretical reflection (for instance, purely instinctive, or emotional, or interest-driven political behaviour). These links between political theorizing and political practice can take a plurality of forms: a text can bear witness to the spirit of its times; it can inspire and motivate distinct forms of political commitment; it can prompt specific practices of loyalty, of voice, or of exit; or (perhaps the ultimate consecration) serve as a fetish, as when King Gustavus Adolphus carried in his saddlebag a copy of Hugo Grotius' *De Jure Belli Ac Pacis* as he laid waste and conquered Europe.[5]

Grotius and his followers effectively provide a vivid example of a mainstream political tradition in action, and of the value of studying such a tradition through the use of primary sources. The Dutch international lawyer Hugo Grotius (1583–1645) was a prolific writer and pamphleteer, and the major thrust of his work was to concentrate the legitimate recourse to war from private to public hands. More broadly, his political philosophy was summed up by the search for a 'middle way' between a pessimistic, authoritarian view of politics and an optimistic, libertarian one. Taken up by successive generations of publicists, this median approach spawned one of the most influential paradigms in international law and international relations in the modern age, most notably in its approach to war.[6] The Grotian tradition of war, drawing from his works, developed between the mid-nineteenth and mid-twentieth centuries in the context of the framing of the laws of war. Its core purpose, which was successfully pursued by Grotian publicists and international lawyers in their

---

[5] Nabulsi, *Traditions of War*, p. 129.　　[6] Ibid. 128–76.

writings, speeches, and especially in the international diplomatic exchanges which led to the adoption of the modern laws of war, was to confine the right of belligerency to armies and states, and to deny any such rights to ordinary members of society. War was thus restricted to soldiers, and the notion of an armed citizenry was rejected as an unacceptable and dangerous challenge to international order.

Such a doctrine, grounded in an ideology which prioritized the notions of order and state sovereignty, naturally favoured the dominant imperial powers in Europe, whose soldiers would thus be protected against acts of civilian resistance undertaken against military occupation. Grotianism, as a political tradition, was thus a political philosophy which was 'index-linked' to existing power structures.[7] These conclusions emerge not only through a close reading of the texts of Grotius and his followers but after a thorough analysis of the tradition in which they were embedded—and archival sources are invaluable in this exercise. Grotius himself devoted his life to providing advice to the powerful, and tailoring his counsel to address their interests. His successors faithfully followed this tradition. Diplomatic correspondence, for example, revealed the consistent obsession of Grotians with the exercise of state power and the preservation of existing order—a conservative ideological disposition which ran counter to their typical self-presentation as advocates of 'progress' and 'humanity'. Grotian political philosophy was also shaped in response to the events on the ground, and particularly the rise of popular democratic political movements which sought to challenge the status quo—most notably the political traditions of republicanism, which we shall now turn to for further illustrations of achivally grounded political theorizing.

4

Republican political theory has enjoyed a considerable renaissance in recent years, above all thanks to the work of Quentin Skinner, whose contributions have redefined our understanding of early modern republicanism;[8] Philip Pettit's work has also sought to restore republican political philosophy as an alternative to the liberal and communitarian theories which have come to dominate the field.[9] Our own research has focused on the development of republican political thought between the second half of the eighteenth century and the mid-twentieth century—a critical moment in modern republicanism, which inspired and decisively shaped the theory and practice of democracy as

---

[7] Ibid. 77.

[8] See Quentin Skinner, *Liberty Before Liberalism* (Cambridge: Cambridge University Press, 1998).

[9] Philip Pettit, *Republicanism: A Theory of Freedom and Government* (Oxford: Oxford University Press, 1997).

we know and understand it today. During this period, republicanism represented a frontal challenge to the ordering of the international system of states. Its core principles of freedom defined as autonomy, equality, and popular sovereignty simultaneously challenged: the overarching principle of legitimacy upon which international order was founded; the practices of imperialism, expansion, hierarchy, and conquest to which dominant powers had frequent recourse, both within and outside Europe; and the internal constitutional principles of states. Inspired by a rich corpus of Enlightenment thinking and practice, republicans in Corsica, America, and France rebelled against their rulers and established new political systems which sought to promote greater political freedom and civic equality. Elsewhere in Europe, and most notably in Poland and Italy, republicans waged an ardent battle against their imperial rulers (Russia, Germany, and Austria, respectively), and spawned an insurrectionary tradition which illuminated the European skyline at regular intervals during the nineteenth century. This rich, elaborate, and complex political tradition provides a fertile terrain for exploring the value of primary sources for the political theorist—especially in light of the inherent interdependence within republicanism between theory and practice.

To illustrate the heuristic potential of this methodological approach, let us start with how the concept of a republican tradition can shed new light on the interpretation of classic texts. The example is a key passage in one of the seminal works in the republican canon, Jean-Jacques Rousseau's *Du Contract Social*, where war is defined in the following terms: 'war is then not a relationship between one man and another, but a relationship between one state and another, in which individuals are only enemies accidentally, not as men, nor even as citizens, but as soldiers'.[10] From the mid-nineteenth century onwards, this passage was generally taken to mean that Rousseau believed war to be a matter for states alone, and that its conduct should be left to its officials and professional soldiers; indeed, in the context of the history of the laws of war, this passage was frequently cited by Grotians as the authoritative source for the legal distinction between combatants (soldiers) and non-combatants (citizens, or in their language, civilians).[11] This view is still routinely offered by historians of modern war.[12] As against this orthodoxy, however, other readers of Rousseau have maintained that such an interpretation is fundamentally inconsistent with Jean-Jacques's aversion to tyranny, most notably the servitude resulting from the occupation of one's land by a foreign power (which he also denounced in his writings on Poland and Corsica). How, then, should such a 'battle of interpretations' be resolved in a way which might reveal the

[10] Jean-Jacques Rousseau, 'Du Contrat Social', *Oeuvres complètes* (Paris: NRF-Editions de la Pléiade, 1964), volume 3, p. 356.

[11] For examples of this view, see Nabulsi, *Traditions of War*, pp. 184–5.

[12] See, e.g., David A. Bell, *The First Total War. Napoleon's Europe and the Birth of Modern Warfare* (London: Bloomsbury, 2007), p. 47.

true intentions of Rousseau and a philosophy of justice, freedom and the role of the state? Some commentators have tended to seek refuge in the notion of Rousseauian 'dualism' (a combination of pessimistic realism and unrealistic utopianism)—an interpretative solution which has the virtue of simplicity, but creates artificial tensions and polarities in his political thought. Others, more wedded to the analytical method, have resorted to reading the passage over and over again, in order to find out what Rousseau really meant by the word 'accidentally'.

A more promising option would be to try and understand Rousseau's thinking in the context of its time, by comparing this passage to others in which he discusses the issue of citizen involvement in armed conflict (indeed the very next passage, rarely cited, sheds considerable light on Rousseau's own interpretation), by identifying the body of thought with which he was engaging critically, and (this is where the archivally grounded 'political tradition' element comes in) by uncovering what republican leaders and associations on the ground, from whose practices Rousseau drew upon as sources for his work, were both saying and doing. Once these steps are taken, it transpires that Rousseau's main purpose in this passage was threefold: categorically to deny the legitimacy of conquest; to appeal to, and further elaborate, a republican conception of citizen involvement in civic militias to protect the liberty of the *patrie*; and finally, in articulating a law of war that would protect citizens participating in the defence of their country from reprisals by a conquering army.

Far from being an advocate of the distinction between combatant and noncombatant, therefore, Rousseau emerges as a promoter of popular resistance to military occupation, and indeed one of the founding fathers of a tradition of republican war.[13] It should be noted here that the framework of a 'republican tradition' not only sheds light on continuities in patterns of thought about war over time and space; focusing on how Rousseau's work was both inspired by and inspired political practices in Europe also helps us to arrive at a conclusive interpretation of his original writings.

Those who identified with the republican tradition across the nineteenth century thus championed resistance to oppression in the name of the ideals of liberty, equality, and fraternity, and as the Rousseau example shows, frequently drew inspiration from the writings and heroic practices of previous generations. Indeed conceptualizing the relationship with the past was one of the cornerstones of the theory and practice of republican citizenship throughout this period, and in this respect too archival sources can provide fascinating insights into the continuities and changes in republican civic cultures. In France, the revolutionary past provided a source of direct inspiration for republican groups after 1830: during the July Monarchy, when the newly

---

[13] See Karma Nabulsi, ' "La Guerre Sainte". Debates about Just War amongst Republicans in the Nineteenth Century', in S. Hazareesingh (edited), *The Jacobin Legacy in Modern France: Essays in Honour of Vincent Wright* (Oxford: Oxford University Press, 2003).

constituted sections of the Société des Droits de l'Homme chose names
evoked key events in the early revolutionary years; under the Second Rep
when radical republican groups in the legislature explicitly called thems
'Montagnards' in honour of their revolutionary ancestors in the Convention;
in the years of the Second Empire, when some republican groups invoked the
spirit of the 1790s as a talisman to resist the Bonapartist regime (Delescluze's
newspaper *Le Réveil* was even dated according to the revolutionary calendar);
and under the Third Republic, which in 1880 instituted the celebration of
14 July as France's national day publicly to symbolize its ideological lin-
eage in the tradition of the French Revolution. In all these spheres, primary
sources provide essential material for understanding the shaping of republican conceptions of citizenship: the proceedings and pamphlets of republican
associations, republican newspapers, parliamentary debates, police and
municipal records. But traditions—and this is especially true of republicanism and democracy more generally—are also sites of contestation, and these
sources also show that many republicans strongly criticized the tendency
among their comrades towards the 'fetishism' of the past. During the second
half of the nineteenth century, many republicans thus became increasingly
critical of the violence which had accompanied the Revolution, and which had
most notably manifested itself in the Terror;[14] the memory of the failures of
the Second Republic also prompted many republicans to reject any commem-
oration of this regime during the 1860s and 1870s. Indeed one of the most
notable features of the Paris Commune during its short-lived existence in the
spring of 1871 was its aspiration to 'break with the past'[15]—a common, and
arguably defining, feature of radical republican traditions across Europe.

Between these two republican mindsets of mimetism and complete rup-
ture with their own history, there was room for a great many variations and
nuances. The most interesting, perhaps, from the point of view of ideological
analysis, is invention. The 14 July anniversary, for example, was not merely
a return by the Third Republic to the revolutionary past: it was a deliberate
attempt to bypass the previous half-century of republican political history,
which was largely perceived as one of failure,[16] and to create in its stead a
new consensual civic identity, which drew upon the memory of the early
years of the French Revolution—and in particular the celebration of 14 July
1790, one of the last poignant moments of revolutionary unity. This dual
strategy of memory and 'forgetting' comes across very powerfully during the
parliamentary debates of 1880 which preceded the adoption of 14 July as

---

[14] See, e.g., Edgar Quinet's writings in the 1860s, and the debate they generated; reproduced in
François Furet, *La gauche et la Révolution au milieu du XIXe siècle* (Paris: Hachette, 1986).

[15] Speech by Ranc, reported in *Procès-verbaux de la Commune de 1871*, edited by G. Bourgin and
G. Henriot (1924), volume 1, p. 42.

[16] See Émile Littré, 'Expérience rétrospective au sujet de notre plus récente histoire', *La Philosophie
Positive*, July–December (1879).

France's new national celebration; this more generally underscores the fertile terrain offered by ceremonies for our theoretical understanding of how political communities collectively engage in constructing the ideas of patriotism, collective citizenship, and nationhood. In analytical terms, taking the archival route to the study of 'nationalism' also has the advantage of going beyond the commonly accepted approach of national identity as a construct which is primarily fashioned by the state, and showing that popular practices (of acquiescence, of celebration and of contestation) can significantly shape the intellectual and, perhaps more importantly, the institutional articulation of the 'nation'.

The complexities of this engagement (both in substantive terms and in relation to the republicans' links with their own past) emerge in even sharper focus when the discourses and practices of patriotism among republican associations in nineteenth-century Europe are explored. Let us consider the example of the international society called *Young Europe*, whose aim was to create democratic republics throughout Europe. Its founding charter, *The Pact of Fraternity*, was signed at Berne in Switzerland in the spring of 1834; *The General Instructions for Initiates* emerged rapidly afterwards.[17] These two documents represented radical shifts in both the ideas and practice of European republicans on the principles of liberty and equality, and in the conceptualization of a trinity that linked republican patriotism to both nationalism and internationalism. As understood by *Young Europe*, patriotism was a doctrine which combined the workings of international, national, and local organizations as the blueprint with which to construct republics. Accordingly, the emergence of *Young Europe* highlighted a change in both the ideological language and core values of republicans. It also represented a break from the past in other ways: in its organizational principles and the practical means with which to achieve republican goals (namely the importance of democratic structures); in its conception of the nation and the nation's role within the republic; in the appreciation of the intrinsically international role of republicans, and the mapping out of a structure within which to operate internationally.[18] This debate about patriotism (within *Young Europe*, and between this organization and other republican groups) was part of a tradition of thought

---

[17] Mazzini's own, much abridged, translation of the *Pact of Fraternity of Young Europe* can be found in G. Mazzini, *Life and Writings of Mazzini* (London: Smith, Elder & Co, 1866), volume 3, pp. 26–34. Original copies of both the *Pact* and the *General Instructions for Initiators* are in the papers of Alexander Dybowski, BP 486, Bibliothèque Polonaise, Paris. The first imprint of the *Pact of Fraternity*, signed in Switzerland by representatives of *Young Poland*, *Young Italy*, and *Young Germany*, can be found in J. E. Roschi, *Rapport fait au Conseil Exécutif de la République de Berne Concernant Les Menées des Réfugiés Politiques et Autres Étrangers* (pièces-annexes) (Berne, 1835).

[18] On *Young Europe* and *the Pact of Fraternity*, see William Linton, *European Republicans* (London: Smith, Elder & Co, 1893); Paul Harro-Harring, *Mémoires sur La Jeune Italie* (Paris: Derivaux, 1835); and E. E. Y. Hales, *Mazzini and the Secret Societies: The Making of a Myth* (London: Eyre and Spottiswoode, 1956).

and practice that has been elided, and which could be recaptured only through archival sources. One of the critical contributions of primary sources here was to allow the portrayal of the very moment and the means by which influential ideas first emerged in the public sphere—what Franco Venturi described as the 'active moment' of an idea. This quest could not be concluded by relying upon 'seminal texts', but rather by an approach that located these debates within the political and intellectual spheres where they came alive: both the locally based republican societies and associations, and their pamphlets, declarations, and doctrines, as well as the actual physical battlegrounds of insurrection, rebellion, conspiracy, and other arenas where the practical attempts to apply republican principles were made. Furthermore, this was not a conversation that was being held exclusively within closed political communities, but across national and state boundaries. Thus what the archives revealed in the case of *Young Europe* was a form of patriotism not rooted in national primacy or transnational cosmopolitanism, but rather in an entirely new conception of the nation—enhanced yet entirely subsumed within the universalist framework of republicanism.[19] We argue therefore that retrieving sophisticated theoretical models of democratic practice and principles from the crucial period when democracies were emerging and becoming institutionalized is essential in order to be able to engage with contemporary philosophizing, since it assumes understandings of the nature and purpose of democracy.

No less important than the ideals of resisting oppression and celebrating (and redefining) patriotism was the aspiration among republican thinkers to promote a theory of the good life. This is perhaps the aspect of republican doctrine which has received the most scholarly attention in recent years.[20] Archival sources have much to offer here. Consider the example of Jules Barni, one of the leading republican political theorists of the Second Empire and early Third Republic. Barni was the author of several works on republican political philosophy, and one of the major theoretical expositions of republican doctrine in the nineteenth century, *La Morale dans la Démocratie* (1868). In this work, based on a series of lectures delivered in Geneva, he articulated a vision of republican politics which was grounded in a theory of the virtues. But this was no abstract treatise: as he put it, 'this is not a piece of idle speculation or theoretical curiosity, it is an eminently practical work'.[21] 'Practical' had several overlapping meanings in this context, and they can be uncovered by establishing the immediate contexts in which Barni was writing, and his

[19] See Stuart White, 'Republicanism, Patriotism, and Global Justice', in Daniel Bell and Avner De-Shalit (edited), *Forms of Justice. Critical Perspectives on David Miller's Political Philosophy* (Lanham, MD: Rowman & Littlefield, 2003), pp. 251–68.

[20] On the French case, see, e.g., Claude Nicolet, *L'idée républicaine en France* (Paris: Gallimard 1983); Philip Nord, *The Republican Moment: Struggles for Democracy in Nineteenth Century France* (Cambridge, MA: Harvard University Press, 1995); and Jean-Fabien Spitz, *Le moment républicain en France* (Paris: Gallimard, 2005).

[21] Jules Barni, *La morale dans la démocratie* (Paris: Germer Baillère, 1868), p. 15.

purposes in producing this work at this specific political juncture. First—and this was a common trait of republican philosophical writing in the nineteenth century—the book was addressed not only to intellectual elites but also to all sections of society. Barni's vision of the republican virtues was also steeped in his struggles as a republican opponent of Bonapartism: refusing to swear the oath of allegiance to Napoleon III's regime, he resigned from his post as a teacher, and he spent the rest of the 1850s and 1860s working to rebuild the intellectual and political foundations of the republican movement in France. His vision of the republican virtues, and in particular his celebration of 'civic courage', was drawn directly from his own campaign against the despotism of the Second Empire. This publication was in this sense a work of active resistance, written with the practical political objective of helping French citizens overthrow Napoleon III's 'Caesarist' regime—a point made by Barni not in the book itself (he could not state this explicitly for fear of incurring the wrath of imperial censorship), but in a private letter to his friend Edgar Quinet[22]—a vivid example of how archives can illuminate an author's intentions.

In addition, the book's moral philosophy, and its delineation of the republican virtues—self-respect, temperance, probity, and courage—expressed the republican critique of the Second Empire's public morality (or rather the lack of it), which had led to the corruption of the civic fabric. But further layers of meaning emerge when the text is confronted with the author's personal experiences as an exile in Geneva, his efforts to find a place for himself in the shifting political configurations of the republican movement in France in the 1860s, and above all his practical involvement in the Ligue de la Paix, a European anti-militarist organization which campaigned for international peace from a republican perspective. French and Swiss public archives, and the records of Barni's correspondence to his friends, reveal the numerous difficulties he encountered in these practical endeavours; these, in turn, place his writings about morality in a more revealing light. Archival sources, in short, allow for a complex and multidimensional reading of *La Morale dans la Démocratie*, which emerges as much more than an anti-Bonapartist tract.

Like his fellow-republicans across Europe, Barni's republicanism was grounded in a dialectical conception of political theorizing and political practice: the purpose of theory was to mobilize society towards specific republican ends, and these normative ends were in turn shaped by the particular forms of political and intellectual sociability within which republican politics crystallized: salons, clubs, leagues, and associations; printing presses and newspapers; exiled communities; secret societies; and even prisons. In these organizational settings, republicans of all ilks—the Carbonari in the 1820s, the Young Europe movement in the 1830s, the grass-roots local and masonic movements and the

---

[22] Letter of 20 March 1868, BNF; NAF 20781.

Ligue de la Paix in the 1850s and 1860s—came together to debate about tactics and strategy, and the underlying principles of the good life; and again, archival sources provide critical insights into this process. A useful conceptual example here would be the republican notion of liberty, which appears repeatedly in discussions about how the monarchical and imperial adversaries of democracy had stifled freedom, and how republicans should organize to restore it; what position liberty should be accorded in their scheme of values, especially in relationship to equality; and above all how freedom could be achieved by drawing men and women together across territorial boundaries, be they local, national, or international. Through these discussions, we can view how liberty was defined not only as a political ideal but also as a concrete principle, which influenced (and was in turn shaped by) the problematic of institutional design, the current concerns of the political theorist.

5

We began with the concept of a political tradition, and showed how, as an active site of political theorizing, traditions could offer a useful framework for thinking about political ideas and concepts through the use of primary sources. This broad framework was then concretely illustrated by drawing upon the modern republican tradition, and showing how a number of key questions about republican ideology and doctrine—from issues of intentionality and textual interpretation to substantive questions concerning the relationship with the past, the practices of citizenship, the justifications for resisting oppression, and the definition of the good life—can be fruitfully explored with the help of archival documents. To conclude this exposition, we shall now move to a more specific level, and illustrate the theoretical potential of primary sources through the presentation of a single document. Although we will initially focus on the contingent characteristics of the text, it will rapidly become apparent that its true nature can only be understood through the framework of the wider republican tradition of war—which will, quite neatly, take us back to our earlier discussion of Rousseau's political philosophy.

The text is a proclamation issued in October 1870 by a republican grassroots military organization based in Marseille, the Ligue du Midi. This association had been founded a few weeks earlier by the newly appointed prefect of the department, Alphonse Esquiros, in order to energize France's war effort against the invading Prussian army. As the opening sentence revealed, the situation on the ground was getting increasingly desperate, with French military forces suffering a series of setbacks; the ostensible aim of the Ligue du Midi was thus to rally the populations of southern France in defence of the Republic.

Paris and Lyon appeal to all the public-spirited forces of the country.

The central government asks everyone to co-operate without delay in the defence of the nation through the spontaneous initiative of departments.

The Ligue du Midi has come into existence to respond to these patriotic expectations. It places at the disposal of the valiant defenders of Paris, and of all the defenders of the Republic, its popular organization, and its autonomous activity. Fifteen departments, as well as Algeria, have come together, in this hour of peril, to attempt a supreme effort in order to deliver Paris and Lyon.

The Prussians are to-day around the town of Besançon and are threatening the valley of the Rhône.

There is no time to lose! The republican populations of the Midi have to organise a levée en masse to prevent the invaders from defiling the soil of the Fatherland any further.

French citizens of the Midi, to Arms!

The Central Committee of the Ligue du Midi, represented in Marseille by the delegates from fifteen departments of the Rhône valley and Algeria,

DECREES

Article 1: In every department which has affiliated to the Ligue du Midi, all citizens should be ready to leave their homes at the first signal, and to march, under the banner of the Republic, against monarchical and Prussian despotism.

The departmental delegates are hereby appointed as General Commissioners of the Ligue du Midi. They will proceed to the departments forthwith to preach holy war, to form local Republican Committees, and to act in conjunction with them to bring about, by every means possible, a general uprising.

Article 2: A national public subscription, freely agreed by each department, each municipality, and each citizen, will be launched to obtain the weapons and supplies necessary for the Ligue's activities. The proceeds of this subscription will be paid in to the treasury of the Ligue, through the Central Committee of each department.

Article 3: The General Commissioners will, in concert with republicans of their department, appoint a delegate from every canton. These delegates will all travel to Marseille to attend the General Assembly of the Ligue du Midi, which is scheduled for 5 November [1870]. This manifesto should be displayed by all patriots of the Midi, in every canton and every commune in the 15 departments and in Algeria.

Article 4: The citizens of each locality should inform the offices of the Ligue du Midi, in Marseille, of the results of their individual endeavours to facilitate the work of the General Commissioners. They should, in addition, keep in permanent contact with the Central Committee of the Ligue, which is based in Marseille.

In the name of the **one and indivisible** Republic, members of municipal and administrative authorities owe it to the nation to offer their most loyal and efficient support, as citizens, to the members and delegates of the Ligue du Midi, created for the defence of the Republic.

Alphonse Esquiros,

President of the Ligue du Midi and Regional Prefect of the Department of the Bouches-du-Rhône

The first thing which is striking about this proclamation is its appearance: it is printed on white paper, normally reserved for official proclamations.[23] This is already, to anyone familiar with French administrative practice, an oddity: how could an association, which is by definition part of civil society, also claim to speak on behalf of the state? In fact, even without any prior knowledge of the context in which this document was written, it is clear that this text is brimming with political vigour and ideological tensions. Its appearance and content seem to suggest that Esquiros and his colleagues in the Ligue du Midi were acting in an official capacity, and in concert with the central government—an implication which is strengthened by reference (in bold) to the 'one and indivisible Republic' at the end of the proclamation. However, this audacity is somewhat tempered by the injunction to local municipal and administrative officials to offer their loyal support to the Ligue—which suggests an uneasy awareness on their part that such support might not be readily forthcoming. More fundamentally, the text is manifestly an appeal to the populations of southern France actively to defend their sovereignty, if necessary by a 'general uprising'—hardly the language commonly used by states when addressing their own citizens.

In truth the Ligue was seeking to operate in parallel to the established Republican government led by Léon Gambetta, and—not surprisingly—its scheme for popular mobilization and grass-roots empowerment was received coolly by the authorities. This proclamation effectively reflected major divisions among French republicans in the autumn of 1870: a political cleavage between centralists and decentralists over the locus of sovereignty in the new order; a functional disagreement over the proper prerogatives of the administration in a Republican state; and an ideological division over whether the Army or the citizenry should have primary responsibility for conducting military operations in times of war and occupation. It is worth noting, in this context, that the proclamation made no explicit reference to the French army—an absence which was not at all fortuitous. The Ligue's language plainly implied that the future of the nation's territorial defence (and perhaps the very future of the Republic) lay in a massively mobilized, ideologically fervent, and militarily trained and armed citizenry.[24]

Alongside its importance in making sense of the political strains among French republicans at a particular historical juncture, this type of document— a proclamation of a republican grass-roots organization—also provides a fruitful source for thinking about the more general theoretical questions which have been discussed throughout this chapter. First and foremost, this manifesto highlights the force but also the ambiguities in the republican

---

[23] Archives départementales du Rhône, Lyon, 1 M 118.

[24] See Sudhir Hazareesingh, 'Republicanism, War, and Democracy: The Ligue du Midi in France's War Against Prussia', *French History*, 17/1 (2003), pp. 48–78.

conception of freedom. The Ligue portrayed itself as an exemplar of freedom because of its autonomy ('libre activité'), which is to be understood both in terms of its independence from the arbitrary will of others and its capacity to act in accordance with the edicts of reason. Liberty is also (and this too is a characteristic feature of the republican tradition) defined in terms of its opposite: freedom from monarchical and Prussian despotism. It is interesting to note, as well, that republican freedom is presented here in the context of patriotism. Indeed, patriotism arguably frames the Ligue's entire conception of liberty, which anchors it in a notion of sovereignty whose very purpose is collective liberty. Yet at the same time it highlights potential limits and contradictions in its conception. It is not clear, for example, what it would mean for a department 'freely' to contribute to the public subscription mentioned in article 2; nor is it apparent whether it might be permissible for an individual citizen to choose to stay at home instead of 'marching under the banner of the Republic' against the invading Prussian army, as seems to be mandated by the first article. What does this document therefore tell us about the republican conception of freedom? That it is a bold, participatory, and almost martial notion, grounded in a distinct conception of what it means to be a human being and a citizen. Above all, the Ligue's proclamation shows that freedom is neither a fixed nor an abstract ideal, but (as we noted earlier in the case of Young Europe) a political value whose very shape comes into operation through active moments, during which the concept is articulated and tested against competing notions.

Furthermore, the Ligue's proclamation sheds interesting light on the issue of individual and collective leadership in democratic politics. Esquiros is an emblematic figure here, not least because of his own personal trajectory in republican politics since the 1840s, and his historical reflections on the French revolutionary experience (he was the celebrated author of a history of the Montagnards).[25] But his spell as a local republican leader in Marseille in 1870, and the wording of this particular proclamation, also tells us a great deal about such issues as how political legitimacy is constructed from the ground up, how far it is reliant upon a capacity to mobilize social actors, and in particular what might be the limits of individual action in the constrained settings of war and political revolution. The proclamation of the Ligue du Midi also invites consideration of one of the critical issues in democratic theory: the nature of sovereignty. The text signed by Esquiros is, in this respect, profoundly dualistic, for he writes both as a prefect (and thus as a representative of the French state) and on behalf of an association which claims its legitimacy from the 'patriotic populations of the Midi', and ultimately presents itself as the voice of the 'true' Republic. Under what circumstances does a state—even

[25] See Esquiros entry in Eric Anceau, Sudhir Hazareesingh and Vincent Wright, *Les préfets de Gambetta* (Paris: Presses Universitaires de Paris-Sorbonne, 2007), pp. 195–8.

a Republican state—lose its capacity to represent the general interest, and conversely, under what conditions can a local association assume this capacity? These questions, which mattered to the republicans of the Ligue du Midi in those fateful weeks of October 1870, are of universal significance—especially when the institutions which collectively embody the sovereignty of a people are threatened, weakened, or even dissolved. The architecture of modern democracies has replicated this dispersal of power among local, regional, and executive authorities, and was institutionalized through these types of civic practices.

The significance of the Ligue du Midi's proclamation emerges in a wider light when viewed from the perspective of the broader republican tradition of war. Indeed when the language of the manifesto is compared to the theory and practice of insurrectionary war waged by republicans against monarchical and imperial forces in Europe, it becomes plain that Esquiros and his colleagues were operating within a commonly understood framework of what it meant to be a republican, especially in times of military conflict and foreign occupation. Drawn from the writings of Rousseau, and in particular from the passages in the Social Contract which denied the possibility of any legal foundation to slavery, as well as the practices of republican insurrection in Corsica, France, Italy, and Poland, this tradition of republican war remained a thriving force in European democratic politics. Its re-emergence in the guise of the Ligue du Midi in 1870 demonstrated the profound elements of continuity in the traditions of radical republicanism in Europe across the nineteenth century. More fundamentally, this example of the Ligue du Midi and its political and ideological antecedents show yet again that political theorizing could occur not only across time and across space but also in a wide range of arenas: in pamphlets, in parliamentary debates, among associations and organized groups, on battlefields, and in besieged towns. This ceaseless activity underscores the intimate link between theory and practice in republicanism, and thus highlights the intrinsic value of using archival sources for our understanding of democratic political theory—most notably with respect to the framing of democratic principles such as freedom, equality, and justice. The current normative debates about deliberative democracy could draw fruitfully on these examples, which demonstrate the role played by citizens in the construction of today's democratic order.

6

This chapter has sought to show, through a small (and certainly not exhaustive) sample, how primary sources can contribute to political theory, and we conclude by focusing briefly on the three core elements with which our

argument has been concerned: archival sources; the concept of political traditions; and the nature of political theorizing.

Primary sources, as we have demonstrated, can stimulate, enrich, and
broaden political theorizing. Of course, not everything found in an archive
will be of interest to the political theorist, and it is even less the case that the
use of primary sources provides a magic key to arrive at the 'truth'. A source
is an instrument, a means, and as such its properties are similar to all the
others canvassed in this book: used appropriately, it can help enhance our
understanding of a system of political ideas, and thus illuminate a political
text, concept, or theory. But archives no more provide an automatic route
to the 'truth' than ideological or conceptual analysis, or analytical political
philosophy: sound political theorizing is a matter of choosing a method in
light of the sort of questions one is seeking to answer, and then deploying it
sensitively, with integrity, and above all with an understanding of the potential perils which might be encountered along the way. In this context, the
limitations of using archival sources are well rehearsed and appreciated by
those scholars who draw upon them routinely (for example, in history), and
the political theorist should always remain sensitive to these potential pitfalls.
Primary sources can be incomplete, fragmentary, or simply not available; the
status of a document may be unclear (it may lack any reference to the time,
the place, or the purpose for which it was written, or even a signature); it may
be biased from a particular ideological perspective (a recurring problem with
the use of police archives); or, alternatively, it might be so open-ended and
malleable as to invite the imposition of our own scheme of values, world view,
and interpretative frameworks and questions upon it. Even a set of sources
which is complete, unambiguous in its status, and unbiased (for example, the
record of a parliamentary discussion) might contain omissions, tensions, and
contradictions, and will therefore require interpretation and analysis. If we
draw upon a parliamentary debate on the issue of detention without trial as
a means of analyzing the public discourse about freedom in modern Britain,
for example, we will not get to the 'truth' by reading the relevant issues of
Hansard: we will have to explore what parliamentarians say, but then compare their utterances to their public statements and writings elsewhere, and
also explore how far their discourse might be inspired by (or might deviate
from) established patterns of political thinking about freedom. Archives, in
short, rarely do the trick by themselves: they generally need to be used sensitively alongside other instruments of institutional, historical, and conceptual
analysis.

This is where the concept of political traditions comes into play. In this
chapter we have defined traditions as active sites of political theorizing, whose
agents and bearers operate within a triangle consisting of a distinct (if constantly renegotiated) relationship with the past, a set of formal and informal
institutions and practices, and a doctrinal component which can provide

both a source of identity and an object of intellectual contestation. Because it operates both synchronically and diachronically, and posits a dialectical connection between political activity and political thought, the framework of political traditions offers a distinct set of advantages to the political theorist. Thus, traditions enable an analysis of how patterns of thought evolve over time. This temporal dimension is critical in at least three respects: as a way of recovering what has been lost, or written out of our theoretical narrative (like all forms of history, the history of political thought is generally written by victors); as a means of recapturing the breadth and vigour of past traditions of thought, which were often bolder, more creative and more imaginative in their thinking than we appreciate (just one example: the history of democratic theory); and above all as a corrective against the tyranny of the present, which manifests itself in the assumption—as blithe as it is foolish—that the theoretical challenges we face today are unique.

Traditions also allow for these political variations to be mapped out not only in terms of breadth but also depth (and also, to stretch the metaphor, height). Understanding republican freedom, for example, is not merely a matter of reading the *Social Contract* properly, but appreciating the context in which the text was produced (and in particular who Rousseau was arguing both for and against), in appreciating how republican political activists inspired him, and how those he in turn inspired interpreted his writings, and gave voice to it in their speeches, pamphlets, and practices; this 'voice' could well take transnational and international forms, and result in traditions of politics which cut across national boundaries. When we define traditions as active sites of political theorizing, accordingly, the 'active' part refers to several mutually reinforcing elements: traditions are active in the sense that they are dynamic, but also in that they come to life in particular moments, when theoretical endeavour is conjoined with, and energized by, political activity. Indeed one of the major advantages of using political traditions as a source of political theorizing is that they allow for the identification of patterns of thinking which are more 'practical', and may be almost entirely lacking in canonical texts—for example, martialism and Bonapartism.[26]

Which brings us back, finally, to the nature of political theorizing itself. Archives, deployed within the framework of political traditions, offer a particularly useful vantage point from which to engage in the study of political theory. From this position, theorizing about politics can be analysed and conducted in an intellectually inclusive way, which incorporates the heuristic insights of other social scientific approaches (as opposed to sitting in a closed seminar of methodological purists), as an activity which is carried out at all levels of society, in a wide range of social, political, and cultural settings (as

---

[26] On martialism see Nabulsi, *Traditions of War*, pp. 80–127; and on Bonapartism, see Hazareesingh, *From Subject to Citizen*, pp. 29–95.

opposed to the narrow confines of the university), and within a historical framework which critically defines the very meaning and purpose of political discourse (as opposed to an ahistoricism which is in fact a thinly disguised form of parochialism). This view is hardly unique to our approach; indeed there was a time when such a view of moral and political theorizing was routinely taken in Oxford, notably by the likes of G. D. H. Cole, Bernard Williams, John Plamenatz, and Isaiah Berlin. In fact, most of the issues which are addressed through the political traditions framework are questions which are of general concern to political theorists and philosophers all over the world—questions about textual intentionality and context, about the recovery of hidden patterns of thought, and the classification of ideologies, about the definition and meaning of substantive concepts such as freedom, equality, and social justice, and about the principles of national belonging, patriotism, and citizenship.

What then—apart from a lot of dust and chaos, a great deal of labour, and an opportunity to travel—do archives bring to the political theorist's table? The short answer is that they enable a broader, richer, and more robust understanding of the nature of political thinking, and in particular its critical connections with political practice.[27] A more radical way of making this claim is that political activity is often theorized by those political activists, and thus the purpose of political theorizing should be as much to identify and recover patterns of thought as to reconstitute the ways in which normative political ideas and values can become attached to, and find their ultimate expression in, individual and collective political practices. This delicate balance, as indispensable as it is elusive, is precisely what the French republican philosopher Etienne Vacherot had in mind when he congratulated a colleague on the most remarkable feature of his latest book:

the first, and the greatest feature of your work is something very difficult to demonstrate, but nonetheless essential: to reveal the logical order of ideas in a particular sequence of events, and to show not the pure thought, nor the intelligible reality, but the idea as it comes into realisation, and the reality as it begins to take an ideal form.[28]

---

[27] Karma Nabulsi, 'Patriotism and Internationalism in the Oath of Allegiance of Young Europe', *European Journal of Political Theory*, 5/1 (2006), pp. 61–70.

[28] Vacherot letter to Halévy, 19 July 1854. Bibliothèque de l'Institut de France, Paris, MS 4490 (letters to Halévy).

9 Political theory and the boundaries of politics

Elizabeth Frazer

1

The problem of the boundaries of politics exercises many political theory students trying to find a properly political topic. Of course, it is a problem shared by all humanities and social sciences graduate students, struggling to comply with departments' and institutions' views about what's properly disciplinary. But the politics case is especially interesting because ordinary political actors too, worlds away from academic work, face the challenge that they are not *properly political* actors. Their claims can be depoliticized, by being redefined by powerful others as personal, not political, for instance. Their speeches aren't heard; their actions don't count. Conversely, sometimes people find themselves on the receiving end of censure because they *are* behaving politically. The implication, of course, is that they are not behaving in a principled fashion, or that they are not attending to the merits of an issue so much as to the issue of who rules. Or, perhaps, they have broken a taboo and are talking out loud about matters of conviction and disagreement, rather than protecting the possibility of relatively friction-free social interaction by leaving certain tacit agreements intact.

Such censures closely parallel those that can be visited on political theorists who can be accused of doing politics rather than political theory, or attending to issues that don't count or aren't interesting politically. There does seem to be a distinction between 'theory of politics' and 'political theory'. Terminology here is by no means fixed, but we can take it that the grammatical locution *theory of politics* connotes a certain theoretical (contemplative, or scientific) distance between the theorist and her activity of theorizing, on the one hand, and the object of her theory, on the other. *Political theory*, by contrast, seems to make political a predicate of theory. That is, it seems to emphasize the extent to which the theory has political effects, or a political context, or constitutes a definite political intervention. It can soberly be argued that academic argument is completely independent of, and distinct from, social and political argument. Equally soberly it can be argued that academic discourses are discourses. They might or might not have an effect on social and political thinking and argument, but they can't be said to be socially or politically innocent, and no more can be the exclusion of certain topics from their purview. For these reasons, the question of the boundaries of political theory's subject matter really matters.

But what is the 'politics' that we might have a theory of? What does it mean to describe something as 'political'? Politics encompasses analytically, but often not empirically, distinct elements. First, there is policy, which is itself a complex matter of ends and means, or goals and strategies. Second, there is the competition for the power to govern, which is to have a particular kind of control over policy. In what follows, I consider a range of disagreements about whether politics is just a matter of means, or is also a matter of ends. These disagreements resolve themselves, in my understanding, into consideration of what, if anything, is distinctive about what we might call 'the political way'. This question involves consideration of the relationships between politics, society, public, and private life.

We must be aware, to begin with, that in ordinary language the *concept* 'politics' is very complex and encompasses more than one ambiguity. In German, French, and Italian, there is one word to cover what in English is expressed in two. *Die Politik, la politique, la politica,* mean both policy and politics. Policy encompasses both goals and some programme of means to achieve those goals. 'Programme of means' encompasses both principles of philosophical anthropology, or theories about what's possible, what human beings are like and so on, and more practical techniques and technologies. As soon as we attend to all that the concept 'policy' encompasses it is obvious that there must be, in almost any possible world that we can imagine, a politics, as we might put it, of policy. That is to say, what the goals, and the means, and the underlying presuppositions, of policy are will inevitably be a matter for dispute. This dispute will be connected to the competition for the power to govern, and hence to preside over policy.

What is it to describe some thing as political (*politische, politique, politico/politica*)? Beyond the vaguest meaning—that a political action, institution, ideal or anything else has either a context or effects 'to do with' policy or the competition for the power to govern—it's difficult to say in the abstract. In some strands of theory, political action is related to manipulative cunning and ruthlessness. In others, it is related to open, deliberative, persuasive, cooperative talk and decision-making. According to some thinkers, engagement in politics involves engagement with violence; for others, politics entails the eschewal of violence. For some, politics and political rule imply top-down domination and authoritative closure on decisions. For others, politics implies that the questions 'who rules' and 'how they rule' are always open. Let us not forget that meaning of politic, as in 'politic speech', or politic action or conduct, which stresses care, consideration of all the possible upshots of what one says or does, prudence.

Is it a bad thing to be a politician (*ein Politik, un politique, uno politico*), or a good one, or neither? Well, as the previous paragraph makes clear, this is disputed. There is, to begin with, an idea of politics with neutral value connotations. Politics is just all those processes pertaining to the power to govern—competing for it, getting it, keeping it, influencing it, and losing it. Second, there is the pressing idea that politics is negatively valued. In politics, truthfulness is compromised in favour of rhetoric or strategic speech; morality is compromised by the need to make coalitions with people whose views are unsavoury or even unacceptable; authenticity is compromised by the need to act in a way that departs from one's true motives. But, third, there is the equally pressing idea that political action and conduct, political institutions and processes, embody specific positive values—openness and publicity, decisiveness and effectiveness, plurality and encounter.

Who does the label 'politician' cover? There can be a less and a more extensive account of this. We distinguish between those politicians who run for and are elected to or otherwise selected for public office, in contradistinction to people who are appointed by politicians, and those who are relatively permanent public servants, and in contradistinction also to the citizens and denizens who select or elect them and who are ruled by them. On the other hand, we can think of politicians more extensively as people who act in political roles—whether the role of ruler or ruled, elector or elected, winner or loser, sovereign or adviser, subject or citizen. In such political roles, we might say, we are called upon to act politically, and can be held to account for our standards of political conduct. To be sure, this being held to account is, or should be, more severe if we are an elected representative than it is if we are an apathetic citizen. Although, note, the question of the extent to which citizens should rightfully be held to standards of political conduct is itself a theoretical one. Further, and this fact can muddy the analytic waters considerably, but cannot be denied, we can also act more or less 'politically' when we are in other roles in personal, economic, and cultural settings.

This thought raises the question of the relationships between political as opposed to personal and social settings and conduct, and the question of how these map on to the categories of 'public' and 'private'. For many thinkers, political roles, conduct, institutions and processes are more or less coextensive with 'state'. What goes on at the level of, or in the domain of, a state is political just as what goes on in society is social, in an economy is economic, and so on. In some strands of thought, politics and political are confined to 'internal' relations between a state and its citizens and denizens, while 'external' relations between states are treated as if they are something else—pre-political, or non-political, or simply 'international'. In opposition to such restricted usage, an alternative line of thinking associates politics with power. Wherever power (rule, domination, structured inequality of advantage or welfare) is in question, there is politics. Hence, we can appropriately talk of politics in families, civil associations, and in networks and markets, and, of course, between states and societies. A third, distinctive, strand of usage restricts the concept of politics somewhat, insisting that not everything that happens in power situations is political. Where politics is there must be a public process of contestation. Perhaps all power settings are politicizable, but it cannot be inferred that they are all political.

2

I shall return to some of these significant conceptual and theoretical lines of disagreement about the scope of 'politics' and cognate terms. But first I discuss a particularly significant competition over what counts as politics—that between *academic disciplines* and, within disciplines, between *methodologies*. The 'science of politics' has ebbed and flowed in prestige, in relation to the rival disciplines of sociology and economics.[1] Interest in political matters, broadly speaking, has waxed and waned among philosophers and theoretical thinkers.[2] It has often been argued that law, rather, is the discipline that can and should get to grips with the workings of government and politics; or that economic theory and method are the most powerful tools for understanding all social institutions, including government. Depending on one's loyalties and interests in this academic competition, one will be inclined to think that political theory has a very specific subject matter—politics—or that it doesn't and that political theory is really ethics, law, economics, or a broadly conceived social theory. This is not just a matter of personal inclination— as I go on to discuss, certain disciplinary frameworks can effectively eclipse any perception, any conceptualization, of politics or political things, as such, at all.

A complexity, as far as academic work is concerned, is that the discipline of political study including political theory has, at different times and in different places, been very much a state-oriented enterprise. Accordingly its horizon of interest, at such times, is determined by the horizons of interest of

---

[1] Peter Wagner, *A History and Theory of the Social Sciences: Not All That is Solid Melts into Air* (London: Sage, 2001), part 1.

[2] Isaiah Berlin, 'Does Political Theory Still Exist?', P. Laslett and W. G. Runciman (edited), *Philosophy Politics and Society*, second series (Oxford: Basil Blackwell, 1962), pp. 1–34; Paul Kelly, 'Political Theory: The State of the Art', *Politics*, 26/1 (2006), pp. 47–53; Brian Barry, 'The Strange Death of Political Philosophy', *Democracy and Power: Essays in Political Theory 1* (Oxford: Clarendon Press, 1989), pp. 11–23.

that state itself.[3] At some times, in some places, training for social scientists including political scientists, and that for governmental administrators and aspiring rulers, is the same training, and hence the interests of the second group very much shape the interests of the first. At other times, the administrative training that governments and modern states need is organized quite separately from university and academic discipline. At some times, university departments', and hence academic disciplines', horizons of interest have been very strongly shaped by government demand for research into problems, and possible solutions, relevant to public policy. At other times, governments have set up their own research units, and accordingly a divergence between academic and official research—subject matter, philosophical frameworks, explanations—opens up.

Now, of course, such is also the case for other academic disciplines. Physicists', engineers', and medical scientists' relations with public policy projects of armament, civil engineering, and public health, are similarly subject to these ebbs and flows, institutional innovations, and declines. Accordingly, what counts as a good research project from an engineering student's point of view is subject to the contingencies of politics, state, and government. But there is, surely, a significant difference in the case of politics, because the academic discipline's focus is, in part, government itself. On one view of the subject, a political theorist's conclusions about justice might, or might not, be of help to government in exactly the same way as a civil engineer's conclusions about coastal defences might be. There may, or may not, be the 'technology' as it were, and the necessary public resources, to realize a theory of justice, just as there might or might not be the technology and resources to realize a particular coastal defence design.

On another view, though, the issues that are relevant to political theory as an academic enterprise are just those which are relevant to the problems of government and state. This means that the relationship between government and academic political theory is accordingly more complex. According to intellectual historians, there is a complicated relationship between two analytically distinct phenomena. On the one hand, there is the development of distinct academic disciplines with their distinctive foci of study. For example, academic lawyers study codes and cases, while political scientists and theorists study policy, elections, and governmental institutions. On the other hand, there is the crystallization of distinct domains of life. These correspond to specific institutions. As far as my health goes, I am oriented to and by doctors, hospitals, medical research, public health policy. As far as my law-abidingness, or criminality, goes, I am governed by, and I am interested in, police, courts, prisons. As a citizen, I am oriented by the tax authority, the electoral system, what passes for the public debate about policy, and so on. These relationships

---

[3] Wagner, *History and Theory of the Social Sciences*, pp. 18–22.

are not simple or mechanical, and will invariably encompass contestation. I might, for instance, be oriented to ways of thinking about health that are distinct from, or even in opposition to, the institutions that are close to the state and its health policy. It is not possible to say quite unambiguously what the relationship between citizenship and criminality is. However, let us note, taxation and criminal law are conventionally thought of as two distinct bodies of law, although to be sure they will overlap in certain cases. They are governed, in most jurisdictions, by separate bureaucracies and agencies. They are both matters of state. And as such, most people will think of them as distinct from, say, their world of friendships with others who share cultural commitments. They are distinct from people's tastes for commodities and their typical market behaviour. They are, further, the objects of study for distinct academic disciplines, in different departments. Where they are studied together that would be because some university or research agency has made a special effort at interdisciplinarity.

A particularly contentious feature in this intellectual and social process is the separation of politics from the rest of life. People can avoid or evade involvement in the competition for the power to govern, or be excluded from it, just as they can, under certain conditions, 'enter' politics or public life. From numerous critical perspectives, including Marxism and strands of feminism, this separation of politics from the rest of life is a symptom and mechanism of alienation and illegitimate structures of domination.[4] Any clear distinction between public life on the one hand and social or private on the other distorts the possibility of truly human social relations; furthermore, it is artificial and can only be held in place by an exerted, violent, power. From rival perspectives, this distinct status of politics and political institutions and relations is a simple fact about the world. Yet again, it can be thought of as primarily normative—it ought, or ought not, to be the case that we make this distinction, that we locate politics and policy in specific institutions. Of course, given human capacities for designing and building institutions, an earlier era's 'ought' can become a later era's 'is'.

This turns our attention to another set of academic divisions. Within the discipline of academic post-Second World War political science, as every student knows, there is competition between methodologies.[5] Here, I want

---

[4] Marx, famously, looks forward to a post-revolutionary time when 'the public power will lose its political character' and states, class antagonisms, and all the rest will be replaced with 'an association' of social individuals. Karl Marx and Friedrich Engels, *Manifesto of the Communist Party* (Moscow: Progress Publishers, 1977), pp. 59–60.

[5] By 'methodology' is meant a philosophical account of knowledge (epistemology) and reality (metaphysics or ontology), as that is relevant to scientific and scholarly explanation (which also involves logic). It should not be muddled up with 'method' which covers the variety of ways of doing research, including the use of surveys, interviews, archive research, analysis of discourses and texts, and so on. There are, to be sure, some established connections between particular methods and particular methodologies. For instance, statistical analysis of large data-sets, often constructed by way

to discuss how rival methodologies issue in very different understandings of what is political.

In a broadly *positivist* framework, we can identify and study political facts—facts about political institutions, actions, events, and processes, and we can attempt to formulate testable hypotheses in the projects of explanation and, possibly, prediction. One interesting question for this kind of social scientific study is whether political facts are explained by other political facts—that is, the extent to which there is a level of positive political reality, so to speak, which has its own dynamic and workings. In the tradition of Comte and Durkheim, researchers for the most part expect that both the things they study, the explananda (what is to be explained) and the explanans (the explanations), belong, as it were, within the social sciences, and that they do not have to go outside—to biology, or physics—for explanations of what is observed.[6] Numerous economists locate both the explananda and the explanans firmly within the discipline of economics, and numerous political scientists take it that political facts are explainable by other political facts.

However, this view of the matter is by no means uncontested. From the point of view of *rational action theory*, broadly conceived, the answer to the question whether there is a *sui generis* level of positive political reality must be 'no'. According to this methodology, the explanation of political facts and phenomena must lie in individual actions. In turn, these can be related to individual psychology—to cognition and reasoning in interaction with emotion and habit.[7] According to some strands of this methodology, we should take the model of rational action by an individual more or less realistically. Individuals have ordered preferences; and they have mostly well-founded beliefs about the option set that faces them, and about the likely outcomes of alternative courses of action. Together preferences and beliefs will generate rational action. Of course, in some cases actors will not be rational, because of information deficits, or systematically false beliefs, or emotions interfering with the rational action mechanism, or because of preference adaptation.[8] But these are exceptions, and do not detract at all from the validity of the basic model, nor from the scientific view that rationality is the statistical norm of action at the aggregate level. In other versions, this more or less 'realist' account is rejected. The point of scientific models is not to produce accurate

of the survey method, is sometimes identified with the positivist tradition because it treats statistics as facts. But as a rule, and in this case, it is my view that there can be no straightforward inference from methodology to method or vice versa.

[6] Auguste Comte, 'Cours de Philosophie Positive (the "First System")', in G. Lenzer (edited), *Auguste Comte and Positivism: the Essential Writings* (New Brunswick: Transaction, 1998), p. 243 and Émile Durkheim, *The Rules of Sociological Method* (Basingstoke: Macmillan, 1982).

[7] Jon Elster, 'A Plea for Mechanisms', *Alchemies of the Mind* (Cambridge: Cambridge University Press, 1999).

[8] Jon Elster, 'The Nature and Scope of Rational Choice Explanation', in M. Martin and L. C. McIntyre (edited), *Readings in the Philosophy of Social Science* (Cambridge, MA: MIT Press, 1994).

descriptions of how the world is, but to produce simplified models which will be explanatorily powerful to the extent that it is 'as if' the world is as it is in the model.[9] On such a basis, some political scientists want to say that the events and phenomena that they study are explained by individual rational action—it is as if the actors involved were acting rationally—without committing themselves to the proposition that actors are, as such, rational.

From the point of view of *structuralism*, all social regularities and social appearances are to be explained by structures which are hidden to mundane human cognition, but nevertheless retrievable by scientific methods.[10] An example is Marx's account of the workings of capitalist exploitation, hidden though these are behind the appearance of wages, rent and profit, and voluntarily struck bargains and contracts between free individuals. Accounts of an originary difference in separation which resolves itself into sexual difference, and then structures the common sense world of social institutions and individual motivations are another pertinent example.

These three distinctive methodologies are in turn challenged by phenomenological and post-structuralist, post-positivist projects, to which I will return. But now let us note the implications for the boundaries of politics. Structuralist approaches, for instance, are inclined to eschew any focus on any one kind of institution or action—economic as opposed to political as opposed to legal, and so on. This is simply because the whole point of 'structure' is that what look like distinct phenomena are, as scientists can tell us, at a deeper level generated by common mechanisms. So, although we might attempt to change educational institutions and outcomes, or patterns of crime and law, or to redistribute material resources, such manipulations often won't work because we are mistaken about causal efficacy. The underlying structure just will reassert itself—change will come only if there is structural change. In particular, structuralist theorists are likely to be critical of a certain view of action or agency. Political theorists, in particular, frequently focus on individual and collective actions—deliberations, decisions, agreements, the framing of goals, and the pursuit of policy. But, in some varieties at least, structuralists are likely to take the view that individual actions are vehicles for the reproduction of structures. From this point of view, the ideal of political action as deliberate collective effort decisively to change the status quo looks vain and delusive. At the very least, our philosophical analysis of action is dramatically changed.

---

[9] Milton Friedman, 'The Methodology of Positive Economics', Martin and McIntyre (edited), *Readings in the Philosophy of Social Science*.

[10] Claude Lévi-Strauss, *Structural Anthropology*, 2 volumes (Harmondsworth: Penguin, 1963–76); see especially 'The Scope of Anthropology', volume 2, chapter 1. A wonderfully readable and accessible example of structural analysis is Pierre Bourdieu, 'The Kabyle Household, or the World Reversed', *The Logic of Practice* (Oxford: Polity Press, 1990), pp. 271–83. Elsewhere in this book Bourdieu explains why he now thinks that structuralism is wrong.

Interestingly, this general drift of scepticism about the particular distinctiveness of political institutions or action is shared with approaches to political theory and science that are, in other respects, rival to structuralism. Of those we have already met, the rational action, economistic, tradition of social science is associated with the view that we must try to get to grips with underlying power without being dazzled by so-called intellectual projects that divide the world, quite artificially, into discrete chunks—social, political, economic. Typical accounts of power, institutional change, and so on, use typologies and analogies that can be applied to the archetypically political setting of a decision-making body whose decisions will be binding on all. But they apply equally to interpersonal relations such as those of parent and child, or friends, to the worlds of gangs, mobs, and parties, to the interstate settings of firms and armies, and, of course, to markets and the actions of monopolists. It applies where the stakes are economic, cultural, sexual, or political. There is just nothing particularly special, explanatorily speaking, about politics.[11]

Post-structuralist and *post-positivist* theory equally collapse political action and political institutions. The disciplinary and normalizing uses of knowledge are all uses of power. Among numerous pertinent examples, we can mention accounts of how a certain kind of means–end rationality becomes non-optional in a world of bureaucracy and the capitalist profit motive, and of the individual's hygienic disciplining of his own self in processes such as self-cultivation and character building.[12] In so far as we wish to think of politics and things political as those processes, actions, and institutions in which power is implicated and is at stake, then it's all political. Indeed, the main difference between this approach and the economic approach outlined in the previous paragraph is that whereas there 'rational individuals' are a given, axiomatic starting point for theory, here the view is taken that power is needed to shape the subjects who can either exercise power or have it exercised over them. Both, equally, have to be subjects of power in the first place.

From all these methodological points of view, states, political institutions, may look special, different, set apart from the rest of society. It may feel as though we, as citizens, are constrained by different forms of power, subject to specific duties, and afforded particular privileges. It may seem that agency,

[11] Notable works which take 'political' phenomena and processes and explain them reductively this way include James Coleman, *Foundations of Social Theory* (Cambridge: Harvard University Press, 1990), especially chapters 7–9; Thomas C. Schelling, *Micromotives and Macrobehaviour* (Toronto: W. W. Norton, 1978); and Barry, *Democracy and Power*, chapter 8.

[12] This account of 'discipline' is associated with Michel Foucault. See Michael Foucault, *The History of Sexuality*, 3 volumes (Harmondsworth: Penguin, 1990–98) and 'Governmentality', in J. D. Faubion (edited), *Essential Works of Foucault 1954–1984* (Harmondsworth: Penguin, 2002), volume 3: *Power*, pp. 201–22. We cannot assimilate Max Weber into this 'post-structuralist' account but it is notable that this kind of account of 'rationality' appears in *The Protestant Ethic and the Spirit of Capitalism* (first published 1904). Historical accounts of new forms of rationality and the general process of rationalization also pervade *Economy and Society* (Berkeley: University of California Press, 1978).

intentionality, and deliberateness have a place in political action that is distinct from these phenomena in other forms of action. In the marketplace, we think only about the effects of our transactions on ourselves. Sometimes, we are in a situation when we have to do whatever it is that we do next because we are at the behest of physical forces. Compared to these, it seems to be an amazing characteristic of political action that it is deliberate, and involves consideration of the upshot not just for ourselves but for all those involved. In politics, we act prudentially.

However, according to the sceptical view, these appearances are only epiphenomenal. The separation of politics, from economy, from law, from culture, kinship and household life, from personal and intimate relationships, from the individual herself, looks like a very curious affair. Reductivist social scientists insist that such understanding of discrete spheres is just a sign of an incapacity to get to grips with the scientific understanding of how things really work; it is a non- or anti-scientific naivety. Critical theorists argue that the segmentation of the world, and knowledge of it, into separate domains can be analysed as corresponding to a particular social, and political, power impulse which is not innocent in either class or gender terms. The peculiarly bourgeois, and peculiarly male, instinct is to deny the systematic nature of power and disadvantage. So, giving people the vote, that is a form of political power, can be thought of as liberation, or equalization, only because economic, cultural, and domestic disadvantage can be overlooked.[13] Similarly, academic or scientific focus on political institutions can be criticized for taking inadequate account of underlying and causal economic and cultural factors.[14]

Here, then, we have a range of academic and intellectual accounts of politics which refuse, for one reason or another, to treat it as clearly demarcated from other kinds of activity, or from the generality of human institutions.

3

Yet, the idea that 'doing politics' or 'being political' are distinct from the generality of doing and being, that political institutions are a distinct subset of all institutions, and that a political process is a special kind of process, is pressing. In this section, I consider a range of accounts of politics' ends and

[13] The original criticism of 'political emancipation' reflected here is by Karl Marx, 'On the Jewish Question', in L. Colletti (edited), *Early Writings* (Harmondsworth: Penguin, 1975), pp. 211–42. The idea that formal public rights and liberties serve only to disguise and deflect attention from real oppression and exploitation is central to feminist critique, e.g., Carole Pateman, 'The Fraternal Social Contract', *The Disorder of Women* (Cambridge: Polity Press, 1989); and Carole Pateman, *The Sexual Contract* (Cambridge: Polity Press, 1988).

[14] For example, Elizabeth Frazer and Nicola Lacey, *The Politics of Community: A Feminist Critique of the Liberal-Communitarian Debate* (London: Harvester Wheatsheaf, 1993), chapter 1.

politics' means. According to one common view, politics consists of 'techniques of government', 'statecraft'; it is 'concerned ... usually ... with means, skills, methods, techniques, "know-how" ', and not with ends.[15] Two alternative accounts can follow from this emphasis on means. Cell 1 in the following table represents the view that politics can be oriented to all kinds of ends, and consists of any means there are. It is consistent with the common view that anything that happens at the level of, or inside, states is political, and nothing else is. More usually, though, theorists imply that although politics might be oriented to any end, it deploys particular kinds of means (cell 2). This, of course, does not settle the question what particular means—cunning and ruthless strategy, or the public conciliation of rival interests, for example.

	any ends	particular ends
any means	1. for example, 'everything is political' or 'everything to do with the state is political'	3. for example, politics is securing the power to govern by any means
particular means	2. for example, 'Machiavellianism' or 'Ciceronianism'	4. for example, ends and means are mutually conditioning

Another view, here represented by cell 3, takes it that politics certainly is a matter of particular ends, but its means are unconstrained. Politics' end is the securing of the power to govern, and hence to control or closely influence policy and its execution. The process of politics encompasses winning it, keeping it, opposing it, or subverting it. Political actors might exploit it, or squander it. Consistent with this expansive view, we can see how plausible it is to consider that political actors, as such, can use all the means there are. In this sense, it seems there are no limits to politics. We see people use purchasing or production power, economic clout, in such a way that they come to a dominant position in states or globally. This can be by the straightforward use of threats, such as the threat to shift production to states with preferable regulatory regimes, for instance. Or it can be simply that a certain view of economic interests—of the state and society as a whole, of the particular constitutional

---

[15] These characterizations are taken from Isaiah Berlin, 'The Originality of Machiavelli', in H. Hardy and R. Hausheer (edited), *The Proper Study of Mankind* (New York: Farrar Strauss and Giroux, 1997), pp. 284, 290, 299. In this chapter, Berlin is concerned to oppose views of Machiavelli that interpret him as displacing ethics with politics, or as favouring 'political ends' over 'moral ends', by arguing that for Machiavelli, as for most sensible people, politics is not about ends at all, but is a matter of means.

government, or of sections of the society, such as employers or workers—is a taken for granted constraint on what governments can do. We are familiar with examples of political set-ups where political authority tracks religious authority, or even where religious power is the power to govern—to legislate and administer, to judge. In some settings the personal power of patriarchs, or patrons, can be a means—in patronal or patriarchal societies, it might be the means—to wider influence in public policy. Conversely, the power of patronage is a critical power of governmental officers like prime ministers, presidents, and department heads. Armies frequently take over governmental institutions. Sometimes societies are highly militarized, which is to say that military values and conduct run through the culture and influence education, and all sorts of social institutions are subject to military discipline and authority. Governments, of course, use military power for public purposes, and they use police power all the time. Dissenting and disaffected groups, meanwhile, have recourse to a variety of violences.

All these means, and others, are political, according to the sense of politics set out, in two senses. First, they have political effects. Military governments are governments which conduct, one way or another, public policy and make decisions which pass for authoritative. Who can doubt that economic power tracks political power, that market interactions structure the order of influence and authority in a society? Civil violence can sometimes turn out to have been political revolution. Second, perforce, they take place in a political context, and the political context has some effect on their workings. For example, the exact nature of an oppressive and unjust political regime undoubtedly has some effect on exactly how disaffected groups engage in violence. Market transactions—who trades what goods with whom under what conditions—are themselves affected by the order of government and constitution, and by the conduct of the competition for the power to govern. These kinds of considerations lead many thinkers to resist the idea that there are clear limits to the concept of politics with regard to how it is done: it can be done by just about any means humans have at their disposal. It is difficult to think of any action, individual or collective, that does not have political effects or could not be recognized, in some circumstances, to be straightforwardly political.

To say that politics is unconstrained is not, of course, to say that it should not be constrained by ethics or morality. Indeed, one dominant view is that political philosophy is just ethics applied to the question of governmental and other political conduct. This view—that there is ethics on the one hand and politics on the other and that, if we are ethical, we aim to bring them into a proper consistency with one another—contrasts with an alternative view that there is a set of values and norms, ethical standards that are internal to politics, not externally related to it.

At the same time as we take it for granted that religion, economy, culture, violence, and all the rest are, in these senses, political, we also know that they are not. Because our ordinary language, commonplace political discourses and, as I shall go on to set out, political theory and philosophy, also articulate the view that the political way is a distinctive way. It's a better way, by far, than civil and social violence. Military means, at best, have to be followed up with political processes and political solutions. We can't allow markets simply to decide who gets what, where and when, and how. We need political solutions to market failures and market injustices. Sure, the extent to which individuals should be free to do just what they wish, or desire, or choose to do, is a pervasive and continuing concern. Perhaps we can allow personal powers like patronage and patriarchy to operate, up to a point. But we certainly can't accept that it is the proper way to run states and societies in general, or the relationships between states. So, my suggestion is that we do plausibly and intuitively think of political actions and institutions as different from the other economic, social, religious, and cultural institutions and actions that are important for our lives, collective and individual. We think of political means as constrained; and not just by ethical values which are external to it. Cell 4 in the diagram, if we take it that these are the particular means of politics, implies the position that politics cannot be oriented to just any end. These specific political means themselves embody values which are a constraint on possible political ends.

In the remainder of this section, I trace some of the ways these questions and positions have been developed by a selection of political thinkers. The discussion is not chronological—rather it is thematic, and presents similarities and discontinuities in a range of accounts of politics' limits. It also adverts to the value ambiguity in the idea of politics. In setting out how politics' means, ends, and values have been conceived, the questions of the relations between state, society, and individual arise. These issues connect in turn to the problem of publicity and privacy, which I go on to discuss in Section 4.

The idea of politics as specifically political action, and as instrumental, is inspired by a particular, and it has to be said tendentious, reading of Niccolò Machiavelli.[16] We are all familiar with the idea that to act politically is to act, above all, strategically, to deploy a series of human capacities and faculties like ruthlessness and cunning, to be prepared to use even cruelty if necessary, and to act in a disciplined and controlled fashion. The political actor had better be thick skinned and not mind if others don't love him or her. He or she understands human nature and how people really, not ideally or imaginarily, act and react. Machiavellians, in this construction, are able to manipulate the weaknesses in other people's characters. Two points are particularly important. First, this kind of action is consistent with any end—including personal

[16] Niccolò Machiavelli, *The Prince* (Harmondsworth: Penguin, 1961) and Niccolò Machiavelli, *The Discourses* (Harmondsworth: Penguin, 1970). On Machiavelli and politics, see also Gisela Bock, Quentin Skinner, and Maurizio Viroli (edited), *Machiavelli and Republicanism* (Cambridge: Cambridge University Press, 1990).

ones like revenge. Second, political action is above all occult, hidden. The gap between appearances and reality is exploited to conceal the real workings of power.

This interpretation of Machiavellianism is invoked frequently in connection with the so-called political realist tradition. Weber made explicit reference to Machiavelli, and strands of his account of the conduct of 'the politician' (*der Politike*) has some affinities with the Machiavellian Prince.[17] Weber's politician has a specific kind of wisdom—he knows how the world works, has a good understanding of cause and effect, and is therefore able to foretell the likely outcomes of his and others' actions. The place of violence in Machiavelli's account is also reflected here. The politician has the courage to face up to reality. Weber insists that politics is defined just by its means; and the specific means of politics is violence.[18]

Weber explicitly says that politics cannot be defined in terms of its end, because history shows us that political actors have sought all the ends there are, good and bad, personal and public, material and spiritual. But there is a problem with his argument here. Certain ends, if not 'ultimate' ones, definitely are central to Weber's account of political actions and institutions. Whatever else they aim for, political actors have as a goal the governmental domination of a territory. Weber is at one with Marx on certain aspects of politics in conditions of capitalism. Weber's optimistic, liberal view is that the way that will best secure government of a territory properly speaking is that of liberal rights, freedom, and equality. These, after all, are all of a piece with modern states' (but not other kinds, such as patrimonial, feudal, or imperial states) rationalist conception and institutions of law. However, his pessimistic view is that mass societies could equally, probably will, be dealt with by political and economic power together by way of mass servitude and impoverishment: capitalist exploitation could be allowed to have its way; the state bureaucracy could be put at its service.[19]

Weber also draws a boundary to political action that runs counter to much common sense talk. According to him, political action, properly speaking, can only be engaged in by rulers and their agents.[20] A political organization, of which the modern state is one distinctive kind, is one that seeks to dominate, exploit, and administer a territory, the people in it, and its natural and other resources. On his account, political action is confined to state actors. Weber acknowledged that people who organize campaigns, or journalists who write persuasive pieces in defence of some public policy or another, consider

[17] Max Weber, 'The Profession and Vocation of Politics', in P. Lassman and R. Speirs (edited), *Political Writings* (Cambridge: Cambridge University Press, 1994), pp. 309–69. Weber certainly is not guilty of any partial reading of Machiavelli; he is, e.g., aware of Machiavelli's republican ideals (see ibid. 366).

[18] Weber, *Economy and Society*, p. 54.

[19] Weber, 'Suffrage and Democracy in Germany' and 'On the Situation of Constitutional Democracy in Russia', in *Political Writings*.

[20] Weber, *Economy and Society*, pp. 54–6.

themselves to be engaging in political action. But, he said, the conceptually correct way of characterizing what they are up to is 'politically oriented social action', a mouthful which he cheerfully enough acknowledged would not find its place in ordinary talk. People would continue to think of demonstrations and the like as political action, although strictly, scientifically, wrongly.

However, there is another line of thinking in Weber's work which resolves this issue differently.[21] In modern states, with anything like liberal or democratic ideas of citizenship and democracy, there cannot be anything like the very clear distinction between rulers and ruled that we associate with, for example, Plato's republic, or small feudal states, or monarchies. Rather, in modern conditions it is difficult wholly to resist the view that citizenship must be universal in its reach. Weber resisted ideas like that of popular sovereignty; and his liberal democratic vision, as his critics repeat, has a decidedly hierarchical aspect. Nevertheless, Weber did believe that in industrial societies rights must be secured and that government legitimacy will stem only from institutions and procedures such as elections with mass or universal suffrage.[22] When demonstrating against current government policy, or when joining in the activities of a pressure or campaigning group, citizens and their fellow denizens are acting politically, according to Weber's core meaning.

Social groups are political actors, and social relationships are relevant to political organization. By implication, the distinction between 'state' and 'society' is not crystal clear. Critics say, of course, that ends and means cannot be separated as clearly as Weber's methodology implies. Means condition the ends in view as well as the ends attained. And the goal of orderly domination implies that there must be limits to the use of violence.

The Machiavellian and Weberian ways of thinking about politics associate government with domination and, hence, with conflict. This association contrasts with an alternative line of thinking that emphasizes the ideal of government without friction. This and justice as harmony are of course pronounced in Plato's vision. In *Republic*, *Laws*, and *Statesman*, he offers three models of rule. In *Republic*, philosopher kings who take up the role of guardians for the *polis*, form a kind of caste apart. They are intellectually superior, and physically separate with a completely different way of life from that of ordinary *polis* life.[23] Second, in *The Laws*, he puts forward the idea that a legislator, again independent of the ordinary lives and views of individuals inside the state to be governed, should produce an exhaustive code of laws, regulating all aspects

---

[21] In 'The Profession and Vocation of Politics', he defines political action in a way nearer to the 'competing for the power to govern' formulation that I began with. See Weber, *Political Writings*, p. 311.

[22] See, e.g., 'Suffrage and Democracy in Germany', *Political Writings*, p. 129.

[23] Plato, *Republic* (Cambridge, MA: Harvard University Press, 1950–35), p. 417.

of life from population structure and economy to marriage and individual education.[24]

Significant for my purposes in this chapter is that both of these visions from Plato can be characterized as anti-political, in the sense that they take government out of the *polis* and separate it from *polis* life. Plato took the condemnation to death of Socrates to show, among other things, that rule of a state, including judgement, should not be left to ordinary people. In one famous image, he likens this arrangement to the incompetent unruly sailors not allowing the captain to steer the ship, and condemning a true navigator as a 'stargazer'.[25] Life, certainly, with all its uproar and disagreement, will proceed in the Platonic state, but it will be life which does not include as part of its very fabric politics and government. And government, similarly, is depoliticized in the sense that it stands apart from *polis* life. It must be noted, here, though, that Plato proposes a third programme for the improvement of government. That is the work of '*politikos*', generally translated as 'the statesman'.[26] Let's insist, though, on a measure of literalness and take it that we are here talking about a politician, albeit one who reaches the highest levels of public office and exhibits to the utmost the virtue of wisdom. Unlike Plato's other two pictures, of the philosopher kings and the law bringer, while *politikos* is not an ordinary guy or a man of the people, there is, nevertheless, not the same distance between him and the *polis* he governs. Plato's aspiration is for rule without clamour, the attainment of a harmony of ruled with rule. As well as the philosophical education for rulers Plato envisages the use of socialization, and more importantly 'opportune falsehoods' and 'a noble lie' so that citizens would accept their status and role in the *polis*.[27]

In the Platonic and the Weberian views, we have two contrasting depoliticizations, then. Weber, in one strand of his thought, reserves political action for dominators, the members and staff of the political organization which governs and is distinct from the society it dominates. In the Platonic view, too, the governors are quite distinct from the people they rule. But in this case, politics is eliminated altogether in favour of philosophically informed wisdom which allows the guardians to rule in accordance with justice. These contrast with yet another approach which we can loosely call 'Aristotelian'. Here, political action and institutions are tied to political life which is to say '*polis* life'.[28] In Aristotelian philosophy, in general, ends are at the centre of understanding and reasoning. The overall aim to which *polis* life is oriented,

[24] Plato, *The Laws* (Harmondsworth: Penguin, 1970), p. 488.   [25] Plato, *Republic*, p. 488.

[26] Plato, *The Statesman* (London: Bristol Classic Press, 2002).

[27] Plato, *Republic*, pp. 414B–15D.

[28] Aristotle, *Politics* (Cambridge, MA: Harvard University Press, 1932); Aristotle, *Nicomachean Ethics* (Cambridge: Harvard University Press, 1934); Cicero, *On the Commonwealth and On the Laws* (Cambridge: Cambridge University Press, 1999); and Cicero, *On Duties* (Cambridge, MA: Harvard University Press, 1913).

in Aristotle's view, is human excellence or its possibility. Politics as a field of study and thought is distinct from ethics, physics, aesthetics, biology, and other branches of learning and practice. Life in the *polis*, also, is different from life in the wilderness. It is also different from life in the village simply—life in which people attend primarily to the reproduction of the body and are engaged with each other in the close bodily relations of neighbourliness and kinship. In the *polis*, by contrast, there is a public world that is distinct from the household; the people who live together in a *polis* do so, in some sense, by choice. They don't engage with each other simply because of the accidents of geography, or because they have a purely instrumental interest in exchange and other forms of cooperation. The *polis* is a defended organization, and hence its members have to care about it and care about each other. In the public space *polis* members have the capacity, and they set up institutions so that they can further this capacity, to make decisions about matters of public concern, to discuss with each other what can be done, to set up offices to make sure that public matters are properly attended to and administered. In this account, *polis* life—political life—has specific ends in view: human excellence and, also, of course, the stability of the state. It also consists of specific means—a particular way of living and mode of conduct.

Famously, Aristotle has it that 'man is a political animal': *zŏon politikon*. Equally famously, in the medieval period and later this is translated as man being a social animal. What happened? One line of explanation is that what Aristotle meant by '*politikon*' is closer to what we mean by 'social' than what we mean by 'political'. But, of course, this takes for granted what I am trying to question in this chapter. It seems that what is at stake in the translation of *zŏon politikon* to 'social animal' is a concern to distance the model of human life from concern with affairs of state and government, just as what is at stake in the translation of '*politikos*' to 'statesman' is a concern to distance this figure from the Machiavellian political manipulator. But, I am trying to argue, it is by no means settled what we mean by 'political'.

Aristotle clearly does not have in view a number of problems that are central in modern political philosophy and theory, such as how to justify state government, or the limits of governmental interference with individual life. Whereas a number of modern discourses take for granted, and then with more or less precision seek to specify, a distinction between 'political' and 'social', this is not a distinction that the Greeks and Romans themselves drew. Aristotle does, to be sure, talk a good deal about things that we think of as social things—friendship, patterns of sociability, public forms of culture like religious observance, theatre going, parties, and the baths. All this was absolutely central to his idea of *polis* life, what makes forms of rule like oligarchy and democracy work, and the responsibilities of citizenship and governmental power. These are matters of conduct, and character, and for Aristotle (and Cicero) they are at the centre of philosophy of the *polis* or republic.

Polis life, in this tradition, is a good thing. It is the good end to which our endeavours should be directed, according to Aristotle, in our efforts to conduct ourselves, to live, to organize our collective existence, so as to bring it to full realization. Aristotelian ethics explores what are the necessary conditions for such an organization to be possible. It asks about how the ends of the *polis* are related to the ends of life for individuals. It enquires into what kinds of institutions and constitutions safeguard the state and its political life in this sense. There can, to be sure, be tensions between being 'a good man' and 'a good citizen'. But the Aristotelian hope is that life can be harmonized.

Of course, there are many grounds on which this Athenian political life, and the subsequent Roman version of it, can be criticized.[29] Notably, it has been asked whether in this model of *polis* life the full political existence of some necessarily relied on the servitude, slavery, or otherwise second-class status of others. Others focus on the instability in public policy that resulted from the particular way the popular voice was articulated. The personalization of political power—the spending of private funds on public goods—is a problem. And this is connected with the highly personalized competition between individuals and their factions.

Later on, any assumption that *polis* life is a good thing becomes deeply problematic. By thinker after thinker, in tradition after tradition, the point of view of the individual or group in conflict with the state, with those who run things, is taken up. The initial set of considerations comes, of course, from Christian thinkers wrestling with the problems of living under the Roman state. With obvious differences of detail, the contours of the problem are then delineated in different contexts. Can the religious individual think of himself as a citizen? How can he be constrained by the laws of a state that does not observe (the correct) religious principles? The same difficulty can face individuals with not religious but secular ethical principles that are at odds with the dominant ones. So liberals, like Christians, might find themselves happily enough obeying the laws of a state, just because the laws are in accord with what their own principles prescribe anyway. But that is not the same as obeying the laws because they are the state laws. So, there is a problem of authority.

However, those who reject the identification of 'man' with 'politics' in this sense of fully paid up membership of, and wholehearted participation in, a state, frequently do nevertheless want to hold on to the idea that 'man' is a 'social' animal. The Christian approach to philosophical anthropology, for example, emphasizes love, the construction of fellow human beings as such as neighbours, and also the importance of collective and communal existence in congregation. Aquinas certainly wanted to hold on to these as religious ideals

---

[29] M. I. Finley, *Politics in the Ancient World* (Cambridge: Cambridge University Press, 1983) and M. I. Finley, *Democracy Ancient and Modern* (New Brunswick: Rutgers University Press, 1985).

and as the grounds for human life on earth, while dealing with the ʌ
of certain orders of political authority for Christian life.[30] There is
with later tendencies to value human social relations, whether they are
of as voluntaristic as in some strands of liberalism, or involuntary a
views of many of liberalism's critics, while taking a generally hostile, or ʌt ieast
sceptical, attitude to state and public power.

Any clearly drawn distinction between 'political' and 'social' can cut, as it
were, both ways, valorizing either the political or the social side of the divide.
I want finally in this section to turn to the distinct account from Hannah
Arendt which privileges political vis-à-vis social, economic, and cultural life.[31]
Arendt insists that when we characterize or seek to understand politics any
emphasis on instrumentality—whether politics is seen as involving specific
ends or only means—is a mistake because political action is creative and open-
ended. Thinking in terms of ends and means is the mark of administration or
management, of domination and exploitation, of work and production, not of
politics properly speaking. We can locate Arendt in our diagram of positions
regarding ends and means (in cell 4); but not if we think of ends conceived
of absolutely independently of the means (political process) by which they
are to be achieved or realized. For her politics properly speaking is a public
encounter between individuals who are severally and collectively ready to take
responsibility in making decisions about the shared world. In political life we
can realize freedom—crucially, in public political life we act into an open
future. And in these contexts of political action we must be equalized. This
is not to say we are the same as others, nor do we have equal amounts of
goods and resources. But the concerned action of affirming and maintaining
the world we share (the 'public thing') has to involve, according to Arendt, a
political project of equality. In these and other ways, Arendt makes a strong
demarcation between political and social life. In public life, we do not and
cannot assume that others are just like us. Instead, our assumption should be
that they are not like us, that we have to be prepared to stand in their shoes
and see the world from their standpoint. This is Arendt's version of 'plurality'.
By contrast, in our social lives the assumption that others are like us might
well be central to our capacities for sociability.[32]

Arendt is critical of attempts to depoliticize either government or human
life—critical of Plato's depoliticizing project and of modern social scientists',
and lawyers', attempts to take government out of *polis* life. She is critical of
the numerous variations on the view that if only we get our social relations
right everything else will be right. In connection with this commitment—
methodological and ethical—to the distinctiveness and value of political life,

---

[30] Thomas Aquinas, *Political Writings* (Cambridge: Cambridge University Press, 2002).
[31] Hannah Arendt, *The Human Condition* (Chicago: University of Chicago Press, 1958).
[32] Arendt, *The Human Condition*, pp. 22–32, 51–76, 175–89.

she is concerned to think of how there might be public life without the deadly
levels of competition that we see in ancient Athens and Rome, how there
might be public policy without those bizarre patterns of spending. In Arendt's
view even Aristotle is guilty, in developing political philosophy, of presuming
that philosophers have some kind of special authority in political matters,
whereas the whole point of political decision-making is that it is decision-
making by the people directly involved in an issue, deploying just ordinary
human faculties. She singles out our capacities to promise and to forgive as
the two that keep us in a proper relationship between past and future. A
real problem with visions like Plato's, in which government and the state or
society it governs are radically separated from one another is that it issues in
patterns that conform to those of the worst excesses of the nineteenth and
twentieth centuries: colonial and imperial domination of a territory, people,
and resources; the uses of violence, exploitation, and corruption to shore up
that domination; the widespread uses of bureaucracy and the routinization of
administration which make people and life into objects, and at the limit of
course are marryable to the most deadly—genocidal—projects.[33]

4

In the analysis and discussion to this point, there have been a number of
adversions to the relationship between state and society. First, we saw that in
certain settings a more or less clear distinction between politics and the rest
of life can emerge, and politics can be identified with state institutions and
process. Numerous analysts insist, though, that there can be nothing specific
about political or state power, about political as opposed to the generality of
social action. Furthermore, social resources can be used for political purposes.
Some institutions are clearly state institutions, for instance, defence departments which organize and deploy armies. But in most states some public
resources are also organized and deployed by agencies which are 'social', such
as voluntary organizations. Some organizations are located in both state and
society, and organize both social and state resources—for example, schools
and trades unions.

Second, there can be an assumption that when we consider the nature of
political action or conduct, we must be talking about politicians who, by
implication, are a distinct group. Opposed to this is the view that everyone
does or might act politically. The capacity for political action is a human
capacity. In this sense when we talk about political operators in a firm, or

[33] Hannah Arendt, 'Philosophy and Politics', *Social Research*, 71/3 (2004), pp. 427–54; *The Human
Condition*, pp. 195–6.

the politics of a street gang, we are not engaging in metaphorical extension, but rather we are referring to human action which is strategic and oriented to the power to govern, or which is conciliatory and oriented to decisive order, or which encompasses both of these to some degree. Further, in modern states with widespread suffrage and other political rights, relative status equality, the relative openness of office and so on, we can look at the roles of voter (and even non-voter) as a kind of political office. So it is not metaphorical to say that all are political actors.

Third, the distinction between politics and society also arises in those projects which are concerned to expunge politics (and all its ethically dubious tendencies) from social and interpersonal life. Numerous theorists aim for a politics and state power free zone which is left for the individual, or for social institutions like families and firms, or for communities. These and other lines of thought, then, both take for granted and at the same time problematize a boundary between state and society. Such a boundary inevitably is blurred and shifting.

There is a similar problem with the distinction between public and private.[34] Some times, and from some points of view, economic transactions including employment have been thought of as private, at other times as public. At some times, private indicates simply not being under the purview and legal regulation of a state. At other times, it has fuller meanings, such as a property of an individual or a group of individuals, or carries the connotation of unseen, not to be seen, hidden. As with state and society, and political and social, these distinctions are not only shifting but contested. Quite simply, at some times and in some places it will be in the interests of particular people for the boundary to be located in a particular place. There are obvious examples. State legislation impacts on patterns of domestic labour, on sexuality, on parenting. At some times in some places, the status quo on such matters is contested, propelled onto the public agenda and subject to campaigns for legal changes, changes in established social expectations and norms, changes in culture. It will be in the interests of some to oppose such changes, and one counter they have is to invoke the normative concept of privacy arguing, for example, that childrearing is a matter of private decision for parents, or that sexual relationships are a matter of private agreement between adults.

There is no space here thoroughly to explore the ways these boundaries have been drawn and maintained in popular thinking, in law, according to rival ideologies, and by rival interests. I can only briefly sketch here a suggestion that focus on the category 'polity' might be more helpful for the analysis of normative problems than any attempt to settle the public and private, political

---

[34] See Jeff Weintraub and Krishan Kumar (edited), *Public and Private in Thought and Practice: Perspectives on a Grand Dichotomy* (Chicago: University of Chicago Press, 1997), for some relevant conceptual and historical analyses.

and social, state and society distinctions. By polity, we mean a society which is organized politically. How else could it be organized? Well, it could be left to nature, or the domination of the stronger; communities could just carry on doing what they have always done; market transactions and exchanges could determine all distributions; those who have religious or magical power could dominate. And so on. In this connection, to govern politically implies governing by way of a public process of conciliation of competing views and interests.[35] On its own, this does not entail democratic procedures as such—polity is consistent with a certain kind of monarchy, for example, as well as a certain kind of republican rule. There are, though, other kinds of government or domination that are definitely ruled out. And this kind of society is not governed entirely by politics: of course personal, religious, economic, familial, and other forms of power will be significant in any real society. But in a polity specifically, political processes both are significant and also have a special kind of legitimacy.

In any kind of society—a theocracy, say, or some kind of totalitarian authoritarian regime as well as a polity—individuals and groups, issues and situations, can be politicized. By the politicization of an individual or group, we mean roughly a consciousness of some aspect of their situation or fate as related to government and the power to govern (not necessarily to do with anything like a state as such) and some kind of theory and practice of public action related to changing the situation or fate. By politicization of an issue or situation, we mean roughly the propulsion of talk and action about it onto a public stage. This tendency to politicization is distinctively an aspect of human life and society. Human individuals, in particular, will tend to ask questions about organizations of rule. Implicit in such questioning, which may under some conditions turn into full-blown demands for legitimization, or change, and might take a turn to action, is politics.

In a polity, of all forms of human society, there can be no immediate assumption that politicization is illegitimate, or immoral, or dangerous. By contrast, we know of regimes which devote huge amounts of resource to ensuring that there is no questioning, let alone action in connection with, the organization of rule. To say that politicization is legitimate in a polity is not to say that there can be any assumption that 'everything is political'. But what is, and what ought to be, political, is one point on which liberals, libertarians, socialists, communitarians, conservatives, anarchists, feminists, and adherents to other 'isms' part company. The 'ideologies' that are a familiar feature of the political theory landscape offer rival accounts of the range of issues that should be depoliticized one way or another. They also offer rival accounts of how their politicization is to be preempted—for instance

---

[35] This analysis broadly follows the approach of Bernard Crick, *In Defence of Politics*, 4th edn. (Harmondsworth: Penguin, 1992).

by being settled legally and constitutionally, or left to individuals to decide for themselves, or left to individuals to treat with each other over, or to religious communities, or families, or the state authorities.

It leaves to be considered what constraints on or standards of conduct should govern those who participate in various institutions and settings when they are acting politically. We have also met a range of disagreements about this. Max Weber, for instance, emphasizes that the politician (which in modern societies includes all those who attempt to influence policy and government) must recognize that they are dealing with forces that are almost diabolic. Political organization, in the end, is held in place by violence, as well as agreement, ideology, material constraint, and so on. Individuals need to cultivate a particular kind of character, courageous, realistic, knowledgeable, if they are to be able to cope with the uses of political power.[36] Hannah Arendt's account of political conduct emphasizes that when engaging in public political life we must act freely, encountering our fellows as equals, prepared to welcome newcomers, bringing with us our human capacities for promising, forgiveness, and judgement. Perhaps above all, for Arendt, political action absolutely eschews violence.[37] Theorists of deliberative democracy offer a distinctive account of political life, centred on communication and persuasive speech, and rational modes of decision-making.[38] This is by no means an exhaustive account—again, it is always worth the student's while to ask what rival political theories prescribe, exactly, as regards political conduct.

Some theorists resist the idea that there is anything special to political conduct, as opposed to personal, economic, social, cultural, and so forth, at all. It might be argued that our conduct should be consistently governed by a set of ethical principles or prescriptions, for example; or that across settings human behaviour can be consistently understood as calculative maximization of self-interest. I discussed this kind of thinking earlier. By contrast, those who argue that there are, and should be, standards of conduct specific to politics, presume a picture of diurnal life as a series of boundary crossings which involve changes in demeanour, and in our treatment of others. Arendt, for instance, argues that in political life we encounter others as completely separate from ourselves, across a gulf as it were. We ask of them, if anything, 'who are you?'—not, 'what are you?' or 'where are you from?' In other settings, the 'gulf' would be quite destructive of life and relationships—in our intimate

[36] Max Weber, 'Profession and Vocation of Politics', pp. 359–69.

[37] Hannah Arendt, *The Human Condition*; and *Between Past and Future* (New York: Viking Press, 1968).

[38] John S. Dryzek, *Deliberative Democracy and Beyond: Liberals, Critics, Contestations* (Oxford: Oxford University Press, 2000); Amy Guttman and Dennis Thompson, *Democracy and Disagreement* (Cambridge MA: Harvard University Press, 1996).

worlds for instance; and there are settings where it is perfectly appropriate to ask where people are from, or what they do.

5

At this point, we have by no means settled the question of the boundaries of the set of things political, the point at which the study of political organization or action ceases, or the limits of interest of the discipline of political theory. But some of the complexities that attend consideration of these questions, and some of the points about which thinkers disagree, have been brought into view. These points of contention might helpfully be seen as dimensions of the complex concept 'politics'. The first dimension is '*state-society-individual*': for some politics is coextensive with the state; for others it extends into society and other aspects of human lives. The second dimension is '*publicity-secrecy*'. For some political action, conduct and procedures are characterized above all by visibility and an associated conciliatory impulse to treat with all one's fellows. For others, politics is defined by manipulativeness, cunning and an occult quality. The third dimension is '*deliberation*'. For some theorists, political action is above all deliberate, prudential, and decisive. Human beings can decide how to decide—this is an astonishing capacity that seems to set us apart and make us, exactly, a political animal. For others, arguing from theories of power and structure, voluntarism can only be an illusion or wishful thinking. What happens in the world is decided really by economic forces, or contingent shocks, or irrational processes. A fourth dimension might be '*openness-closure*'. For some theorists, the point of politics is that decisions are endlessly revisitable, there is and can be no final settlement. For others, political decision-making is so decisive as to constitute a form of violence; and contrasts with the openness and indeterminacy of 'hidden hand' mechanisms like the vast number of individual transactions that determine price in a market. (Interestingly, both these—mutually opposed—understandings of politics can constitute a reason for people to dislike it!).

The account of politics that has been developed and problematized here is consistent with the broadly constructivist view that not all human societies will think of politics as distinct from other aspects of life. Not all human lives will have policy as even a possibility, let alone an institution or an articulated concept. One central question for theory and intellectual history regards the conditions under which this idea, and the institutions that embody it, are possible or probable: what are the historical contingencies under which we can even have politics? And, by extension, what are the historical contingencies under which we might have political theory?—that is, hypothetical enquiry about the implications of this or that kind of government, this or that structure of power and authority, this or that goal and means to attaining the goal. There are two questions here. First, when do ideas in people's heads become specifically political ideas? That is, when do they become used as counters in the competition for the power to govern, ideas that might become ideas about what policy ought to be? Second, under what conditions do the particular reasonings of political theorists about the merits of those ideas, about the conditions of the possibility of their realization, come to have any force? That they do, in our own time, have force is, of course, one reason why political theory, what it deals with, and how it conceives of its subject matter, really matters.

10 Thinking politically and thinking about politics: language, interpretation, and ideology

Michael Freeden

1

Everyone engages in political thinking at some level or other, although at different degrees of sophistication, intensity, and frequency. We are all concerned with our relationship to authority, with notions of good social arrangements, with hierarchies of urgency and significance in deciding whether to support or resist public policies, with ways of asserting our will over others, and with the need to succeed or defend ourselves when faced with competing views in those areas. But political theory has not always been at its best in identifying, capturing, interpreting, and analysing those ubiquitous thought-practices. Now matters have begun to change. The field of studying political thought has opened up considerably over the past decade, and the methods employed in its pursuit have become more diversified.

The main reason for that is the growing recognition that understanding political thought cannot only be achieved through two of its main, and celebrated, approaches. The one approach has encompassed normative constructions and prescriptions (for example, the best form of participatory democracy) or ideal-type conceptual clarification (for example, what is justice?), and is located principally in the domain of political philosophy and ethics. Normative perspectives usually attempt to impose value structures that emanate from the dictates of reason, that appeal to general human ethical intuitions, or that ensue from the reflective deliberation of a group. The world from that standpoint is flawed, though improvable, and the remedies proffered are frequently intended to hold irrespective of time and space. The second approach, located principally in the domain of the history of ideas, has explored notable trends of thinking over time—say the idea of a social contract—or has investigated the thinking of major individual theorists and what they intended to say through their culturally salient texts. It weaves narratives about the development of ideas, and identifies contexts in which ideas make sense. Both those intellectual and academic traditions remain indispensable to further our understanding, to sharpen our critical faculties, to inspire our political imagination, and to highlight central concerns that connect or divide societies. But there is undoubtedly additional space along-side those two scholarly traditions. With all their richness, they leave a large gap that takes insufficient account of the ordinary and normal manifestations of concrete political thought in any given society, its patterns, its subtleties, its languages, and the processes it permeates. Put simply, political thought always displays two characteristics: thinking *in* a political way—that is to say, thinking politically—and thinking *about* politics. If we ignore those important features of human conduct, we will perilously impoverish our views of politics and of political thought. No student of society can keep a finger on the pulse of her or his subject matter without, among others, examining the attributes and forms of political thinking that human beings and human collectivities exhibit, and which are so obvious—and so common—a part of our public as well as private lives. Those modes of thinking are not marginal activities, and should not be a matter for optional research. They go straight to the heart of analysing political thought. We may take a leaf out of the pages of political scientists, sociologists, or anthropologists in reclaiming those empirically ascertainable aspects of political thought for the social sciences, even as we may gratefully utilize the analytical sharpness that philosophers offer, and the contextual awareness that historians cultivate.

2

I propose to characterize political theory—as distinct from political philosophy—as the *study* of actual political thinking (or thought). It is a second-order discipline that investigates two dimensions of political thought as its subject matters: first, the features that distinguish thinking *politically* from other kinds of thinking; second, the ideational configurations—known as ideologies—that shape existing patterns of thinking *about* politics.

Thinking politically refers to a range of particular thought-practices of, and concerning, collectivities. They include the construction of collective visions of a good society, the exercise of power through speech and writing, the distribution of significance and the ranking of priorities, the languages through which support for political entities is offered or withheld, and the endeavours to justify the exercise of ultimate control over the boundaries and jurisdictions of all fields of social activity. The creation of a welfare state, for example, began as a vision of a reformed relationship between state and individual. Every debate, such as over congestion charging in town centres, is an attempt to exercise power, given that total agreement on any decision is highly unlikely. The advocacy of human rights is always a verbal prioritization of what we regard as most important about our flourishing, contestable though it may be. Oaths of allegiance and arguments over civil disobedience are instances of mobilizing or refusing support. And the outlawing of some kinds of sexual behaviour is a political intervention in a particular domain of social conduct. Human thinking always revolves around such issues, though of course not exclusively. As political theorists interested in what thinking about politics *is* and *can or cannot be*, we need to understand, analyse and categorize the properties of our subject matter.

The second dimension signals that we cannot solely relate to what counts as thinking politically. We also need to look more closely at the characteristics of thinking *about* politics: the patterns and ranges of views that people hold when their thoughts concern the central issues and challenges their societies encounter: the core domain of politics. Those ideological configurations appear in various identifiable arrangements through which we access the meanings they carry. Ideologies reflect, and attempt to determine, substantive, collectively held interpretations of the political world, such as: what change is legitimate? How and with whom should we encourage social cooperation? What constitutes fair distribution? They compete with each other over the control of political language necessary to further their views of the good society and of the public policy that will realize those views. That control is no symbolic sideshow but a vital means of moulding and directing a society. To monopolize, channel, or contain the understandings prevailing in that society's language is also to preside over its practices and processes. People are propelled above all by the oral and written expressions of thinking. That is more prevalent and more efficient than hitting them over the head with a cudgel.

We all engage in the practice of thinking politically. But thinking *about* politics—relating to and forming ideological frameworks—is a practice in which most of us engage, at least intermittently, albeit at different levels of sophistication. All those everyday practices include description, prescription, and interpretation. Political theory is a complex and reflective mode of conceptualizing politics, and it includes theorizing about the two forms of concrete political thinking. To make matters slightly more complicated, some aspects of political theory also *display* descriptive, prescriptive, and interpretative thinking and preferences—that is to say, they are themselves ideological. For example, if we assume that ideologies normally mutate and are multiple, our methodology is embracing some liberal assumptions. Moreover, political theorists are themselves limited by the constraining features of language (whether or not they recognize those constraints). Therefore good political theory needs also to theorize about itself, that is, to be introspective and self-critical.

Put slightly differently, both dimensions of political thought are expressed through *language*, verbal and written, and are structured through political *concepts*, political thought's basic units of meaning. All political thought operates within a dual set of constraints: semantic—referring to meaning—and structural (or morphological). The restrictions on the meanings political thought can embody and convey result from the permanent properties of political concepts: ambiguity, indeterminacy, inconclusiveness, and vagueness.[1] The structural constraints on political theory relate to the ineliminable properties of political discourse, to be explained below: essential contestability, decontestation, and fluid configurations, both over time and across geographical and cultural space.[2] Unless political theory can develop methodologies that offer satisfactory accounts of how the production, transmission, and reception of political thinking are crucially contained and enabled through those linguistic and conceptual features, it will remain incomplete. The anatomy and morphology of political thinking affect every aspect of the semantics of political thought. For instance, an ideational structure closely linking liberty with release from stunting hindrances—such as discrimination or poverty—creates a very different field of meaning from one that links liberty with private property rights. The manner in which clusters of political concepts are ordered, weighed, and prioritized must be a matter of central interest to political theorists. Investigating the morphology of political thinking is imperative if we wish to understand how its raw material behaves, how it may be moulded, and what its limits are.

3

Some forty years ago, the 'linguistic turn' popularized the notion that words and language were indeterminate. Theories about semantic openness, the constant mutation of language, and the imprecision of its usage pushed aside views that ideas had essences that could be rendered in absolute and universal terms or that there was a correspondence between language and reality, and challenged the finality that political decisions and visions frequently demanded. Whereas even ambiguity can be disambiguated once clarity of

[1] Michael Freeden, 'What Should the "Political" in Political Theory Explore?', *The Journal of Political Philosophy*, 13/2 (2005), pp. 113–34.
[2] Michael Freeden, *Ideologies and Political Theory: A Conceptual Approach* (Oxford: Clarendon Press, 1996), chapters 2–3.

expression is brought to bear on an utterance—thus race could be made contextually to signify a nationality ('our island race'), an 'ethnic' grouping (the Aryan race), or a competition (a race against time)—indeterminacy dismisses the possibility of interpretative closure. For example, the complex of ideas and practices known as 'democracy' embraces core components such as equality, participation, accountability, and self-determination. But the relative weight assigned to each is in continual flux and knows no final resting point.

If democracy is an instance of an indeterminate concept, important conclusions follow about how we can and cannot think about it. It then lacks two features that many political philosophers value: it is not amenable to a precise definition, thus frustrating some analytical ambitions; and it cannot be the object of a moral consensus, thus disappointing ethicists who pursue the global acceptance of what they see as fundamental social truths. Definitional precision has been a goal of careful philosophical thinking as well as of some comparative politics analysts.[3] But as Becker noted, 'Unfortunately, we cannot make our concepts precise and at the same time keep the full range of evocative meaning they have acquired in ordinary discourse.'[4] Precising requires simplifying assumptions that are inadequate for thinking about the controversial and contested arena of good, let alone correct, democratic practices. It is highly likely that a *number* of definitions of democracy are intellectually valid and politically legitimate interpretations of the relationships among its components. That would appear to endorse the validity of pluralism. But indeterminacy is more than that. It indicates the ineluctable contingency resulting from the permanent slipperiness of interpretations. Of course, not all interpretations of democracy are acceptable: past attempts to include 'guided' democracies by non-elected elites do not hold water. There certainly exist both logical and cultural constraints on extreme relativist interpretations that declare that 'anything goes'. That said, we can never nail down the intricate meaning of political concepts for once and for all. Consequently, we need—as scholars—to develop tools that will specifically assist us in coping with conceptual indeterminacy, rather than force an artificial determinacy on an unwilling subject-matter or foster the illusion of fixed universalizable meanings. More of that is discussed below.

As for moral consensus, it can be retained only on macro-levels, too general to be of specific, or cross-cultural, application. We may all support human rights as a regulative ideal, but differ over the ranking of their priority (liberty or food?), over the urgency of their realization (education or housing?), and over their range and detail (does the right to health include an indefinite right to very expensive treatment in a world of limited resources?). Moreover,

---

[3] On 'precising' in comparative politics, see David Collier and Steven Levitsky, 'Democracy with Adjectives: Conceptual Innovation in Comparative Research', *World Politics*, 49/3 (1997), pp. 430–51.

[4] Howard S. Becker, 'Notes on the Concept of Commitment', *American Journal of Sociology*, 66/1 (1960), p. 40.

we may object to some human rights (freedom of expression or of dress), as potential violations of ethical codes to which we subscribe, or prefer to redescribe them as religious or cultural duties, detached from the individualism that underpins much rights theory. In other areas, theories of deliberative democracy have frequently foundered on the unequal distribution of articulateness and participatory skills that hinder the egalitarian formation of a moral consensus. And the study of ideologies often exposes consensus as involuntary and as biased, and the proclaiming of truth as a form of rendering dogma unchallengeable.

Political concepts are not only indeterminate, they are also vague. That is to say, their boundaries are porous and open to challenge. Liberalism may gently shade off into libertarianism, if liberty is inflated at the expense of other liberal core notions such as individuality or progress. Socialism may slide either into social democracy or into communism, libertarianism into anarchism, allegiance into obedience, persuasion into coercion, and so forth. There are no clear cut-off points, no relations of complete mutual exclusiveness, no instances of conceptual purity in actual utterances and texts. To the contrary, the structures of many concepts intersect unavoidably: justice, for example, contains important components of equality and of legitimacy. There is little point in bemoaning those permeable boundaries. The alternative focus on starkly segregating boundaries—reinforced by the rediscovery of Carl Schmitt's much-echoed distinction between friend and enemy[5]—merely disables us from recognizing vagueness as a key attribute of political concepts, theories and ideologies.

Indeterminacy and vagueness are accordingly features of language rather than defects in thinking. Of course, we can create temporary oases of precision and clarity, but we cannot hold them constant for any lengthy period, or across cultural space, because understandings and epistemologies change over time. There is no evidence whatsoever in the course of human history for an absolute freeze on meaning. More significantly, we may be encouraging the illusions of precision and of agreement on meaning by oversimplifying, by ignoring contesting interpretations, or by a non-critical adherence to a point of view. But there is no cause for alarm. Those illusions, miscomprehensions, or inaccuracies are perfectly normal in the realm of political thinking. In fact, they are necessary for political decisions to be made: precision may be the kiss of death for attempts to fashion viable policies that possess sufficient support to make them workable. Negotiation is rarely successful unless each side can broadcast an interpretation of an agreed, yet inescapably polysemic, text that pulls it in the direction most likely to be accepted locally, while obscuring or minimizing the differences it camouflages. Our task as political theorists is to become acquainted with these 'imperfections' and to bring the full weight

---

[5] Carl Schmitt, *The Concept of the Political* (Chicago: University of Chicago Press, 1996).

of our analytical capacities to bear on them, irrespective of our moral and intellectual positions.

The linguistic constraints on what concepts cannot do are matched by what language *does* enable concepts to do. First, it introduces semantic flexibility; that is, a capacity to convey multiple meanings extracted from different contexts both through the features of concepts mentioned above and through the constant rearrangement of sentences and arguments. The changing fortunes of words such as 'fascist', between the 1930s and the 1970s, or 'federal' in European Union parlance, or 'liberal' in British and American contexts illustrate that capacity. Second, its polysemic capacity becomes a tool of immense innovative force, serving human imagination and political vision. Consider the ways in which 'power' as the positive 'empowering' of women has developed in feminist discourse. Exploring such conceptual potential and uses are rewarding areas of research. Third, we may focus on diverse aspects of the process of disseminating language. For the main part, students of political thought have concentrated on the production of texts and arguments. Some scholars consider a substantive argument to be the crux of academic interest, and one that obtains a life of its own to be explored, dissected, and criticized. Others regard the reconstruction of authorial intentions as the historical challenge they must meet. Both are important ends of research. But language is consumed as well as produced—that is incontrovertibly essential to the process of communication—and for students of society the circulation, impact, and comprehension of political ideas must also be of vital concern. Any given linguistic expression will be consumed differently, so that we need to understand how epistemologies at the disposal of the recipients sieve meanings as a preliminary to appreciating the various ways words, texts, and arguments are absorbed and interpreted even within the same society. That becomes an important end of political theory.

The study of meaning is known as hermeneutics. One of its insights is that significant elements of the meaning of political concepts and texts are unintended by their authors, yet may nonetheless be discerned both by their target audiences and by scholars analysing them (perhaps in dissimilar ways). Paul Ricoeur's felicitous phrase 'the surplus of meaning'[6] drew attention to the inability of authors fully to control the literal language they employ and its interpretation, thus diluting the focus—so prominent in Anglo-American philosophy—on the individual as a purposive agent. The notion of unconscious meaning also drew sustenance from psychoanalysis, taking into account human drives and latencies expressed in conduct and language. Whereas some theories of rationality dismiss unintended meaning as insignificant, the switch to the impact and translation of utterances and texts acknowledges the

---

[6] Paul Ricoeur, *Interpretation Theory: Discourse and the Surplus of Meaning* (Fort Worth: Texas Christian University Press, 1976).

importance of *what is comprehended or internalized* by political and cultural communities in extending our understanding of political language. Here we investigate evidence—the particular types of understanding people actually hold, and that we as scholars attempt to decode. The messages the text diffuses are assimilated in fluid and variable ways that reveal something about the political thinking of its readers and of the groups—social, national, ethnic, religious—to which they belong. Political thought then becomes importantly (though not exclusively) the outcome of diverse interpretations, and the study of ideologies becomes a vehicle for exploring the group consumption as well as production of political viewpoints.

In parallel, whereas some *intended* meanings may be dismissed as dissimulative smokescreens obscuring reality—as they are in Marxist theories of false consciousness—the student of actually existing political thought needs to investigate the malicious, the wrong, and the inadvertent, not only the inspiring and the virtuous, as part and parcel of run-of-the-mill thinking about politics. Consequently, in contrast to Marxist views of (ideological) thinking, the *decoding* of messages replaces the aim of *unmasking* them. Decoding relates to the eliciting of meaning; unmasking relates to the outing of falsehood and the recovery of true essence. When we engage in decoding, those questions of truth become irrelevant because we have no means of establishing their truth status (as in 'does unalienated man have true consciousness?'). Instead, their meaning lies within a cultural context (as in 'the notion of alienation is underpinned by the belief in a human essence, independently of whether such an essence "really" exists'). Alternatively, truth becomes lowercase and to some extent relative, as in the following argument: 'Our current understanding is that human rights are universal. Arguably all human beings want to preserve areas of choice or need that could be reformulated as entailing rights. However, different epistemologies, ideologies and value systems might query the *centrality* of any given right and whether the choices or needs it protects are indeed *universal*'.

4

A key challenge in theorizing about political thought is to identify what constitutes thinking politically and then to develop research sensitivities as to how that thinking presents itself in utterances and texts across the political spectrum. As suggested above, we think politically when we contemplate issues pertaining to collectivities in the following areas. First, the distribution of significance is a central form of thinking politically because it allocates value, gravitas, priority, or urgency to the components of social life and to the policies we support or oppose. A political act always entails ranking, weighing, and expressing preferences, and political thought-practices and discourses always contain reflection on those issues. Thus, a right is a ranking device that proclaims the priority of certain values (say, life, or liberty) over other human ends, goods, or preferences. Or, in an emergency, the conventional cry of 'women and children first' details obligations towards those assumed to be the physically more vulnerable members of society—a complex mixture of communal altruism, social self-protection, and male chivalry. Second, human beings have views about what constitutes the good life in conjunction with others (not necessarily in cooperation with them!). In making policy decisions for a social grouping, they construct shared plans and, more ambitiously, project collective visions of a good future (which may relate to admired or detested presents and pasts). Utopian (perfect or ideal), messianic (redemption through religious salvation), ameliorative (welfare state), or traditional (family-based or class-based) designs of desirable social arrangements are commonplace types of political thought.

Third, thinking politically revolves around the acceptance and justification sought by the governing units of collective entities for their existence and their procedures. The securing of allegiance, obligation, loyalty, and respect for authority requires forms of political language that impact on the fundamental legitimacy of the power wielders who attempt to mobilize support. Such support is a crucial fuel on which a political system runs and involves constant dialogue between leaders and populace. That dialogue need not, of course, be democratic; it could equally involve the continuous assertion of the unchallengeable status of religious texts and edicts, or myths concerning the founding of a society. Fourth, thinking politically articulates cooperative, dissenting, or conflictual arguments and conceptual arrangements concerning collectivities, a feature that involves not only leadership but the various groups in a society who provide or withhold such support. Stability, instability, and struggle are manufactured through such thought-practices. Schemes of securing or challenging law and order, revolutionary plans and goals, beliefs in fraternity or community, ideologies of patriotism and nationalism, all discharge those roles.

Fifth, thinking politically is distinguished by its attempts to trump and regulate the competing claims of other forms of publicly relevant thinking. From King Creon's insistence on the priority of the laws of the *polis* over Antigone's devotion to her dead brother, to the regulation of civil society practices in the world of banking, the political sphere 'arrogantly' assumes its own pre-eminence in dictating who does what (though not necessarily how). In clashes between competing allegiances, the political domain is charged with making and effecting the choice through invoking theories of sovereignty and authority. That feature of thinking politically concerns the construction and maintenance of symbolic, conceptual, and practice-determining boundaries between different forms of human and social activity. It parcels out and regulates domains of competence, for example between families, markets, and states. In sum, the political domain is privileged as including, among others, all human activity that determines boundaries, arbitrates, and intervenes.

All those features of thinking politically demand close scrutiny if we want to unpack actual political thinking and ask ourselves: Which typical things go through people's minds when they think about politics? That must be a major research objective of political theorists. If we fail to identify the various levels of complexity and the diverse conceptual forms in which those central modes of thinking about politics occur, and if we are not prepared to acknowledge their assorted written, verbal, and non-verbal forms, their rational and emotional dimensions, and the multiple seductive rhetorics they employ in different contexts, we will ignore a vast amount of what political thought embraces. On this understanding, even the normative is a standard feature of political thought that requires empirical and interpretative analysis. Normative political theory exhibits the conceptual, linguistic, morphological—and ideological—characteristics we find in any instance of political thinking. Arguably, normativity may be better defended and preserved if it acknowledges that it does not deal with uncontestable ethical universals, not even with 'best practice'—a meaningless category unless we assume that the best of all possible worlds is attainable. The usefulness, efficiency, and relevance of normative prescription would be considerably enhanced if conducted within an understanding of the nature, and the limitations, of its subject matter—political thought itself. Normative theorists—political philosophers and ideologists—need to know what can and cannot be done with political thought, and consequently to what political theory can aspire. If the responsibility to obtain such knowledge currently weighs more on normative theorists, it is because many of them are relatively disengaged from methodological reflections. Concurrently, the scholarly interpretation of actual political thinking must acknowledge that the drive to recommendation and to improvement is, and always has been, one of its central—though not sole—features, irrespective of whether the proffered solutions are realizable or even desirable. Consequently, prescription may be *normative*, in endeavouring to construct universal rules of desirable and virtuous conduct, but it may more modestly refer to recommending *preferred* positions, values, and policies that do not aim for universality. One of the duties of the interpretivist is to advance the linguistic and ideological transparency of epistemological frameworks and conceptual structures in order to assist the task of political philosophers.

5

How do we approach the analysis of concrete thinking *about* politics? When it comes to the features of political thought-practices, they are found in very diverse locations: first, traditionally, is the text authored by an exceptional theorist or philosopher, but the manner of reading those texts can vary greatly. They may be seen as superior examples of common thinking at a particular time (Mill's *On Liberty* is an unusually polished statement among generally held mid-nineteenth century British liberal ideas), or as genres of acceptable political argumentation (Machiavelli's *The Prince* as a 'mirror for princes' guide), or as reflecting unconscious cultural constraints and assumptions, including silences (on matters of gender equality, for instance). Second, they may be found in more obviously political writings such as constitutions or party manifestos. Notions of public duty, systems of (re)distribution of wealth, pronouncements on the realm of the private, schemes for social change or equilibrium, all leap out from such documents. Third, parliamentary debates provide endless sources of political argumentation, on both domestic and international policy, that bridge elite and popular political thinking and serve witness to the mores outlining the permissible and the knowable in a particular context. Fourth, newspaper editorials offer clear evidence of informed and less-informed public and intellectual opinion as running commentaries on the issues of the day. Fifth, popular literature, pamphlets, even belles lettres provide insights into the political mindsets of a society. Sixth, everyday conversation—mainly the province of discourse analysts—is replete with political attitudes and prejudices. Finally, visual and aural displays (advertising, military marches, public architecture, national anthems, uniforms, the body language of officials) transmit political stimuli and symbols that are easily grasped or unconsciously internalized.

On the whole, we assume that the texts we peruse—and all the above examples are 'texts', whether written, oral, or visual—are authored by someone, whether individual or group, and we may attribute varying degrees of importance to knowing something about the author (attempts to reconstruct an author's intentions, or to identify an author's status, aspire to such knowledge). But texts are also treated as 'authorless' for two very different reasons. A conventional practice among political philosophers is to 'raid' a text for a type of argument, or a substantive assertion, that is then made to withstand the ravages of time, and treated as an abstract assertion requiring analysis. That form of decontextualizing is part of the philosophical processes of assessing arguments or establishing truths, as truths are by their very nature assumed to be unconstrained by time or space. The second reason is a very different one, namely, a process of (permanent) recontextualization of texts in order to establish particular, if fluid, meanings they may accrue among

significant social groups and that are therefore of importance to s(
research. Mill's *On Liberty*, for instance, has been subject to chains o
terpretation: as a libertarian text extolling liberty above all else, as a 1
text asserting the necessary link between liberty, individuality and progress, or
as a social democratic text emphasizing human development, well-being and
participation. The emphasis is on the reception and consumption of texts that
shape, and are shaped by, the shifting cultural and ideological frameworks at
the disposal of a society.

In addition to scrutinizing a complete text we may wish to focus on an
argument obtained from a given text as the appropriate unit of analysis. But
rather than doing that in the abstract—say, the changing conceptualizations
of equality since the French revolution—the emphasis would be on the work
a particular theme does with respect to specific political understandings;
for example, how changing views on nationalism and globalism colour re-
conceptualizations of immigration in the public discourse of a given society. Finally, we could focus on the concept—the building block of political
thought—in order to establish how it is moulded by cultural as well as logical
constraints and how conceptual combinations map out ideological fields of
meaning oriented towards public policy. Thus, human rights have been presented as logically arising from needs or interests. Culturally, they have in the
past been seen as natural and hence to be discovered; but more recently have
been regarded as the products of intense social preferences that are invented
or that evolve. And the attachment of a right to a particular good, such as
liberty, life, or property, prioritizes and protects that good by ranking it above
non-rights-protected goods.

6

The relationship between studying political philosophy in its normative and
analytical modes and studying concrete forms of political thinking has been
problematic. In paradigmatic form, Anglo-American political philosophy
concentrates on high-quality, analytical, and normative political thinking,
seeking to establish criteria for truth statements concerning what is valuable and ethically desirable, making distinctions and clarifying the rules of
good argumentation. As is often the case with philosophers of that school,
they expect their subject matter to meet the same intellectual standards they
impose on themselves; in effect they produce a (one-way) discussion with
the objects of their interest, a monologue dressed up as a dialogue. That
conversation eliminates the *epistemological* distance between scholar and text,

although a *critical* distance is maintained in the same way as it would were the philosopher to debate with a colleague.

But in the study of concrete political thinking, particularly in studying ideologies, an epistemological and methodological fissure opens up. The scholar is not necessarily committed to the same understandings, or arguing at the same level, as the individual and groups being investigated. When exploring populism you do not have to be a populist, or adopt its language. Even when the objects of investigation are themselves political theories or ideologies of high sophistication, there is no direct conversation between the researcher and the researched. The language is dissimilar, the criteria of analysis, of assessment, and of verification may vary and, above all, the questions will be different. The aim of the student of ideologies is to reveal and decode patterns of thinking rather than to argue with, promote, defend, or reject substantive ethical and intellectual positions. Most analytical political philosophers assume that political thought is, or should be, the product of rational autonomous agents. They tend to overlook or ignore political thinking that fails to reflect that purposive model, as being outside the remit of political philosophy. In contrast, the study of actual political thought will respect instances of reflective and purposive agentic thinking but will equally wish to be knowledgeable about four other very typical types: (*a*) bad and indifferent purposive agentic political thinking; (*b*) irrational or emotionally infused thinking; (*c*) unintentional and unconscious conceptual and discursive meaning; and (*d*) group generated political thinking. Without those categories, the study of political thought cannot offer a proper account of the nature of thinking about politics and of the ideological patterns it always displays.

Finally, on that theme, political philosophers are prone to assume that bad political thinking cannot be studied well. That is a serious misconception. Political philosophy utilizes complex and refined tools well-suited and admirably honed over the years to the research and epistemological ends it pursues, but it is not well-equipped methodologically to investigate and analyse the normal political thinking that exists beneath the radar of analytical philosophy. Conversely, the contemporary study of ideology has introduced subtle scholarly tools designed specifically to deal with types of thinking that philosophers overlook, but that students of politics just cannot afford to. In other words, what constitutes good theorizing about ideology is rather different from what constitutes good philosophizing. Good theorizing about ideology includes the capacity to unpack ideological beliefs, to 'denaturalize' ideological language when such language endeavours to put an argument beyond contestation, or to lay out alternative argumentative paths that result from the malleability of conceptual configurations and reconfigurations. To illustrate, such theorizing may decode a call for increased freedom and democracy as sustaining a free market in which economic elites vie for popular support;

or as sustaining a more participatory society in which individual development and social justice are the goals. It may expose universalizations of arguments as reflecting a cultural partiality: thus the 1948 Universal Declaration of Human Rights announces that 'The family is the natural and fundamental group unit of society', and contains a liberal-capitalist insistence on private property. Good theorizing about ideology will heed the inescapable rhetoric of any argument. It will also be sensitive to the continuous mutations of ideological discourses. Those mutations have become more rapid in recent decades due, among others, to marketing techniques using 'spin doctors' and the desire—borrowed largely from the advertising world—to repackage messages frequently in order to increase an ideology's mobilizing potential. We need only recall New Labour's move in four years from 'stakeholder society' to the 'third way' to the modernizing and future-oriented promise of the millennium—all short-lived ideological constructs.

Not least, proper theorizing about ideology uses its own rules of assessment concerning what makes for a good first-order ideological argument. Obviously, some criteria employed by political philosophers are relevant—such as a degree of coherence and articulatory cogency. But the stringency of such criteria can be relaxed in favour of other considerations. The test of a first-order ideological text must be whether it meets the purposes and functions ideologies are intended to achieve, even when those purposes are revealed as partial (which they will always be), illusory, or misleading. Actual political thinking may exhibit different assets from the ones analytical philosophers are accustomed to identify, assets that do not suggest the automatic inferiority of such thinking. Rather, it may be more useful, relevant, revealing, inclusive, or inspirational, and many of its instances—liberal and socialist ideologies spring to mind—also display significant complexity.

There are three ultimate tests of an ideology. First, its ability—whether planned or unconscious—to harness the cultural constraints within which it operates in order to legitimate, or delegitimate, a particular configuration of concepts. Second, the difference it makes in exercising persuasive argumentative power to transform or preserve political practices. Third, the attractiveness of its discursive forms not only on the rational but on the emotional and rhetorical, mobilizing, levels. Once reduced to threats, an ideology ultimately becomes more precarious. The ultimate test of *analysing* an ideological text is the ability to make sense of those processes. Making sense of something is quite different from endorsing its validity or moral status. That is why we should invest as much energy in analysing variants of fascism as in analysing variants of social liberalism. Politics covers the entire range of activities and processes pertaining to collective control and decision-making, whether desirable or not, whether productive or not, whether pleasant or not, and the study of ideologies—as a direct branch of the study of politics—must follow suit. We want to know, to assess, to understand, even to anticipate, but we need to leave judging to ethicists, or to ourselves when operating in ethical mode, not as analysts of ideology.

7

The study of ideology has now become the most developed of the genres of exploring actual political thinking, although it can be supported by the important work of conceptual historians,[7] and requires embellishment through the creation of a genuine comparative study of political thinking.[8] Reference was made above to the unmasking role that Marxist approaches adopted with respect to ideology. That involved exposing the dissimulative, exploitative, and oppressive features of ideology as a manifestation of alienation, and of the abstracted and partial consciousness that alienation produced. But this offers no challenges whatsoever to students of ideology. All that mattered was ideology's elimination, once true consciousness had been re-established; consequently, its present variety of ostensible distortions was of little interest to Marxists. Curiously, that dismissal of a major genre of political thinking is shared by Marxists and analytical political philosophers, who otherwise differ on a score of issues. The strong intellectual alliance against ideology helped to maintain the aura of insignificance accorded it—in some circles to this very day—and accounts for the relatively late emergence of sophisticated methodologies that probe into its features. The reluctance to take ideology seriously was compounded by a series of historical events in the first half of the twentieth century that propelled ideologies such as fascism, Nazism, and communism into the public eye as totalitarian, abstract, and highly dangerous ideational systems that threatened civilized ways of life.[9] We now know that those systems were exceptional, not typical, of ideologies.

Antonio Gramsci—although more famous for the 'dominant ideology' thesis—was one of the first to recognize that ideologies are produced simultaneously at different levels, rather than simply being produced by controlling socio-economic groups. As researchers, we need to bear that important insight in mind. Ideologies may be articulated by individuals of great intellectual or rhetorical ability, whether philosophers or members of cultural elites, but, as Gramsci insisted, they are also the result of flashes of understanding, views of

---

[7] See Reinhart Koselleck, *The Practice of Conceptual History* (Palo Alto: Stanford University Press, 2002) and Melvin Richter, *The History of Political and Social Concepts* (New York: Oxford University Press, 1995).

[8] For preliminary thoughts on a comparative theory of politics, see Michael Freeden, 'Editorial: The Comparative Study of Political Thinking', *Journal of Political Ideologies*, 12/1 (2007), pp. 1–9.

[9] For a typical viewpoint, see Karl Dietrich Bracher, *The Age of Ideologies* (London: Methuen, 1985).

the social world held by the 'masses', or what we might now call the general public.[10] Drawing in broader, non-elitist, spheres of social and political thinking is a valuable scholarly practice in itself, 'democratizing' the study of political thought. The study of ideologies is the prime instance of analysing political thought that takes normal and average thinking about politics as seriously as it does high-quality thinking. Paradoxically, if for Marxists ideology is alienated thought, for contemporary students of ideology it is far less 'alienated', far less removed from the realities of social life, than is much political philosophy.

The emergence of theories that regarded ideologies as symbolic maps of political reality signalled an important development in the scholarly interpretation of political thought.[11] The focus now shifted sharply towards assembling empirical evidence for the meanings political thought contained. Mapping of course also simplifies, but some simplification is necessary in the processing and conveyance of research material, and ideological mapping was able to launch a more complex understanding of the structure and flexibility of ideologies than hitherto available. The important thing about mapping is that it is not purely descriptive. Pure description of social and political phenomena is impossible, for we always connect what we see and hear to an interpretative scheme. Interpretation is the art of making something plausible, not necessarily irrefutably correct, and it is always subject to replacement by further and even contrary interpretation.

Ideologies are of special concern to students of politics because they are a prominently public face of political debate and language, competing as they do over communal policymaking, and produced and held as they are by significant social groups. If thinking about politics is a ubiquitous practice, the existence of ideologies is its durable collective form. Ideologies serve as the sustaining structure of the conceptual units that comprise the substance of political thought. They are the only discursive framework through which we access the material of thinking about politics. Key concepts such as liberty, authority, the state, or equality that pertain to the core of the political are always located in a broader ideological pattern. This is not to contend that political thinking is only ideological; that would be unwarranted reductionism. Any instance of political thinking may operate simultaneously at a number of levels: as moral theory, utilitarian preference-uttering, the protection or critique of social arrangements, the conscious or unintentional enunciation of a *Weltanschauung*, the attempt to wield power in a social relationship, the honing of rhetoric. But a speech-act or writing-act of political thinking will always have an ideological dimension. Thus, the statement 'liberalism is neutral among different conceptions of the good' is patently open to ideological

[10] Antonio Gramsci, *Selections from Prison Notebooks*, Q. Hoare and G. Newell-Smith (edited), (London: Lawrence and Wishart, 1971), p. 327.
[11] Clifford Geertz, *The Interpretation of Cultures* (London: Fontana Books, 1993).

decoding. It is couched in terms of an incontrovertible truth statement ('is', not 'may be'); it is already a prioritizing statement (neutrality is a key property of liberalism); its context will dress it up as a desirable or undesirable attribute of liberalism; it is intended to serve as a recipe for advantageous social arrangements; it has a pluralist undertone in recognizing the multiplicity of coexisting ideas of the good life; it assumes that neutrality is a possible feature of political thinking and that procedural stances can rise above power struggles; it implies that conceptions of the 'good' (as distinct from the 'preferred') are readily available; and it is cast in a bold and memorable rhetoric that encourages conclusiveness. All those messages have been *de*contested from ideologically contestable positions.

The role of ideologies in decontesting what is essentially contestable is their most striking feature. Political concepts are essentially contestable for two main reasons: the impossibility of finding an agreed standard of evaluating the worth of political concepts, and the impossibility of any attempt to define a political concept without having to disregard some of its important components. We cannot agree on what value or disvalue to assign to a concept, because there is no sure-fire method of ranking values (when, if ever, is equality more important than liberty or vice versa?). Nor can the compound structure of any political concept be reproduced in any single attempt to define or apply it. Even if we agree on the minimum core of a concept (say, all conceptions of justice revolve around a system of giving people their due), we need to fill that vacuous outline with additional content in order to make sense of it (what does 'due' mean? *What* goods are due? Why are they due?) and from that point on the concept is contestable. Put differently, political concepts have many conceptions, of which quite a few can lay claim to be legitimate or at least plausible meanings of the concept in question. But they cannot all be employed at the same time. Equality cannot concurrently refer to identity, to equality of outcome, and to equality of need. We need to choose among them, a choice that is logically arbitrary though epistemologically and culturally both significant and inevitable. We are back here to the issue of indeterminacy, now applied to conceptual analysis.

Given that concepts have many conceptions, ideologies are clusters of concepts that form particular morphological arrangements in which one conception of a concept is selected, or decontested, through placing it in a particular relationship with other concepts that surround it. Those other concepts, and *their* conceptions, constrain the very large range of possible meanings the given concept could have held. Thus if the concept of citizenship is placed in close proximate relationship with duties, or equality, or participation, or ethnicity, those neighbouring concepts will limit the meaning of citizenship and direct it in each case on to a separate path, just as the concept of citizenship will impact on *them*. Together, however, the structural configuration of concepts forms the field of political meaning that we term ideology, and it constitutes the main method of mapping ideologies. Liberalism, socialism, or anarchism display conceptual arrangements that differ not so much in the concepts they employ but in the prioritizing and different weighting of *shared* concepts.

In thinking about politics, we select from among the competing conceptions of a concept the one that we regard as most appropriate for the task in hand. If that 'condemns' us—as researchers—to relativism, it is a limited relativism. To claim that more than one conception of a concept is plausible is not to claim that they *all* are plausible. Democracy may refer to the will of all or the will of the many (we have to choose the one or the other, as both cannot coexist) but it is unreasonable to 'mistake' the will of a closed elite for democracy, as some totalitarian systems deliberately have.

Tellingly, the act of decontestation is suspended between the need to close meaning for obvious decision-making reasons and the underlying impossibility of doing so with finality. Decontestation is both unavoidable and doomed to ultimate failure. It is unavoidable because language becomes unusable when it contains unmanageable surpluses of meaning. It is doomed because of the plural understandings that human beings possess, and because of the continuous fluidity of the meaning carried by language, over time and across space. As participants in the political system, as ideologues, and even as normative scholars, we suspend our belief in the many interpretations a concept carries, and we suspend our *disbelief* in the possibility that our interpretation is the correct one. In so doing, we often dress up our decontestative thought-practices as social truths on moral or religious grounds. Without the ubiquitous thought-practice of decontestation, we cannot endow our social and political environment with understandable meaning. We would be incarcerated in a perpetual world of indeterminacy, inducing intolerable levels of anxiety and defeating the construction of an epistemology that, like all epistemologies, can quench our thirst for a modicum of certainty. But as analysts of the properties of political language we must accept the inevitability of contestability. An appreciation of the work that decontestation does is therefore fundamental to our understanding of the nature of political thought, particularly of ideologies, with their penchant for naturalizing human and social truths. That appreciation requires incorporation into the sophisticated methods and approaches needed in the analysis of actual thinking about politics, transforming opaqueness into transparency.

Ideologies are important because they navigate through the political world, which would otherwise be too indeterminate to fathom. They are dedicated instruments for selecting both non-negotiable and negotiable collective values. While their study fosters a critical distance from such values that appreciates their contingency, it also recognizes that local ideological variants may share much in common and constrain the more irresponsible kinds of relativism. The combination of reason, emotion, and imagination in political argument constitutes the typically fertile form of political thinking embedded in ideologies, to whose interplay researchers should be sensitive. The multiple conceptual components that ideologies configure are a durable source of great—if occasionally volatile or hazardous—adaptive creativity from which societies draw inspiration and which should increasingly absorb the critical interest of political theorists.[12]

8

Finally, some thoughts on the practical research implications of this chapter. The approach discussed here—studying the two practices of thinking politically and thinking about politics—does not rule out the conventional modes of studying political thought: analytical political philosophy and the history of political thought. One simplified way of looking at the three approaches is to locate them, respectively, in three different disciplines: political studies, philosophy, and history. We can—and do—focus on each separately, but at some cost to an overall understanding of political thinking. The alternative is to work with different combinations of those approaches, depending on the primary target of our research: that is to say, what work do we ultimately want our subject material to perform for us: (*a*) map and interpret the ranges and features of political thinking, the clusters of conceptual combinations they display, and their relative weighting and significance, and engage in comparative analysis of theories and ideologies; (*b*) produce a critique of the logic or ethical content of a political argument and offer justifiable improvements on those; or (*c*) identify the contributions of individuals to the corpus of political thought, and the contexts of their writings, as they have accumulated, or diminished, over time.

The student of (*a*) the actual practices of political thinking would do well to acquire the finesse developed by analytical philosophers in unpacking arguments, clarifying concepts, appreciating the critical ethical issues involved, and exploring the range of normative prescriptions to general political problems. That student also needs to understand the evolutionary, discontinuous, and contextual frameworks that historians bring to bear on concrete thinkers and texts, including the real-world constraints that have in the past shaped the nature of political thought. The analytical philosopher (*b*), in turn, needs to understand the range of possible conceptions that any given concept can contain and the semantic consequences of combining concepts in different patterns. Normative theorists always operate under the general limitations of language and conceptual morphology, and should acknowledge

---

[12] For further discussion, see Michael Freeden, *Ideology: A Very Short Introduction* (Oxford: Oxford University Press, 2003).

the contestability of their normative positions. In addition, their ideal-type solutions should not stray too far from the plausible contexts in which they would be located, nor ignore the experience of the impact of various political theories that has built up over time. The historian of political thought (c) needs to assess the particular evidence at her or his disposal as part of broader comparative patterns of political thinking and to be prepared to accept the levels of generalization and family resemblances that both philosophers and students of political language and ideologies employ.

As an example, let us return to Mill's *On Liberty*. That text has traditionally been read as part of the canon of Western political thought, as the most eloquent nineteenth-century statement of the case for liberty. For some historians (c), it is situated at a transition point in the development of utilitarianism, being a statement about the limits of state intervention that also takes on board human well-being as a first stage in the emergence of modern welfare theory. The differences between the early and the late Mill become one important context in which to read *On Liberty*, as does his background as civil servant and M.P. For (b) analytical philosophers, Mill's harm principle, and his distinction between self-regarding and other-regarding conduct, may be problematic, as is the question of locating his definition of liberty on the much-overrated divide between negative and positive liberty; yet his general argument may be seen as a paragon of reason. For analysts of concrete political thinking and ideologies (a) the specific conceptual combination that Mill offers—linking liberty with individuality and progress—forms a semantic field that excludes other understandings of liberty, but is open to reinterpretation through re-readings (variable consumption) of the text. As ideological evidence, *On Liberty* is an excellent example of the implicit superiority assigned to liberalism as the set of beliefs identified with the march of civilization itself, and its power is augmented by its lucid and committed prose. Ultimately, though we may commence with any one of those approaches to Mill's texts, we will glean considerable additional insight into our chosen research problem when we intersect our preferred approach with the others.

☐ FURTHER READING

In what follows we do not provide an exhanstive bibliography. Instead, we offer a few suggestions for further reading for those who would like to follow up the material covered in particular chapters.

Chapter 1: Analytical Political Philosophy

Jonathan Dancy, *An Introduction to Contemporary Epistemology* (Oxford: Blackwell, 1985).

Norman Daniels, 'Wide Reflective Equilibrium and Theory Acceptance in Ethics', *The Journal of Philosophy*, 76/5 (1979), pp. 256–82.

Peter Godfrey-Smith, *Theory and Reality: An Introduction to the Philosophy of Science* (Chicago: University of Chicago Press, 2003).

Larry Laudan, *Progress and Its Problems: Towards a Theory of Scientific Growth* (Berkeley: University of California Press, 1977).

Philip Pettit, 'The Contribution of Analytical Philosophy', in R. E. Goodin and P. Pettit (edited), *A Companion to Contemporary Political Philosophy* (Oxford: Blackwell, 1993).

John Rawls, *A Theory of Justice* (Cambridge, MA: Harvard University Press, 1971).

John Rawls, 'The Independence of Moral Theory', *Proceedings and Addresses of the American Philosophical Association*, 48 (1974–5), pp. 5–22.

Walter Sinnott-Armstrong and Mark Timmons, *Moral Knowledge? New Readings in Moral Epistemology* (Oxford: Oxford University Press, 1996).

Chapter 2. Political Philosophy for Earthlings

Joshua Cohen, 'Taking People as They Are?', *Philosophy & Public Affairs*, 30 (2002), pp. 363–86.

Jean Hampton, 'Should Political Philosophy be Done without Metaphysics?', *Ethics*, 99 (1989–9), pp. 791–814.

Andrew Mason, 'Just Constraints', *British Journal of Political Science*, 34 (2004), pp. 251–68.

David Miller, *Principles of Social Justice* (Cambridge, MA: Harvard University Press, 1999).

Thomas Nagel, 'What Makes a Political Theory Utopian?', *Social Research*, 56 (1989), pp. 903–20.

Juha Räikkä, 'The Feasibility Condition in Political Theory', *Journal of Political Philosophy*, 6 (1998), pp. 27–40.

Andrea Sangiovanni, 'Justice and the Priority of Politics to Morality', *Journal of Political Philosophy*, forthcoming.

Marc Stears, 'The Vocation of Political Theory: Principles, Empirical Inquiry and the Politics of Opportunity', *European Journal of Political Theory*, 4 (2005), pp. 325–50.

Chapter 3: Political Theory, Social Science, and Real Politics

Benjamin R. Barber, *The Truth of Power: Intellectual Affairs in the Clinton White House* (New York: Norton, 2001).

Harry Brighouse, *School Choice and Social Justice* (New York: Oxford University Press, 2000).

Archon Fung, 'Democratic Theory and Political Science: A Pragmatic Method of Constructive Engagement', *American Political Science Review*, 101 (2007), pp. 443–58.

Thomas Pogge, *World Poverty and Human Rights* (Cambridge: Polity, 2002).

Ingrid Robeyns and Adam Swift (edited), 'Social Justice: Ideal Theory, Non-ideal Circumstances', special issue of *Social Theory and Practice*, 34/3 (2008).

Adam Swift, *How Not To Be A Hypocrite: School Choice for the Morally Perplexed Parent* (London: Routledge, 2003).

Adam Swift, 'Political Philosophy and Politics', in A. Leftwich (edited), *What Is Politics?* (Cambridge: Polity, 2004).

Avner de-Shalit and Jonathan Wolff, *Disadvantage* (Oxford: Oxford University Press, 2007).

Chapter 4: Why Be Formal?

Kenneth Arrow, *Social Choice and Individual Values* (New York: Wiley, 1951).

John Broome, *Weighing Goods* (Oxford: Blackwell, 1991).

Jean Hampton, *Hobbes and the Social Contract Tradition* (Cambridge: Cambridge University Press, 1988).

Daniel M. Hausman and Michael S. McPherson, *Economic Analysis and Moral Philosophy* (Cambridge: Cambridge University Press, 1996).

Shaun Hargreaves Heap, Martin Hollis, Bruce Lyons, Robert Sugden, and Albert Weale, *The Theory of Choice: A Critical Guide* (Oxford: Blackwell, 1992).

David M. Kreps, *Game Theory and Economic Modelling* (Oxford: Clarendon Press, 1990).

John E. Roemer, *Theories of Distributive Justice* (Cambridge, MA: Harvard University Press, 1996).

Robert Sugden, *The Economics of Rights, Co-operation and Welfare*, 2nd edn. (Basingstoke: Palgrave Macmillan, 2004).

Chapter 5: Recognition as Fact and Norm: the Method of Critique

Kenneth Baynes, *The Normative Grounds of Social Criticism: Kant, Rawls and Habermas* (Albany: State University of New York Press, 1992).

Selya Benhabib, *Situating the Self. Gender, Community and Postmodernism in Contemporary Ethics* (Cambridge: Polity Press, 1992).

Pierre Bourdieu, *Language and Symbolic Power*, edited by J. Thompson (Cambridge: Polity Press, 1991).

Jürgen Habermas, *The Inclusion of the Other: Studies in Political Theory* (Cambridge: Polity Press, 1998).

Lois McNay, *Against Recognition* (Cambridge: Polity Press, 2007).

Glen Newey, *After Politics: The Rejection of Politics in Contemporary Liberal Philosophy* (Basingstoke: Palgrave, 2001).

Charles Taylor, 'Language and Society', in A. Honneth and H. Joas (edited), *Communicative Action: Essays on Jürgen Habermas 'The Theory of Communicative Action'* (Cambridge: Polity Press, 1991).

John Thompson and David Held (edited), *Habermas: Critical Debates* (London: Macmillan, 1982).

Chapter 6: Dialectical Approaches

G. A. Cohen, *History Labour Freedom. Themes from Marx* (Oxford: Oxford University Press, 1988).

Michael Forster, 'Hegel's Dialectical Method', in Frederick C. Beiser (edited), *The Cambridge Companion to Hegel* (Cambridge, 1993), pp. 130–70.

Jon Elster, *Logic and Society. Contradiction and Possible Worlds* (London: John Wiley & Sons, 1978).

Jon Elster, *Making Sense of Marx* (Cambridge: Cambridge University Press, 1985).

Daniel Little, *The Scientific Marx* (Minneapolis: University of Minnesota Press, 1986).

Georg Lukács, *History and Class Consciousness. Studies in Marxist Dialectics*, translated by Rodney Livingstone (London: Merlin Press, 1971).

Georg Lukács, *A Defence of History and Class Consciousness. Tailism and the Dialectic*, translated by Esther Leslie, introduced by John Rees, postface by Slavoj Žižek (London: Verso, 2000).

John Roemer (edited), *Analytical Marxism* (Cambridge: Cambridge University Press, 1986).

Chapter 7: Political Theory and History

Dario Castiglione and I. Hampsher-Monk (edited), *The History of Political Thought in National Context* (Cambridge: Cambridge University Press, 2001).

John Dunn, 'The Identity of the History of Ideas', *Political Obligation in its Historical Context* (Cambridge: Cambridge University Press, 1980).

Michel Foucault, *The Archaeology of Knowledge* (London: Tavistock, 1972).

Reinhart Koselleck, *The Practice of Conceptual History: Timing History, Spacing Concepts* (Stanford: Stanford University Press, 2002).

J. G. A. Pocock, 'The Concept of a Language and the *metier d'historien*: Some Considerations on Practice', in A. Pagden (edited), *The Languages of Political Theory in Early Modern Europe* (Cambridge: Cambridge University Press, 1987), pp. 19–40.

Quentin Skinner, *Visions of Politics*, volume 1, *Regarding Method* (Cambridge: Cambridge University Press, 2002).

Leo Strauss, *An Introduction to Political Philosophy: Ten Essays* (Detroit: Wayne State University Press, 1989).

James Tully (edited), *Meaning and Context. Quentin Skinner and his Critics* (Cambridge: Polity Press, 1988).

Chapter 8: Using Archival Sources to Theorize about Politics

Sudhir Hazareesingh, *From Subject to Citizen. The Second Empire and the Emergence of Modern French History* (Princeton: Princeton University Press, 1998).

Sudhir Hazareesingh, *Intellectual Founders of the Republic: Five Studies in Nineteenth Century French Political Thought* (Oxford: Oxford University Press, 2001).

Karma Nabulsi, *Traditions of War: Occupation, Resistance and the Law* (Oxford: Oxford University Press, 1999).

Karma Nabulsi, 'Patriotism and Internationalism in the "Oath of Allegiance" to Young Europe', *European Journal of Political Theory*, 5/1 (2006), pp. 61–70.

Philip Nord, *The Republican Moment: Struggles for Democracy in Nineteenth-Century France* (Cambridge, MA: Harvard University Press, 1995).

Grace Roosevelt, *Reading Rousseau in the Nuclear Age* (Philadelphia: Temple University Press, 1990).

Quentin Skinner, *Liberty Before Liberalism* (Cambridge: Cambridge University Press, 1998).

Stuart White, 'Republicanism, Patriotism, and Global Justice', in D. Bell and A. De-Shalit (edited), *Forms of Justice. Critical Perspectives on David Miller's Political Philosophy* (Lanham, MD: Rowman & Littlefield, 2003).

Chapter 9: Political Theory and the Boundaries of Politics

Hannah Arendt, *The Human Condition* (Chicago: University of Chicago Press, 1958).

Hannah Arendt, *Between Past and Future: Eight Exercises in Political Thought* (New York: Viking Press, 1968).

Bernard R. Crick, *In Defence of Politics* (Harmondsworth: Penguin, 1992).

Elizabeth Frazer, *The Problems of Communitarian Politics: Unity and Conflict* (Oxford: Oxford University Press, 1999).

Elizabeth Frazer and Nicola Lacey, *The Politics of Community: A Feminist Critique of the Liberal-Communitarian Debate* (London: Harvester Wheatsheaf, 1993).

Bonnie Honig, *Political Theory and the Displacement of Politics* (New York: Cornell University Press, 1993).

Chantal Mouffe, *On the Political* (London: Routledge, 2005).

Max Weber, *Political Writings*, edited by P. Lassman and R. Speirs (Cambridge: Cambridge University Press, 1994).

Chapter 10: Thinking Politically and Thinking About Politics: Language, Interpretation, and Ideology

Michael Freeden, *Ideologies and Political Theory: A Conceptual Approach* (Oxford: Clarendon Press, 1996).

Michael Freeden, 'What Should the "Political" in Political Theory Explore?', *Journal of Political Philosophy*, 3 (2005), pp. 113–34.

W. B. Gallie, 'Essentially Contested Concepts', *Proceedings of the Aristotelian Society*, 56 (1955–6), pp. 167–98.

Antonio Gramsci, *Selections from Prison Notebooks*, edited by Q. Hoare and G. Newell-Smith (London: Lawrence and Wishart, 1971).

Karl Mannheim, *Ideology and Utopia* (London: Kegan Paul, 1936).

Noel O'Sullivan, 'Difference and the Concept of the Political in Contemporary Political Philosophy', *Political Studies*, 45 (1997), pp. 739–54.

Paul Ricoeur, *Lectures on Ideology and Utopia* (New York: Columbia University Press, 1986).

Teun A. van Dijk, *Ideology: A Multidisciplinary Approach* (London: Sage Publications, 1998).

☐ INDEX